Change and Stability in Foreign Policy

Change and Stability in Foreign Policy

The Problems and Possibilities of Détente

Kjell Goldmann

Princeton
University Press

Published by Princeton University Press, 41 William Street,
Princeton, New Jersey 08540
In the United Kingdom: Princeton University Press, Guildford, Surrey

LIBRARY OF CONGRESS CATALOGING-IN-PUBLICATION DATA

Goldman, Kjell, 1937–
Change and stability in foreign policy : the problems and possibilities of détente
/ Kjell Goldmann.

p. cm.   Bibliography: p.   Includes index.
ISBN 0-691-07778-9 (alk. paper)
  1. Detente. 2. International relations. 3. United States—Foreign relations—Soviet
Union. 4. Soviet Union—Foreign relations—United States. 5. Germany (West)—Foreign
relations—Soviet Union. 6. Soviet Union—Foreign relations—Germany (West) I. Title.
JX1393.D46G63 1988
327.1'12'0904—dc19   87–35542   CIP

This book has been composed in Linotron Sabon

Clothbound editions of Princeton University Press books
are printed on acid-free paper, and binding materials are
chosen for strength and durability. Paperbacks, although satisfactory
for personal collections, are not usually suitable for library rebinding

Printed in the United States of America by Princeton University Press,
Princeton, New Jersey

CONTENTS

LIST OF TABLES

THE OBJECT of this study is the tension between two ways of accounting for political action: in terms of situations, and in terms of traditions. In the former, actions are interpreted as adaptation to the environment and are thought to be explicable and predictable in terms of the situations in which actors find themselves. In the latter, it is presumed that actions can be explained and predicted in terms of the way in which the actor traditionally behaves. In the former perspective, U.S.-Soviet relations develop in accordance with action-reaction dynamics. In the latter perspective, they reflect U.S. and Soviet foreign policy traditions. The foreign policy of my own country, Sweden, can similarly be seen as adaptation to the situation obtaining in its environment or as the continuing pursuit of a policy with deep historical roots.

In fact it is both. Action must be assumed to be determined by both situation and tradition—by tradition, but modified by situational demands, or by situations, but constrained by tradition. The problem is to go beyond this truism to a theory of the relative importance of situations and traditions. The theory of foreign policy stability sketched in Part One of the present study is a modest effort in that direction.

The idea of thinking about détente in these terms originated when I was invited to present a paper to a panel about East-West relations while being preoccupied with the theoretical problem of stability and change in foreign policy. This resulted in Parts Two and Three of the book. I hope the reader will agree that it adds to our understanding of the problem of détente to think of it as a question of the establishment of a tradition strong enough to withstand the pressure from challenging situations.

Among the many people who have helped me along, two colleagues at the University of Stockholm have been particularly important: Jan Hallenberg and Bertil Nygren. They both wrote their doctorates with me as their adviser, and their impact on the book will become obvious to the reader. Another Stockholm colleague, Bengt Sundelius, made comments on an early paper, which proved to be so important for my further work that this must be explicitly acknowledged. The Stockholm Department of Political Science, with its Group for Research on Peace and Security Policy, generally functioned as a stimulating home base for my research effort.

You need more than a home base, however. It was crucial for this study that I was able to spend a sabbatical term at Princeton University's Center of International Studies. Moreover, thanks to my friend William K. Domke as well as other friends and colleagues, I was able to present my thoughts to several other audiences across the United States. The interest I met and the criticism I received at Princeton and elsewhere were of great importance.

In order to carry out the détente part of the study I needed to interview people in Washington, D.C., as well as in Bonn. I am greatly indebted to Erik Pierre, then at the Swedish Embassy in Washington, and to my old friend Sven G. Linder, then Minister at the Embassy in Bonn, for their invaluable help with making the arrangements. Thanks are also due to those busy American and German policymakers and scholars who took the time to let me interview them.

This study, which was completed in 1985, has been supported by a grant from the Swedish Council for Research in the Humanities and Social Sciences. Preliminary versions of parts of the argument have been published in *World Politics* and *Cooperation and Conflict* as well as by the Swedish Institute of International Affairs and the Center of International Studies at Princeton. The détente scenario outlined in chapter 10 is included in *Rivalitet och samexistens*, which is being published for the above-mentioned research group by Studentlitteratur.

Häkan Karlsson helped me to edit the manuscript: his assistance was doubly valuable, since he combines attention to details with a profound knowledge of U.S. foreign and defense policy. Daniel Goldmann and Karin Wiberg assisted with the word processing. Donald Lavery solved a large number of linguistic as well as practical problems, as he always does.

Stockholm
April 1987

ABM	Antiballistic missile
APNW	Agreement on the Prevention of Nuclear War
BPA	Basic Principles agreement
CDSP	*Current Digest of the Soviet Press*
CDU	Christian Democratic Union
CIA	Central Intelligence Agency
CMEA	Council for Mutual Economic Assistance
COPDAB	Conflict and Peace Data Bank
CPSU	Communist Party of the Soviet Union
CREON	Comparative Research on the Events of Nations
CSCE	Conference on Security and Cooperation in Europe
CSU	Christian Social Union
DIA	Defense Intelligence Agency
DIW	Deutsches Institut für Wirtschaftsforschung
DSB	*Department of State Bulletin*
FDP	Free Democratic party
FRG	Federal Republic of Germany
GATT	General Agreement on Tariffs and Trade
GDP	Gross domestic product
GNP	Gross national product
ICBM	Intercontinental ballistic missile
IIM	Interagency intelligence memorandum
IMEMO	Institute of World Economy and International Relations
INR	Bureau of Intelligence and Research
KCA	*Keesing's Contemporary Archives*
KGB	Committee of State Security
NASA	National Aeronautics and Space Administration
NATO	North Atlantic Treaty Organization
NIE	National intelligence estimate
NSA	National Security Agency
OECD	Organization for Economic Cooperation and Development
OPEC	Organization of Petroleum Exporting Countries
PLA	People's Liberation Army (China)
SALT	Strategic Arms Limitation Talks
SNIE	Special national intelligence estimate
SPD	Social Democratic party

Introduction

ASSUME THAT A NATION is pursuing a given foreign policy and that we are concerned with the way in which it will act in the future. We may want to make a forecast—but then, to what extent is the present policy of a nation a valid guide to its future behavior? Or we may want the nation to change its course—but then, would an influence attempt be likely to succeed? In other words, is the policy with which we are concerned stable or unstable, invulnerable or vulnerable?

A variety of factors may have an impact on whether a specific foreign policy is likely to endure or to change. The chief objective of the present book is to bring them together into a theory of foreign policy stability, or an outline of such a theory.

The question of change and stability in foreign policy is vital for peace and security. In order to improve relations between long-standing adversaries it is necessary to destabilize their mutual policies of enmity. Once this has been achieved, the task is to stabilize their emerging policies of amity—that is, to make it possible for an initially fragile détente to survive the stresses and strains that are bound to occur. This book is concerned not only with the general problem of change and stability in foreign policy but also with the specific problem of détente stabilization.

A theory of change and stability in foreign policy is sketched in Part One. Its core is an inventory of what will be called the "stabilizers" of foreign policies, that is, of phenomena tending to inhibit change in foreign policy even when there is a pressure for change. The theoretical sketch is offered as a basis for further research, but it is also meant to serve as an aid in the analysis of immediate issues. Hence, I hope to pave the way for the improvement of foreign policy theory, but I also have a more practical objective: how, with a limited yet systematic effort, can we examine the extent to which a foreign policy is in fact vulnerable or invulnerable to pressure for change? The inventory of stabilizers may be useful as a checklist for such purposes.

The checklist is applied to East-West relations in Part Two. The period from the late 1960s to the late 1970s can be seen as an experiment with what became known as détente. Both the East and the West began to pursue, or declared that they intended to pursue, a policy of restraint, arms control, and cooperation. Leonid Brezhnev and Richard Nixon embraced at meetings in Moscow and Washington.

SALT I was put into effect and SALT II was negotiated. East-West trade multiplied. A document was signed in Helsinki in which the further development of détente was mapped in detail. It seemed to many that a new era had begun in world politics.

Détente proved to be an unstable feature of Soviet-American relations, however. It was clearly undermined already by 1975 and was generally referred to in the past tense by 1980. Do we have to conclude from this experience that stable détente is impossible? That is the question I address in Part Two of this book, in which Soviet-American relations during the 1970s are compared to those between the Soviet Union and West Germany, where détente fared better.

Applying the theoretical sketch introduced in Part One to this problem is meant to serve two purposes. First of all, the empirical application of a theoretical sketch is a device for improving it—for examining its plausibility as well as for exploring operational problems and possibilities. At the same time, even in a preliminary version a theoretical sketch may help the analyst to select, order, and interpret his or her data. The theory sketched in Part One suggests that we examine the extent to which "stabilizers" emerged to protect the new relationship of détente, and in Part Two an attempt is made to map systematically the extent of détente "stabilization" in Soviet-American and Soviet-West German relations. This may be useful for evaluating the détente experiment: What went wrong, what went well, and what can be learned from the experience?

In Part Three I take the further step of using the theoretical sketch in conjunction with the empirical results for an analysis of the general problem of "peaceful coexistence," or "détente." A core problem in international politics is whether stable, reasonably amicable policies are possible between adversaries in a system whose basic feature is anarchy. Some suggestions about the problems and possibilities of détente stabilization in anarchy are made in Part Three. They are inspired both by the general argument about change and stability in foreign policy and by the specific observations about East-West relations in the 1970s.

Formulating a theory, relating it to data, applying it to a specific problem—this order of presentation does not accurately represent the actual sequence of research. The interaction between the three lines of inquiry—foreign policy theory, East-West relations, détente in anarchy—has been considerable throughout. It is reflected in some early publications, in which the basic ideas of the study were tried out (Goldmann 1982, 1983a, b).

Such interaction is useful, but it also carries problems. The attempt to contribute to foreign policy theory may have been overly influenced by the preoccupation with détente. The exploration of East-West relations may have been too circumscribed by the theoretical sketch. The consideration of détente as a general problem of international politics may have laid undue stress on the stabilization aspect.

It should be clear against this background that I have not attempted to carry out a comprehensive analysis of either foreign policy change, East-West relations, or the problem of détente. Instead I have experimented with a particular perspective on each of these. The insights offered are meant to supplement rather than to substitute for those of others—to add to an ongoing discussion, or to three ongoing discussions. If others are brought to ask questions they would not otherwise have thought of asking, the main purpose of this book has been achieved.

PART ONE

Change and Stability in Foreign Policy
A Theoretical Sketch

CHAPTER 1

Foreign Policy Stability as a Research Problem

WE GENERALLY ASSUME that there are patterns in the foreign policy of nations and not just single acts. A knowledge of the pattern—the "policy"—of an actor is assumed to be useful for explaining and predicting actions. If we can show that an action fits into a pattern—that is, that the actor behaves as he usually does, or says that it is his policy to do, we have in one sense explained his action. Similarly, if we know the pattern, we may anticipate what the actor will be likely to do in the future. We know, in other words, about a regular feature of international politics—a feature that may, however, be more or less amenable to change.

The assumption of foreign policy patterns is easy to justify. The arguments commonly put forward range from the imperatives of geopolitics to the standard operating procedures of bureaucracies to the inertia of belief systems. However, analysts also find it easy to explain new departures after the fact by reference to, say, the dynamics of international relations, the flux of domestic politics, or the erratic nature of personalities. Such explanations undermine the very assumption that foreign policy is patterned—unless it can be explained why this particular policy was vulnerable to that particular disturbance.

There is an inevitable tension between viewing international politics as the pursuit of policies and seeing it as variable responses to shifting situations. Yet the tradition in foreign policy analysis is to do both. It was to be expected that the United States and China would remain enemies even after the Sino-Soviet rift: their mutual enmity had deep roots in both countries. It was also to be expected that they would come together as a result of the new triangular balance of power. But if both were to be expected, how can either be explained, and how could either have been predicted? What factors determine whether, when, and to what extent pressure for change in a policy will in fact produce change?

This is an unresolved issue in foreign policy theory. It relates to three key problems in the analysis of international politics:

1. The problem of adaptation. On the one hand, nations—and organizations in general—are under pressure to adapt to changing

conditions in their environment. On the other hand, they have a tendency to stick to their previous policies. What determines the impact of environmental change?

2. The problem of learning. On the one hand, nations—and organizations in general—take into account the way in which the environment responds to their policies; negative feedback is a pressure for change. On the other hand, there is a tendency to continue as before. Inter-nation action-reaction sometimes operates and sometimes fails to operate. What factors account for the impact of feedback?

3. The problem of domestic change. On the one hand, shifts in domestic politics—and within organizations in general—may place new people in positions of power, people whose views differ from those of their predecessors. On the other hand, new people may find themselves to be the prisoners of past policies. What factors determine the sensitivity of a foreign policy to domestic change?

These are three common themes in controversies over foreign policy. How will U.S. policy be affected by long-term changes in the international distribution of power? Would Western restraint have an impact on Soviet arms policy? Is West German foreign policy dependent on who wins the next election? Nations are assumed to pursue identifiable, stable policies. At the same time, a number of factors are assumed to be sources of change in policy. The issue concerns the likely outcome of the confrontation between the two. Foreign policy theory is weak on this point. It is uncommon among foreign policy theorists even to make a strict distinction between pressures for, or motivators of, change and pressures for, or motivators of, lack of change. The theoretical sketch to be presented here is meant to improve our understanding of the stability and instability of foreign policies, and to do it by taking environmental change, negative feedback, and shifts in leadership for granted and focusing instead on the factors accounting for their varying impact.

The term *theoretical sketch* is deliberate. What follows is theory—it contains not merely definitions but also propositions about the ways in which certain phenomena affect certain other phenomena. It is a sketch in three ways, however: its concepts are imprecise, its propositions are weak, and it has not been exposed to a systematic empirical test. A theoretical sketch is a necessary intermediate step between impressions and theory proper. It paves the way for more sophisticated inquiry. It also, however, serves, in the absence of theory proper, as a tool for asking better questions—as a systematic checklist for the analysis of specific problems.

Such a checklist can be useful. If none exists, the analyst has the option of doing the work ad hoc—that is, without considering the meaning and relevance of the concepts. The analysis risks being overly narrow, biased, or prejudiced as a result; whatever comes to mind at the outset is assumed to be the proper object of study. Or the analyst may make his or her own theoretical preparations. This is a big task, however, and it may be out of the question for the analyst who is concerned with a specific case or an immediate problem rather than with the development of theory; those who need to consume theory cannot always produce it themselves. Now, if a theoretical sketch exists, there is no need to choose between being arbitrary and beginning from scratch. Theory proper is better, but a sketch is better than nothing at all. This is the way in which the sketch that is about to be presented may contribute to the analysis of specific problems of foreign policy stability—as a reasonably systematic, considered, and comprehensive list of matters to be taken into account.

The notion of a theoretical sketch is further discussed in the Appendix. A problem with theoretical sketches is how to evaluate and improve them. They are not always strictly testable, especially not by historical case study. Nor are they arbitrary, however. The Appendix includes some thoughts about the way in which a theoretical sketch may be improved by empirical application, and some improvement of the present sketch is attempted in Parts Two and Three of the book, where it is applied to the analysis of East-West relations and the problem of détente.

The outline of Part One is as follows: First, in the present chapter, foreign policy stability is introduced as a problem of research. In section 1.1 a conceptual framework for the analysis of change and lack of change in foreign policy is suggested and the concept of a "stabilizer" is introduced. This conceptual discussion specifies the problem with which the book is concerned. Section 1.2 is devoted to some of the literature expected to be concerned with foreign policy stabilizers. Against this background, an inventory of foreign policy stabilizers is made in chapter 2, and the processes of foreign policy stabilization and destabilization are briefly considered in chapter 3.

1.1. THE FRAMEWORK OF ANALYSIS

The basic structure of the framework of analysis is shown in Figure 1.1. A change in policy has "sources," but sources do not produce policy changes directly. Sometimes pressure for change produces change, but sometimes it does not. That is the problem of stability considered here. Our concern is not with the sources of change in foreign policy but with its stabilizers.

Thus, two intervening variables, so to speak, are assumed between sources and policies. A source of policy change is an event tending to start a process of policy change. A stabilizer is a variable affecting (1) the likelihood that such an event will set a process of change in motion, and/or (2) the extent to which a process of change will be completed and produce a change in policy. The chief questions are: What are the stabilizers, and how do they operate?

A more detailed view of the framework of analysis is set out in Figure 1.2. Three sources of policy change are shown. One possibility is that a change in policy is brought about by a change in the environmental circumstances called "conditions." This is what may be called a process of adaptation. When the United States revised its policy toward the People's Republic of China in the late 1960s, this may be seen as adaptation to a situation in which China was no longer an ally but an adversary of the Soviet Union. Policies may also be their own sources of change in the sense that they may change in response to negative feedback. This will be called learning. A typical case would be the abandonment of a conciliatory policy because the response had been nonconciliatory. Another would be the abandonment of a forceful policy toward an adversary because such a policy had been found to render one's allies uneasy. Some instances of policy change are neither adaptation nor learning, however, and there is therefore a need for the category of "residual factors."

Three processes of change are also distinguished in Figure 1.2. Each policy is assumed to be based on a set of ideas on the part of the policymaking system, and each change in policy is assumed to be based on a change in ideas. The latter change may, however, be of three kinds: rethinking by individuals within the policymaking system (represented in Figure 1.2 by the direct arrows from "conditions," "policies," and "residual factors" to "ideas"); a change in the composition of this system; or a change in the balance of power between the members of the system.

Figure 1.1. The framework of analysis: basic structure.

POLICYMAKING SYSTEM

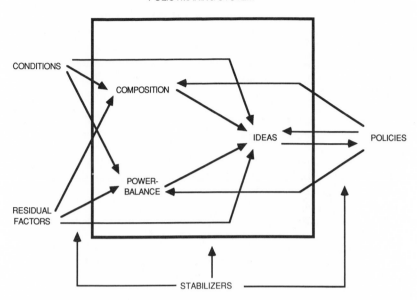

Figure 1.2. The framework of analysis: detailed version.

In the rest of this section, the concepts and relationships in Figure 1.2 will be discussed in more detail.

Policy   It is commonplace to point out that foreign policy research has been imprecise about its dependent variable (Faurby 1976: 141–44, Hermann 1978: 25–32). The same may apparently be said about so-called policy studies. It is emphasized in this literature that the meaning of "policy" is unclear and that "policy" is a "generic symbol pointing toward a field of interest, rather than a scientifically precise concept."[1] A consensus has been suggested to obtain among foreign policy analysts to the effect that foreign policy is "a set of goals, directives, or intentions, formulated by persons in official or authoritative positions, directed at some actor or condition in the environment beyond the nation state, for the purpose of affecting the target in the manner desired by the policymakers"—but this, it has been added, is not to have said very much (Cohen and Harris 1975: 385).

Against this background it has appeared necessary to be relatively precise about what is meant by "policy" in the present study—that is,

[1] Rose 1973: 73. For similar observations, see Anckar 1978: 113–14, Heiskanen and Martikainen 1974: 11.

what the theory about to be sketched is meant to be a theory about. A consideration of this matter now may inhibit confusion later on. An attempt to define the concept of policy in a precise fashion has been made by Kerr (1976), and her definition is useful as a point of departure. Kerr suggests that four conditions are necessary requisites for a public policy and implies that together they are sufficient. Her first condition is:

1. An agent must intend to act in accord with some conditional imperative X, i.e., whenever conditions beta obtain, do action(s) alpha.

Hence, a policy requires both an agent and a conditional imperative. Without an agent, there is no policy, but "some sort of principle." A policy has a specific subject and is not a universal norm.

Kerr then distinguishes between "policy" and "promise." Whereas a promise is specific to one or a specified number of instances, a policy is general:

2. The agent must perceive as likely that the conditions beta will occur more than once or a restricted number of times.

There is, however, one more difference between policies and promises: they are not "equally revisable." To change a promise is to break it. A change in policy does not carry this connotation; "the agent has simply to revise the conditional imperative." Hence this condition:

3. The agent may substitute conditional imperative X' for conditional imperative X, without violating conditional imperative X.

Kerr finally distinguishes between public and private policy by adding this criterion:

4. The agent must declare to the relevant public the agent's intention to act in accord with the conditional imperative X.

The problem of identifying the "relevant" public is extensively discussed by Kerr but is unimportant here. From our point of view, the chief problem is that Kerr defines policies as programs and not as behavior patterns. In foreign policy research, the opposite position is sometimes advocated; the Comparative Research on the Events of Nations (CREON) project has decided "to conceptualize the external actions of national governments in terms of behaviors rather than goal-seeking policies" (Hermann 1978: 32). However, programs are not only very close to what is usually meant by policies but are important objects of study because they can have important consequences. The chief question is whether policies are necessarily programs: major change has occurred in Soviet action on the high seas, but we cannot (for the sake of the argument) find any Soviet document substituting, in Kerr's terms, conditional imperative X' for conditional imperative X. Can we talk of a change in Soviet naval "policy" nevertheless?

One possibility is to assume a change in program behind a change in behavior; Kerr's fourth condition is not met, but the three others are. Allison (1971) and others have demonstrated the questionability of ascribing intentions to complex actors on the basis of their behavior, however. Another possibility is to regard a behavior pattern as a policy regardless of whether it has been the agent's intention to pursue such a policy. In our approach, we shall distinguish between verbalized policy, defined roughly as a publicly declared program, and nonverbalized policy, defined without reference to any program on the part of the agent.

The following definitions are a starting point:

D1. Policy: an agent's line of action with regard to an object.
D2. Line of action: the agent does alpha whenever situation beta occurs; beta will occur more than once or a restricted number of times.

D1 plus D2 is a variation on Kerr's conditions 1 and 2; the "object" has been added to D1 in order to make clear that a policy concerns either a specific issue area (for example, "trade policy") or the agent's relation to some other actor (for example, somebody's "China policy"). Kerr's condition 3 is unacceptable for the purposes of this study, however. It is misleading to distinguish between promises and policies. Policies in the present approach are in fact promises, commitments.

The essence of D1 plus D2 is that a policy is attributed to an agent and that it consists of a line of action. The subclass "verbalized policy" may be defined as follows:

D3. Verbalized policy: a line of action that an agent declares he is following or intends to follow with regard to an object.

A verbalized policy is identified by—and only by—the study of the agent's declarations. D3 refers to the policy as described by the agent. Alpha and beta are specified by the agent himself.

Nonverbalized policy is a more difficult concept:

D4. Nonverbalized policy: a line of action that is in fact followed by an agent with regard to an object.

In this case, alpha and beta are specified by the observer and not by the agent. Moreover, whereas a verbalized policy can apply to the future

in the sense of expressing intentions, a nonverbalized policy is by definition a generalization about past behavior.

Verbalized and nonverbalized policies are different phenomena.
They can exist independently. There may be a causal relationship
between the two, however. Programs may lead to behavior, and
behavior may lead to programs. The correlation is unlikely to be perfect, but it is also unlikely to be zero.[2]

An analysis of policy stability presupposes a definition of policy
change. This concept is considered by Rose (1976: 14–23). However,
his variable is "progress in terms of a policy objective"; he is thus concerned with a change in outcome rather than in policy as defined here.
In terms of the present definition, a change in policy with regard to a
given object can only mean a change in alpha or beta: either a new act
in a given type of situation or a given act in a type of situation previously associated with a different act. Stabilizers inhibit such changes.

Ideas   In the present framework, a change in policy is based on a
change in ideas, on rethinking, on reappraisal. What does it mean to
say that a policy is "based" on ideas? On whose ideas? On what kind
of ideas?

Ideas are related to policies both in the sense of argument within the
policymaking system and in the sense of public justification. The
common dichotomy between "real" and "declared" motives is misleading: the degree of similarity and the amount of interaction between
arguments given to different audiences, and between arguments and
private thoughts, is an empirical question with no self-evident answer
(this is discussed in more detail in Goldmann 1971: 51–53). Policy
change is assumed to be based on a change in ideas, in the sense that

---

[2] It is important to note that no assumption about "real" or "underlying" intentions
is made in definitions D3 and D4. Neither publicly declared programs nor behavior
patterns are presumed to reflect "real" or "underlying" goals and objectives. In terms of
the present definition of policy, whether the Soviet Union pursued a policy of détente in
the 1970s does not depend on the "real" thoughts of Soviet policymakers. This is so
because the object of the present study is to study change and stability in declared programs and behavior patterns—in verbal and nonverbal foreign policy behavior, if you
wish—rather than in underlying intentions, not to mention the conceptual and empirical
difficulties that must be overcome in order to identify the latter.

A different view is put forward by Carlsnaes, who has published a criticism of a preliminary version of the present analytical framework in the form of a review of a book
by my project colleague, Jan Hallenberg (Carlsnaes 1985). Carlsnaes advocates a definition of policy as necessarily intentional in the sense of declared in camera, as he puts
it.

there is a difference between the arguments for the previous policy and the arguments for the new one.

Whose arguments? Part of the answer is simple. Organizations produce not just policies but also authoritative statements about the ideas in which the organization has decided to believe. There is a precise meaning in ascribing such ideas to an organization. Official beliefs do not exhaust the kind of ideas that can be meaningfully ascribed to organizations, however. "Ideas" in our framework of analysis include thoughts that are circulating in the policymaking system without being officially expressed in the name of the organization. This leads to the problem of specifying the border between the policymaking system and its environment. Moreover, individuals within the policymaking system may have different reasons for supporting a policy, and this is one more ambiguity in the notion that an organization's policy is based on the ideas of its policymakers. Both ambiguities are common in foreign policy analysis. For the purpose of the present discussion, it seems possible to live with them. What is important here is that, since a change in ideas is concomitant with a change in policy, the student of the latter must be concerned with the factors inhibiting the former.

Rethinking may take a variety of forms. A policy may be based on: (1) norms laying down goals, (2) a theory according to which the pursuit of a certain policy under certain conditions increases the likelihood that these goals will be attained, and (3) a description of prevailing circumstances according to which these conditions obtain. Hence, a reappraisal may be normative, descriptive, or theoretical. In a normative reappraisal, a shift in policy is rooted in a change in the agent's value system; in a descriptive reappraisal, a shift in policy is rooted in a change in the definition of prevailing circumstances; and in a theoretical reappraisal, a shift in policy is rooted in a change in causal beliefs.

There are several kinds of theoretical reappraisal. A distinction can be made between falsification and extension. In the case of falsification, new evidence causes the agent to cease to believe in a theoretical assertion previously found to be plausible. In the case of extension, the agent adds new variables to his theory. One kind of extension is policy innovation. Another may be termed goal addition: new goal variables are added to the theory, and in this process negative side effects are discovered with regard to goals that were previously not considered to be relevant.

We now have five types of reappraisal on which a policy change may be based (Figure 1.3). They are not equally probable. Hypothetically, normative reappraisal is least likely to occur, and descriptive reappraisal most likely;[3] falsification in the light of new evidence and policy innovation may be more likely than goal addition. This speculation is not central to our present concerns, however.[4]

Composition of the Policymaking System   Reappraisal by an organization need not involve reappraisal by individuals. An organization may "rethink" by changing its policymakers. Even if the beliefs of individuals are constant, the organization's beliefs may change. The new policymakers may have normative, descriptive, or theoretical ideas that differ from those of their predecessors. Falsification in the light of new evidence, policy innovation, or goal addition in the "thinking" of

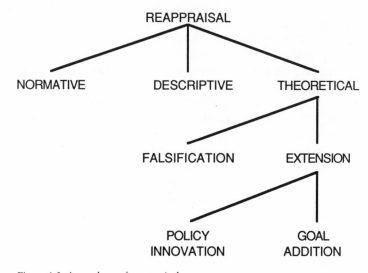

Figure 1.3. A typology of reappraisals.

[3] "Any change in Soviet policy, when acknowledged at all, is described as the natural response of a perfectly consistent program to differences in conditions" (Hough 1980a: 500).

[4] Carlsnaes (1985: 213–14) criticizes our concept of ideas and the way in which it is related to other concepts in Figure 1.2 mainly on two accounts. He maintains, first, that since "policies, however you define them, are . . . replete with ideas," the concept of ideas is not logically distinct from the concept of policy in our framework of analysis, and therefore that the relationship between them cannot be causal. Obviously, however, "ideas" in Figure 1.2 is short for "other ideas than policies"; hence, it is logically possible to talk of a causal relationship between the two. Second, Carlsnaes cannot accept that, as in Figure 1.2, "ideational change is . . . imputed to be the product of factors . . . which are exogenous to human agents"; in his view, ideas by definition cannot be products of noncognitive factors. My persuasion is different.

the organization may take the form not of new ideas in the minds of old leaders but of a change in leadership.

Leadership change does not necessarily imply policy change, however. The significance of the coming into power of policymakers who are either committed to a different policy than their predecessors or uncommitted to any policy is one of the chief objectives of the study of policy stability.

Balance of Power within the Policymaking System   If the policymaking system contains advocates of competing policies, the balance of power between the camps may determine which policy will be pursued. Reappraisal may consequently be brought about by a change in the balance of power within the policymaking system. In an extreme case, no individual within the policymaking system has changed his or her opinion on anything, nor has any individual entered or left this system, yet there has been rethinking on the part of the organization because external events have produced a shift in the balance of power between contending norms, descriptions of prevailing circumstances, or theories. The Soviet Union seems quite capable of changing the balance of power between armers and arms controllers in Washington.

Conditions   We now come to the most difficult concept in the framework of analysis. The framework assumes policies to be rational responses to "conditions." A change in conditions is—in the framework—one of three sources of policy change. The other two are negative feedback and "residual factors."

This distinction between conditions and residual factors is useful but unclear. It is useful for making explicit that policy change may be the result of a process set in motion by events substantively unrelated to the policy. A change in U.S. policy toward the Soviet Union may be brought about by a change in the strategic balance, but it may also be triggered by a Watergate break-in. The precise distinction is difficult, however.

When talking about the "conditions" of a policy, we must first consider whether we have subjective or objective rationality in mind. Would it be useful to regard as policy conditions those circumstances to which the policy is or was originally intended to be a rational response? I think not. An approach in terms of subjective rationality would be operationally difficult: we would need full insight into the calculations of the actor, and this is often unrealistic. There is also the ambiguity of the case where a change in policy is intended to be a rational response to a change in factors that were not taken into account when the policy was originally adopted. Suppose that the leaders of nation A decide to adopt a policy of enmity toward nation B on ideological grounds and without any consideration of the balance of power; suppose further that this policy is revised at a later stage because the balance of power is perceived to have changed; it would be peculiar to regard this revision as if it had been brought about by substantively irrelevant, "residual" factors rather than as adaptation to new conditions.

The assumption of objective rationality makes it possible to avoid this peculiarity. In what follows the conditions for a policy are those features of the environment to which the policy is in fact a rational or "logical" response. A change in objectively relevant conditions, in the present framework of analysis, implies a pressure for adaptation, and a chief concern of this study is with the factors determining the extent to which such adaptation will take place.

The main result of defining conditions in terms of objective rather than subjective rationality is to broaden the scope of the concept of policy conditions and hence of adaptation: A phenomenon may come to be regarded as a policy condition regardless of whether it can be shown that it was taken into account by policymakers.

Now, policy conditions in this sense will vary not only from policy to policy but also from analyst to analyst. The designation of something as a condition for a policy will in large measure be a matter of analytical perspective or preference. A Marxist and a "realist" will likely differ on the question of what are the conditions for, say, U.S. arms policy. However, it must be recalled that we are concerned at this stage with a mere framework of analysis, a mere form that remains to be filled with substantive contents, a mere language for the formulation of research questions. The suggestion is that it may be useful for the Marxist to phrase questions in terms of the adaptation of classes or leaders or governments or elites to changes in economic conditions and useful for the "realist" to formulate concerns in terms of adaptation to shifting power situations. Both would likely find the adaptation of U.S. arms policy to be less than perfect, and consequently both would profit from concerning themselves with the "stabilizers" of U.S. arms policy. There is emphatically no suggestion of a hypothesis that foreign policies tend, or do not tend, to be objectively rational. The only purpose here is to define the concepts of policy conditions and adaptation as usefully as possible.

Residual Factors   The category of "residual factors" includes all those events that may trigger a process of policy change but are neither changes in conditions nor negative feedback. Anything producing not just individual rethinking but changes in the composition of or in the balance of power within the policymaking system can be a source of policy change. Watergate was a source of change in many U.S. policies, both foreign and domestic. It produced rethinking among individuals as well as shifts in the domestic balance of power and, ultimately, changes in leadership. However, it would be peculiar to argue that Watergate represented a change in the conditions for, say, U.S. human rights policy and that the change in human rights policy from Nixon to Carter amounted to an adaptation to new conditions. Watergate was a cause rather than a reason for this and other changes in policy.

Obviously it is worthwhile to theorize about policy conditions and negative feedback and hence about the likelihood that a policy will become subject to a pressure for change from such sources. This is done by both "realists" and Marxists. Theorizing about residual sources of policy seems to be less meaningful. Hence, our ability to predict pressures for policy change is necessarily limited. This is a reason for focusing on the stabilizers rather than the sources of policy. It is unimportant for that purpose to be able to distinguish in a precise fashion between pressures for adaptation, pressures for learning, and pressures from other sources. The task is to identify the factors making policies more or less sensitive to pressure from any of these sources. These are called "stabilizers" in the present framework.

Stabilizers   The chief purpose of the present framework of analysis, then, is to put the concept of "stabilizer" in its proper perspective. This concept can be defined in the following way:

D5.   A stabilizer of policy P of agent A: any attribute of P, of the ideas on which P is based, of A, or of A's relations with the environment that reduces the effects on P of changes in conditions for P, of negative feedback from P, and of residual factors.

The definition indicates several types of stabilizers. The significant point here is the variety of phenomena that may function as stabilizers and not the typology as such.

The threefold role of stabilizers is shown in Figure 1.2. Stabilizers determine whether an input into the policymaking system from one of the three sources of policy change will set a process of policy change in motion. They determine whether changes in the composition of or the balance of power within this system will lead to rethinking on the part of the system. And they determine whether and how such rethinking will change policy.

The assumption is that in the absence of stabilizers, policies are highly sensitive to new conditions, to negative feedback, and to residual factors. Stabilizers reduce this sensitivity. They may (1) block policy change unless removed, (2) reduce the scope of policy change, or (3) delay policy change.

The three functions of stabilizers are not fully compatible. If change is blocked or delayed, the scope of later change may increase (Jones 1981: 24–25). Change is sometimes the appropriate strategy of conservatives, and lack of change the appropriate stategy of radicals. Whether a phenomenon helps to stabilize a policy may depend on one's time perspective. Unless otherwise stated, this study is concerned with the ability of a policy to remain constant under stress rather than with its ability to survive in part by changing in part. In other words, we assume that we have identified a policy pursued by an actor and ask what will happen to this policy in the short run if there is pressure for change.

The essence of the framework of analysis is thus that policies sometimes come under stress from disturbances and that stabilizers reduce their sensitivity to stress. Obviously, policy stability is sometimes desirable and sometimes not. Sometimes stabilizers should be constructed, and sometimes they should be removed. At other times it is difficult to make up one's mind, because the effect of short-term change or lack of change on long-term stability is difficult to predict.

1.2. SUGGESTIONS FROM THE LITERATURE

The task now is to fill the framework of analysis with theoretical contents—to go from defining concepts to suggesting hypotheses. What phenomena function as stabilizers of foreign policies? Is there an earlier body of theory to draw on?

It is necessary at this point to distinguish between theories of foreign policy substance and theories of foreign policy stability. Foreign policy research is usually concerned with explaining substance; hence the preoccupation with what is commonly called the sources of foreign policy. Obviously, as long as the factors that have given rise to a policy remain constant, the policy will tend to remain constant; all sources of foreign policy may function as stabilizers in this trivial sense. If bipolar East-West confrontation is a source of, say, Norway's membership in NATO, the continuation of this confrontation helps to preserve that membership. A theory of foreign policy substance is by logical implication a theory of foreign policy stability.

What makes the concept of stabilizer worthwhile, however, is that change and lack of change in foreign policy may also be affected by factors accounting for stability without accounting for substance—factors that do not explain why a particular policy has been adopted and yet help to explain why it continues to be pursued. "Bureaucratic inertia" is perhaps the most obvious example: any foreign policy is stabilized by bureaucratic inertia. Long-standing commitment may be another example: to the extent that there is such a commitment to a policy—any policy—that policy is protected against disturbances. Even if most of the East-West confrontation disappeared, Norway might remain in NATO because of bureaucratic inertia, long-standing commitment, and a number of other factors. This study is concerned with developing a theory of foreign policy stability in this restricted sense. Even though most theory of foreign policy and international politics is relevant for the question whether foreign policies will change, much of it is irrelevant for this particular concern.

Several works about change in international relations were published in the early 1980s. It has become common to point out that existing theory fails to account for the problem of change and lack of change. However, the perspective of some recent studies is different from the one adopted in this book.

Change and the Study of International Relations: The Evaded Dimension (1981), edited by Buzan and Jones, is primarily intended to "demonstrate the shortcomings of the way in which change is conceptualized in the contemporary study of international relations" (p. 1). The argument is in large measure concerned with epistemology. Some of the contributors employ a mode of thinking reminiscent of the present framework of analysis (chaps. 11–12), but the book is not concerned with more specific problems, such as the question of how to account for the lack of change in a foreign policy.

Change in the International System (1980), edited by Holsti, Siverson, and George, is for the most part devoted to international system transformation rather than to foreign policy change.[5] To be sure, the two levels are connected. Systemic transformation alters the conditions for foreign policy; the present study deals with the question of why the foreign policy responses may be delayed and incomplete. At the same time, systemic change may be triggered by changes in foreign policy; the present study is meant to improve our understanding of the factors that hinder or facilitate such initiation. Hence, the study of systemic

[5] An exception is George's contribution, to which we will refer when considering the question of the way in which domestic politics may affect the stability of a foreign policy (chapter 2).

transformation and the study of foreign policy stability are linked. However, writings about the former appear to contain little that can be incorporated in a theory of the latter.

Gilpin's *War and Change in World Politics* (1981) stands in a similar relation to the present study. Gilpin argues that the stability of an international system depends on "its ability to adjust to the demands of actors affected by changing political and environmental conditions," and particularly by the differential growth of power (p. 13). He is concerned with accounting for the pressures for change; here, the concern is with their impact on foreign policy.

Why Nations Realign (1982), edited by Holsti, is about change in foreign policy rather than systemic transformation, but the focus is on pressures for change rather than on the factors determining the responses to such pressures. None of the six case studies reported in the volume deals with pressures for change that failed to produce change (pp. 198–99). In fact, the inability of the study to explain the lack of change is emphasized in the book, and its theoretical framework does not include what are here called stabilizers (p. 14).

So much for the literature dealing specifically with the problem of international change. Hints about stabilizers may be found in the vast literature about power politics, integration, and international law and organization. However, three research orientations in particular would seem to carry the promise of exploring the stabilization problem more systematically: the study of comparative foreign policy, of organizational and bureaucratic processes, and of the cognitive aspects of foreign policy. Rather than undertaking the Herculean task of perusing three major fields of study in a search for ideas about stabilizers, I will focus on a single representative work from each orientation—representative both in the sense of surveying or synthesizing much of what has been written and in the sense of itself being a major contribution to the literature.

The Determinants of Foreign Policy Behavior   The concept of adaptation is associated with Rosenau, a Nestor in the field of comparative foreign policy. His concept of adaptation is different from that of the present study, however. According to Rosenau (1981: 38), the foreign policy of a "national society" is adaptive "when it copes with, or stimulates, changes in its external environment that contribute to keeping its essential structures within acceptable limits." Thus, while Rosenau relates adaptation to system maintenance, the above definition of adaptation as policy change in response to changing conditions carries no such overtones.

It has been argued that Rosenau's theory of adaptation "does not discuss the conditions under which any sort of change might occur" and that the theory is therefore "basically static" (McGowan 1974: 36, 38). Rosenau has proposed a well-known set of hypotheses about the relative potency of types of explanatory variables, however.[6] There are chiefly three background variables: size, developed/underdeveloped economy, and open/closed polity. There are five types of explanatory variables: individual, role, governmental, societal, and systemic. Rosenau's hypotheses may be seen as suggestions where to look for stabilizers in different types of states. His reasoning suggests, for example, that stabilizers of U.S. foreign policy are likely to be primarily societal (for example, public opinion) and governmental (for example, bureaucratic inertia). In the Soviet Union and China, Rosenau considers individual-level variables to be more important. Since an individual-level stabilizer is something of a contradiction in terms—if the stability of a policy hinges on individual leaders, the policy is best regarded as unstable—it follows that foreign policy is more difficult to stabilize in the Soviet Union and China than in the United States. Rosenau also believes the significance of systemic variables to be a negative function of size; the main difference between the foreign policy of great and small powers would therefore be that systemic stabilizers (for example, international structures and agreements) are more important for the latter than for the former.

These ideas, even though suggestive, are too general to shed much light on the stabilization of specific policies. Let us turn instead to *Why Nations Act* (East, Salmore, and Hermann 1978), a publication of the CREON project. In this book, seven "perspectives" on how to explain foreign policy behavior are examined. Current knowledge is surveyed, and a number of propositions are developed concerning each perspective. I have searched for hypotheses about stabilizers in this material but have found fewer than expected.[7] This result may suggest that the field of comparative foreign policy has been underconcerned with the problem of change and stability. The following propositions deal with this problem, however.

---

[6] The first version was published in Farrell 1964. A revised version can be found in Rosenau 1980: 115–69. For a clarifying interpretation of Rosenau's hypotheses, see McGowan 1974.

[7] Two of the chapters are about sources rather than stabilizers of foreign policy: those on national attributes and on the international system. In the chapter on situations, the likelihood of change is essentially seen as a function of perceptions (e.g., pp. 188–89); this begs the question of what factors have an impact on perceptions.

1. "The more dogmatic the head of state, the less likely his government is to change its position on a well-established policy" (p. 66).
   Interest in foreign affairs strengthens this effect, and training in foreign affairs weakens it (p. 58).
2. Leader-autonomous decision making groups "will tend more frequently to select behaviors involving change from the government's
   previous position than . . . other decision structures," whereas delegate groups and assemblies "will tend to select behaviors involving
   change less frequently than will other decision structures" (p. 98).
3. "Major successful initiatives would likely be taken by unified
   regimes; failures would be higher for initiatives undertaken by fragmented regimes, when taken at all" (p. 115).
4. In the behavior of A toward B, inertia will predominate unless high
   uncertainty is implied in B's signals toward A. Low uncertainty
   results from heterogeneous but reinforcing signals. Crisis implies
   high uncertainty. Pressure of domestic events may decrease the time
   available for foreign policy decision making and may therefore prevent heterogeneous and reinforcing signals from being noticed (pp.
   161–72).

Proposition 1 concerns the stabilizing effects of certain personality
traits on an individual's foreign policy views. One may argue that this
is irrelevant here. This study is concerned with the ability of policies to
survive such disturbances as leadership changes rather than with the
likelihood that individual leaders will change their views. However, it
may be worthwhile to inquire into the conditions favoring the coming
into power of stabilizing personalities.

Proposition 2 is based on a typology of decision structures. There
are nine types. Of these, one is suggested to be destabilizing and two
to be stabilizing. The reasoning behind the first part of the proposition
is that change is facilitated if the leader decides after discussion with a
group whose members are encouraged to advocate different positions
that do not have to be cleared with some outside body; some European
cabinets are mentioned as examples (p. 80). The reasoning behind the
latter part of the proposition is that decisionmaking by groups or
assemblies consisting of instructed representatives of outside entities
inhibits change, because it is difficult "to find a new option from which
everyone benefits" (pp. 81–83, 98).

Proposition 3 relates foreign policy stability to the domestic political
situation. It suggests that domestic fragmentation renders change in
foreign policy unlikely. Examples mentioned are French policy on
Algeria during the Fourth Republic in comparison with the Fifth and

differences between the Johnson, Nixon, and Ford administrations (pp. 115–16).

Proposition 4 has been pieced together from the chapter on prior behavior as an explanatory factor. It seems to imply the following: if B's policy toward A is unchanged, A's policy toward B is stabilized by the combination of three factors: a multitude of interaction channels, consistency in B's behavior, and full attention by A to all signals from B. However, if there is a change in B's policy toward A, the same factors will tend to hasten change in A's policy. In other words, proposition 4 suggests some factors that protect a policy against stress from residual factors but not against stress from changing conditions or feedback. The proposition is suggestive in its emphasis on the interaction between international structures and domestic information gathering.

Cybernetic Decisions   Allison's *Essence of Decision* (1971) is probably the most widely read work about foreign policy as an organizational and bureaucratic process. A work of a similar orientation but more explicitly concerned with the problem of policy change is Steinbruner's *Cybernetic Theory of Decision* (1974).[8] Steinbruner summarizes much thinking about organizations in the form of the "cybernetic paradigm." He compares the cybernetic paradigm with the "analytic paradigm," which is a variation on the rational actor theme, and compares both paradigms with elements from cognitive process theory. Roughly speaking, the analytic paradigm explains why there is always a tendency to change, and cognitive process theory explains why there is always a tendency to stability. The cybernetic paradigm is more clearly concerned with factors that are capable of accounting for variations in change and stability.

In the analytic paradigm, decisionmaking is a relatively successful, intendedly rational adjustment to changing conditions. New information about central variables produces appropriate subjective adjustments (pp. 25–46). Such sensitivity to the environment implies that no defect in the policymaking system leads to inertia. However, it also implies that environmental stabilizers may be important. A change in the conditions for a policy may fail to change this policy because other aspects of the agent's relations with the environment remain constant.

In cognitive process theory, beliefs are stable at the individual level and "changes in the established structure will be unlikely, short of substantial changes in personnel" (pp. 136–37). One destabilizing factor

---

[8] See Cutler 1981 for a critical analysis of Steinbruner's work.

is suggested, however: structural imbalance in belief systems. Cognitive process theory admits that environment affects perceptions (the "reality principle"); perceived inconsistency can therefore develop, and such structural imbalance may destabilize a belief system (pp. 103–9). Conversely, structural balance may stabilize policies. More about this in the next section.

In the cybernetic paradigm, decision processes are assumed to be characterized by highly focused attention and highly programmed response. These concepts promise to be useful parts of a theory of foreign policy stability.

Highly focused attention means that information is neither rationally considered, as in the analytic paradigm, nor systematically distorted or neglected, as in cognitive process theory. Rather, a few critical variables are carefully monitored. Variation within tolerable ranges is neglected and does not produce change. The "selection" of critical variables is characterized by decomposition of the environment: "Whatever the consequences in the larger environment, decisions . . . are controlled by events within the subsystems" (p. 61). Complex problems are fragmented into specific ones, addressed by separate members of the decisionmaking system and treated sequentially at the top of the system.

Highly programmed response means, among other things, that there exists a preplanned repertory of responses to environmental change. If one of the critical variables takes on a value that is not tolerable, the response is selected from this repertory and is not invented ad hoc.

The cybernetic paradigm thus suggests that we look for stabilizers among standard operating procedures for monitoring the environment, among organizational structures, and among response repertories. Two propositions emerge:

1. The larger the degree of organizational fragmentation, the smaller the number of critical variables, and the larger the range of tolerable values for each such variable, the more stable a policy is likely to be.
2. Knowledge of the critical feedback variables and of the range of tolerable values makes it possible to predict under what circumstances policy will change. Knowledge of the response repertory makes it possible to predict the substance of the new policy.

The difference between the cybernetic and the analytic paradigms is a virtual definition of bureaucratic inertia. It will be suggested later on that such inertia is likely to represent late rather than early stabilization. It takes time to create inertia in policymaking systems.

Cognitive Constraints   The literature about the cognitive aspects of foreign policy is fairly large (for a survey, see Holsti 1976). There are two difficulties with applying it to the problem of foreign policy stability. One is related to the level of analysis. The cognitive process literature is about the beliefs, the images, and the perceptions of individuals. However, as pointed out several times already, this study is not concerned with the stability of the views of individuals; an individual-level stabilizer of foreign policy, to repeat a phrase, is something of a contradiction in terms. Here the concern is with organizational rather than individual thinking, and therefore the relevance of psychological theory is limited.

But it is not nil. As suggested above (section 1.1), beliefs can be ascribed to organizations in two senses: by their being officially adopted, and by their being widely shared. Psychological theory cannot be assumed to be valid in the former case. The latter phenomenon is psychological, however. Assuming that such beliefs can be identified, psychological theory may help us to predict organizational behavior.

There is another problem with applying the cognitive process literature to the problem of foreign policy stability, however. As Steinbruner suggests, there is a tendency for the cognitive analysis of foreign policy to assume beliefs to be stable. A standard work like Jervis's *Perception and Misperception in International Politics* (1976) is first a detailed consideration of the mechanisms bringing about this stability—that is, of the various ways in which cognitive processes tend to confirm and reinforce existing beliefs. Jervis thus provides a powerful analysis of a universal source of inertia in human affairs. Beliefs may change under the impact of discrepant information, however, and there is a need for a theory about the kind of beliefs that are particularly likely, and particularly unlikely, to be stable. What determines how sensitive a particular set of beliefs is to stress from discrepant information?

The question is rarely put in this form in cognitive process theory, it appears. The following propositions may be deduced from Jervis's work, however.

There is first the possibility also mentioned by Steinbruner: inconsistency. Beliefs tend to be consistent. For example, the disadvantages of current policies tend to be disregarded, the necessity of trade-offs is avoided as far as possible, and there is a tendency to assimilate new information to preexisting beliefs (chap. 4). The tendency for beliefs to be consistent is partly due to a mechanism described in the theory of cognitive dissonance: beliefs change after a decision has been made so as to make decision makers "feel certain that they decided correctly even though during the pre-decision period that policy did not seem obviously and overwhelmingly the best." This mechanism provides "added force" to the "power of inertia" (pp. 387–88). By implication, were dissonance nevertheless to remain and consistency not to develop, one common stabilizer of policies would be absent.

This feature may stand out more clearly in Festinger's original formulation of the theory of cognitive dissonance. A fundamental assumption of this theory is that "the presence of dissonance gives rise to pressures to reduce or eliminate the dissonance" (Festinger 1957: 18). If this cannot be achieved by adding new cognitive elements, and if the environmental conditions giving rise to dissonance cannot be changed, a pressure to change one's behavior remains. Dissonance cannot always be avoided or eliminated; "the presence of pressures to reduce dissonance, or even activity directed toward such a reduction, does not guarantee that dissonance will be reduced" (p. 23). Hence, inconsistency in thinking (that is, cognitive dissonance) may remain and is itself a pressure for a change in policy; if this pressure exists already, then less additional pressure is presumably needed to bring about a change in policy than otherwise. One question to be considered later in this book is whether détente among ideological adversaries is bound to be based on inconsistent beliefs and whether this is bound to render détente an unstable policy.

A second hypothesis can be directly quoted from Jervis's work: "those parts of the image that are least central—i.e. the fewest other cognitions depend on them—and least important will change first" (1976: 297). The centrality of a belief in the system of beliefs may affect its stability. Jervis suggests that perceptions of hostility are usually central and that beliefs about an enemy are therefore likely to be stable (p. 299). He also emphasizes that the tightness of the connections between central and peripheral beliefs is important: "When these links are weak, the person will be quicker to change individual beliefs—because his views on one question will not be strongly reinforced by his views on others—but for the same reason an alteration in relatively central beliefs will not bring in its train a series of derived changes" (p. 304).[9]

Third, Jervis points at the importance of the extent to which beliefs can be tested empirically. "The degree to which they provide deduc-

---

[9] An important earlier work in which the connection between centrality and stability is demonstrated experimentally is Rokeach 1968.

tions that can be checked against the available evidence" determines how resistant they are to discrepant information (p. 311).

These suggestions may be put in the form of three propositions:

1. If the beliefs on which a policy is based are inconsistent, the policy is unstable.
2. The more central the belief in a policy is for the belief system of an actor and the more tightly it is connected with other beliefs, the more stable the policy.
3. The more testable the belief in a policy, the less stable this policy.

CHAPTER 2

Foreign Policy Stabilizers: An Inventory

WE WILL NOW set out to make an inventory of foreign policy stabilizers. The starting point is to assume that given a disturbance—a change in conditions, negative feedback, a residual event—the stability of a policy is a function of (1) the sensitivity to the environment, (2) the availability of alternatives, and (3) the costs of change. If new conditions or negative feedback are to change policy, they must be noticed and found to be critical. If a change in policy is to be considered, there must be alternatives. If an alternative is to be chosen, the costs of choosing it must be smaller than the benefits. Stabilizers determine how sensitive the policymaking system is to its environment, the extent to which alternatives are available, and how costly the alternatives are.

A preliminary inventory of stabilizers shown in Figure 2.1 lists thirteen phenomena hypothesized to affect sensitivity, alternatives, or costs. The figure also includes the assumption that costs affect the availability of alternatives: the larger the costs of change, the less likely are preplanned alternatives to exist. The several causal links indicated in the figure will be considered in the rest of this chapter.

In the figure, the stabilizers are grouped in four categories. "Administrative" stabilizers are identified by examining the structure and the mode of operation of the bureaucracy. "Political" stabilizers are identified by studying the domestic politics of foreign policy. "Cognitive" stabilizers may be found in the beliefs on which the policy is based. "International" stabilizers concern the state's external relations. The theory of international relations is in large measure concerned with phenomena that may function as international stabilizers, such as international law, transactions, and power balances. There is also a fairly rich literature about administrative and cognitive factors (see chapter 1). What are here called political stabilizers have attracted less attention in systematic theory. There appears to be a contrast on this point between academic theory and the day-to-day analysis of diplomats and journalists: the former is dominated by bureaucracies, cognitions, and international systems and structures, whereas the latter seems in large measure to be concerned with the role of domestic politics.

Administrative, political, and cognitive stabilizers represent what is

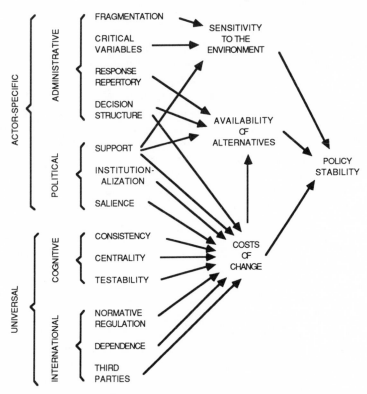

Figure 2.1. Hypothetical determinants of foreign policy stability.

known in foreign policy analysis as "domestic" factors. This is in contrast to the "external," "foreign," "international," or "systemic" factors represented in the present context by the category of international stabilizers.

Another common distinction is the one between "subjective" and "objective" factors. The three cognitive phenomena in Figure 2.1 are subjective in the sense that they refer to features of the actor's own thinking, whereas the remaining variables refer to objective phenomena—administrative arrangements, political conditions, and international structures. The latter can be assumed to have an impact by influencing the perceptions and calculations of actors, but their existence is here presumed to be independent of these perceptions and calculations.[1]

---

[1] In his critique of a preliminary version of the present theoretical sketch, Carlsnaes

A third distinction sets international and cognitive stabilizers against political and administrative ones. The former are universal: they represent mechanisms assumed to operate in the same way always and everywhere. The latter are contingent: the likelihood that they will develop and the way in which they will operate may vary over time and across actors. For example, whereas any foreign policy may be stabilized by international dependence or cognitive centrality, the likelihood of policy stabilization by administrative fragmentation or political institutionalization may vary from one political system to another.

It may be useful to take the further step of distinguishing between two types of contingent stabilizers: those that are policy-general and those that are policy-specific. The former have an impact on the stability of all the policies of a given actor, whereas the impact of the latter may vary from one policy to another. Policy-general stabilizers can be thought of as background variables determining the extent to which policy-specific stabilizers will emerge and have an impact; Rosenau's background variables and the CREON proposition on regime fragmentation are examples (see section 1.2). The stabilizers shown in Figure 2.1 are meant to be policy-specific, but some notes on policy-general stabilizers will be made in the consideration of administrative and political stabilization later on.

At this point the reader may begin to feel that I am arbitrarily singling out some administrative, political, cognitive, and international phenomena, which I call "stabilizers," and that it is artificial to limit the analysis to them to the neglect of other influences on foreign policy. The distinction between stabilizers and other determinants of foreign policy is not arbitrary, however; it was explained in section 1.1, when the framework of analysis was introduced. True, even if the distinction is reasonably clear in principle, it may become blurred in practice; in a study of a particular foreign policy it may not be clear, for example, whether to regard a change in domestic politics as a source of a change

---

(1985: 215) maintains that the cognitive stabilizers and the other three types cannot be categories of the same typology, since they are not "stipulated in terms of the same universe of discourse." The thinking of actors, he writes, "will include—indeed, be dominated by—ideas *about* international, domestic and bureaucratic phenomena; and insofar as this is the case, cognitive factors constitute *second-order* entities in relation to the other types of categories." Similarly, he continues, it seems reasonable to impute cognitive aspects to some of the latter. I obviously have a different view of the feasibility of distinguishing clearly between the beliefs of a given actor about a phenomenon and this phenomenon defined in other terms. However, Carlsnaes is right in pointing out that the cognitive/noncognitive distinction is made at a different level from the other distinctions in the typology. International, political, and administrative stabilizers logically are subcategories of the category of noncognitive stabilizers.

in this policy or as the weakening of one of its stabilizers. However, this ambiguity, which is further considered in section 5.3, is compensated for by the utility of the concept of the stabilizer for theorizing about change and stability in foreign policy as general phenomena. Our object here, to repeat, is to sketch a theory about the factors tending to inhibit change in any foreign policy exposed to a pressure for change from whatever source. The distinction between stabilizers and other determinants of foreign policy is vital to this effort: whereas pressures for change can come from a wide variety of sources, the factors determining their impact appear to be more amenable to generalization.

In what follows, we will consider each of the thirteen stabilizers. The perspective adopted is that of an analyst trying to anticipate what will happen to a policy that is being pursued by a nation, but the reasoning is also applicable (with minor modifications) to the examination of historical cases. The order of presentation will differ from that of Figure 2.1. Some stabilizers, such as international regulation, are likely to emerge early in the life of a foreign policy and therefore to be quite common, whereas others, such as administrative fragmentation, are likely to develop only after a considerable time (see chapter 3). The main pattern is probably from international to cognitive and political to administrative stabilization. Moreover, whereas the international stabilizers are obvious, some of the suggestions about administrative stabilizers may appear less familiar. We will proceed from the most to the least common and obvious: from foreign policy stabilization by international agreement to foreign policy stabilization by administrative structures.

2.1. International Stabilizers

In the course of pursuing a foreign policy, a state may modify its international relations and thereby increase the cost of deviating from it. Suppose—we will continue to use this analogy—that a university professor, who has not been active in politics, is appointed editor of a conservative newspaper.[2] This will likely have three implications for his political behavior: he will be formally committed in his contract to express conservative views; he will grow increasingly used to the

---

[2] I began to use this analogy in 1984 or 1985. In 1986 Hans Zetterberg, an internationally known professor of sociology, was surprisingly appointed editor of *Svenska Dagbladet*, which is the leading conservative newspaper in Sweden. Nothing can be more accidental than any similarity that may obtain between Zetterberg and my imaginary professor.

higher salary associated with his new position; and others will adapt their relations with him to the fact that he is now an active conservative. He will as a result find it to be more costly or risky than before to express nonconservative views. Similarly with nations: a foreign policy may be stabilized by international agreements, by economic dependence, and by relations with third parties.

Normative Regulation   Normative regulation is the traditional method for policy stabilization in international relations. Regulation may take the form of treaties or agreements but also of custom. Norms, whether formal or informal, create expectations that cannot be violated without incurring a cost (Goldmann 1971; Cohen 1981).

There is controversy over the significance of norms in international relations. Some assume the risk of significant sanctions to be so low that the impact of international norms is bound to be small. Others emphasize the rich variety of possible sanctions (Goldmann 1971: 24–26) or argue that threat of punishment is not a prerequisite for norms to be effective (Fisher 1961, 1969).[3] It is difficult to determine who is more nearly correct; historical cases can be mobilized to support either position. Governments, at any rate, evidently believe that it is important what policies do get the protection of international regulation—a large part of international politics consists of bargaining about norms. Whatever the average impact of international regulation, norms are likely to vary in this respect.

In the case of explicit rules, the legal basis may be important. There may be a significant difference in impact between a formal treaty, a nonbinding international document such as a resolution in the United Nations General Assembly, and what is stated in, say, a joint communiqué. The Helsinki Final Act of 1975, the "sanctification of détente" (McWhinney 1978: 148) occupies a gray area between law and nonlaw. It is worth considering whether its impact could have been greater if it had been a formal treaty.

As regards customary norms, their very existence can be seen as a matter of degree. There may be more or less evidence of the existence of a customary norm, and this may affect its impact on policy stability. A Swedish policy of consulting the other Nordic governments on certain matters may be more or less protected by regulation depending on how clear it is that such an inter-Nordic custom exists.

Unilateral international regulation is not a contradiction in terms but a special instance of regulation by custom. By consistently pur-

---

[3] See also the discussion about "focal points" in Schelling 1960: chaps. 3–4.

suing a foreign policy, a country may create international expectations that are costly to violate. Swedish governments keep emphasizing that the policy of neutrality is of Sweden's own choice, and yet it can be maintained that an informal international regulation of this matter has emerged over the years. Unilateral international regulation is difficult to distinguish from the stabilizer here called institutionalization and will be further considered under that heading.

In addition to considering the legal status of an explicit agreement and the amount of evidence of the existence of a custom, it is useful to take into account whether there are contradictions in the normative regulation of the matter with which we are concerned. In the Helsinki Final Act, for example, a tension exists between the principle of non-intervention and the protection of human rights (Schütz 1977: 169–70).

Attention should also be devoted to the problems that may arise when a norm is to be applied to specific situations—difficulties faced by sanctioners trying to determine whether the rule has been violated. Such difficulties may be of two kinds: problems of precision, which result from ambiguity in the rule, and problems of information, which have to do with a lack of reliable data about the situation. The regulation of international violence is often weak in both respects.

It is not necessary to detail further normative regulation as a stabilizer of foreign policies (see Goldmann 1971 for a more extensive consideration). The concept of international regulation has an obvious meaning; its operationalization is relatively easy; the way in which regulation may function as a stabilizer is reasonably clear. These are familiar matters in the analysis of international politics.

Dependence Classical internationalism assumes that interdependence serves to stabilize policies of amity (Lange 1919). In general terms: the pursuit of a policy creates a particular relationship between actor and environment; the actor increasingly depends on continuing this relationship; this dependence helps to stabilize the policy. One problem with this proposition is the ambiguity of its key term, *dependence*. The term is used in writings about international relations to denote anything from North-South dominance to the fact that external events may affect internal conditions. *Interdependence* similarly has a variety of uses (Reynolds and McKinlay 1979; Jones and Willetts 1984). In the present study, the hypothesis that dependence is a stabilizer of foreign policies assumes a narrow definition of the concept.

Suppose that we have decided to conceptualize the "dependence" of an actor in terms of the extent to which attaining his goals depends on the environment (this is not a self-evident assumption; see Dunér 1977: 11–25). Suppose, moreover, that we can calculate what it would cost this actor to attain his goals by three different routes: (1) without interaction with the environment; this will be denoted CA (A for autarky); (2) by interaction with the environment; this will be denoted CI (I for interaction); and (3) by interaction with the environment that, however, is interrupted before the goals are attained; this will be denoted CI/A.

One possibility is to define dependence as the difference between CI and CA. If CI>CA, the actor is independent. If CI<CA, the actor is dependent on the environment, and the size of the difference indicates the degree of dependence. In the extreme case, goal attainment is impossible without interaction, and the actor's dependence is complete. The essence of this concept of dependence is that the actor depends on the environment to the extent that the environment controls what he needs.

Dependence can also be defined as the difference between CA and CI/A. This is relevant under two conditions: CI<CA—that is, the actor can gain from interaction with the environment; and CA<CI/A—that is, it is more costly to interact first and then stop than it would have been not to interact in the first place. The difference between CA and CI/A then represents the additional cost incurred from first attempting interaction and then retreating to autarky. The degree of dependence can be defined as the size of this additional cost. It can be thought of as a measure of structural adaptation: because the actor has adapted to continued interaction, it has become more costly to do without this interaction than it would have been never to engage in it.[4] The difference between CI and CI/A represents what the actor risks losing in the hope of gaining the difference between CI and CA.

If need is the key to the former definition of dependence, adaptation is the key to the latter. The former kind of dependence is not necessarily affected by the amount of interaction between actor and environment. The latter kind of dependence is a consequence of interaction. Dependence in the latter sense is a special instance of dependence in the former sense. It can be called structural precisely because it implies structural adaptation by the actor to continuing interaction.

In the present study a structural concept of dependence is used. That is, an actor's dependence on his relationship with the environment is defined as a function of the cost of goal attainment if the relationship were broken in comparison with the cost of goal attainment if it had

[4] This view of dependence was first suggested to me by Svante Iger; see Iger 1974.

never been established. A wider definition of dependence would have blurred the distinction between sources and stabilizers of foreign policies. Dependence in the sense of need will be conceived of as a source of policy rather than as a stabilizer. "The threat of mutual annihilation has placed the United States and the Soviet Union in a relationship of nuclear interdependence rendering détente inevitable"—this is an argument about dependence in the sense of need. "Increasing economic interdependence serves to preserve détente"—this is an argument about dependence in the stuctural sense. The former is seen here as a statement about a source of détente, and only the latter is regarded as a statement about a stabilizer of it.

Structural dependence cannot be precisely measured, since the measure would have to consist in a comparison between hypothetical situations. As we shall see in Part Two, it is striking the extent to which there has been controversy over whether the Soviet Union has become or can be made dependent on East-West trade; there can hardly be a better example of the difficulty of measuring economic dependence. At the same time, there can hardly be a better example of the importance of trying. Even simple measures like the ratio of imports to consumption and the ratio of exports to production would seem to be worthwhile. More generally, even though a precise answer cannot be given, it is important in any analysis of foreign policy stability to pose the question whether there has developed a significant degree of structural dependence. If we are concerned with, say, the stability of Norway's NATO policy, it is not sufficient to note that Norway was, and is, dependent on the West for protection against the East; this dependence is a source rather than a stabilizer of Norway's foreign policy. We should also consider the extent to which Norway's integration in NATO has rendered other options more costly than they would have been if Norway had not joined NATO in the first place.

Third Parties   The notion of third parties as a stabilizer of foreign policies is taken from traditional power politics reasoning, in which it is generally assumed that the relations between two nations are affected by their respective relations with a third. It became common in the 1970s to conceive of U.S.-Soviet-Chinese relations in this way.[5] According to the theory of structural balance (Harary 1961, 1977; Harary, Norman, and Cartwright 1965; Healey and Stein 1973), some states of such a triad are inherently stable and some inherently unstable.

[5] For attempts at formalization see, e.g., Dittmer 1981 and Goldmann 1979a.

Thus the stability of the policy pursued by an actor toward an object may depend, among other things, on the way in which third parties relate themselves to him and to the object. The theory of structural balance assumes that the state of a bilateral relation can be described as positive or negative. Some patterns of positive and negative relations among actor, object, and third party are stable and others are unstable, according to this theory. The structures shown in Figure 2.2 are thought to be in "structural balance" and are therefore assumed to be inherently stable. In cases I and II, the actor's policy toward an object is stabilized by concern with an enemy third party. In cases III and IV, his policy toward an object is stabilized by concern with an allied third party. All other structures are inherently unstable, according to structural balance theory.

The extent to which the stabilizer here called "third parties" exists may be taken to depend not only on (1) the nature of the relation between actor and third party and on (2) the nature of the relation between third party and object, but also on (3) the weight of the third party. Weight, which is the term used by Riker (1962), is similar to

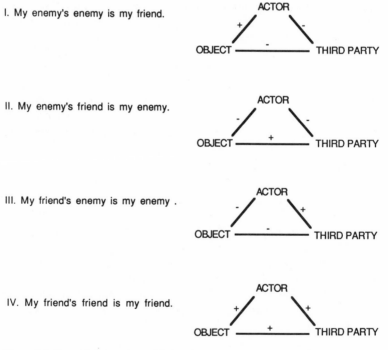

I. My enemy's enemy is my friend.

II. My enemy's friend is my enemy.

III. My friend's enemy is my enemy .

IV. My friend's friend is my friend.

Figure 2.2. Four triads in structural balance.

power. In the present study it denotes the significance to the actor of the third party's relationship to himself and to the object. The importance of the third party as a stabilizer of the actor's policy evidently depends on who the third party is. China is more important as a potential stabilizer of U.S.-Soviet relations than Chad. Precise measurement is impossible, but meaningful judgments can often be made, and it is important to take this aspect into account when exploring the existence of third party stabilization.

2.2. COGNITIVE STABILIZERS

The policy of an organization is based on ideas in two different senses: by the ideas' having been officially adopted, and by their being held by the policymakers as individuals (see section 1.1). The notion that some cognitive structures may help to stabilize a policy is rooted in psychological reasoning. Cognitive stabilizers operate only at the individual level. Hence, the structure of officially adopted beliefs—a foreign policy doctrine, a party program—is relevant only insofar as the official beliefs are also widely shared by the members of the policymaking system.

Whether official beliefs can be taken to reflect individual beliefs is a recurrent bone of contention in foreign policy analysis. The two are not inherently opposed. On the contrary, official and unofficial beliefs are likely to be interdependent. The degree of correspondence is generally unknown, however. Therefore, conclusions about the existence or nonexistence of cognitive stabilizers of foreign policies can hardly avoid having a problematical foundation.

Assume, however, that we do have a basis for making inferences about the unofficial beliefs underlying a policy. There is then reason to consider whether the structure of this set of beliefs is inherently stable. This is so, we shall suggest, if the belief in the policy is consistent, central, and untestable.

Suppose that the university professor who has been appointed the editor of a conservative newspaper expects and is expected to continue the newspaper's policy of advocating the use of nuclear power. Suppose further that nuclear power stations turn out to operate at a loss. The impact of this information on the policy of the newspaper is likely to be smaller if the energy-related beliefs of the editor are internally consistent than if he has long regarded investment in nuclear power as a difficult trade-off between opportunities and risks. The impact is likely to be smaller if the editor views the continued use of nuclear power as essential for the realization of his overall political program than if he thinks that most of what he is striving for can be achieved whether nuclear power is used or not. And the impact is likely to be smaller if his expectations from nuclear power are long-term, abstract, and vague and hence difficult to falsify than if they are short-term, concrete, and specific and include the belief that nuclear power stations will make a profit.

Consistency, centrality, and testability are here assumed to affect policy stability by their impact on the costs of policy change (see Figure 2.1). The costs are psychological (and, indirectly, political, since cognitive and political stabilizers can be assumed to interact); I have borrowed from the literature the hypothesis that it is psychologically more difficult to change consistent and central beliefs than inconsistent and peripheral beliefs, especially if the beliefs cannot be convincingly proven wrong.

Consistency   A fully consistent, policy-related set of beliefs has two features: according to this set of beliefs, the policy is certain to produce the intended result, and it is not thought to have any negative side-effects. Cognitive mapping symbols can be used to demonstrate both aspects. In cognitive mapping, a positive arrow from X to Y means that, in the actor's view, X (or an increase in X) leads to an increase in Y, and non-X (or a decrease in X) leads to a decrease in Y (Axelrod 1976). Consistency in the first-mentioned sense—certainty about the result—is illustrated in the upper part of Figure 2.3. The pursuit of the policy is believed to have a uniformly favorable impact in terms of the objective the policy is intended to serve. All links between policy and goal attainment are believed to be positive. There is no causal route by which the policy is thought to be counterproductive.

The second aspect of consistency is shown in the lower part of Figure 2.3: all side-effects are thought to be favorable.

Consider the view a Swedish peace activist may have of Sweden's arms exports. His main rationale for opposing them is likely to be that weapons tend to produce war and should not be spread around the world; he probably also believes that Swedish arms exports undermine the credibility of Sweden's efforts with regard to peace and disarmament. Suppose, however, that he also accepts the validity of some arguments in favor of exporting arms: domestic arms production improves the credibility of the policy of neutrality; such production assumes export; and the credibility of the policy of neutrality is essential to peace and security. He may believe, in addition, that arms exports have positive side-effects, such as providing jobs and stimulating the domestic development of advanced technology. Thus, his beliefs about

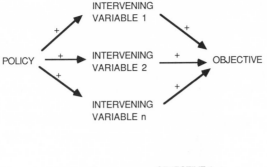

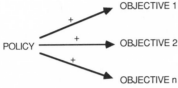

Figure 2.3. Two forms of cognitive consistency.

arms exports are inconsistent in the sense in which this term is used here, and his opposition to arms exports is likely to be more vulnerable than if it had been based on the straight conviction that the export of arms is an obstacle to peace.

Centrality   The belief in a policy may be central or peripheral in the actor's overall belief system. Here, a policy will be regarded as cognitively central to the extent that it is believed to be linked positively to other policies. If the pursuit of policy P1 is thought to facilitate the successful pursuit of another policy P2, then this link between P1 and P2 helps to stabilize P1. The more such links and the stronger they are, the more central and hence the more stable P1.

An adherent of Sweden's present policy of exporting arms to some countries may believe not only that arms exports are essential for maintaining a domestic weapons production and hence for the credibility of the neutrality policy but also that they are important for maintaining the technological level of Swedish industry, for creating jobs, for improving Sweden's balance of trade, and perhaps as a symbol of Sweden's international position and domestic achievements. He may believe, in other words, that several important objectives would be more difficult to attain if the export of arms were to cease. If he does, his support of the policy of exporting arms is likely to be relatively invulnerable to stress from, say, the discovery that Swedish weapons were used in a war somewhere.

Testability   The suggestion that testability be included among cognitive stabilizers is inspired by Jervis's work (see section 1.2). Untestable beliefs are stable because they do not run the risk of being challenged by discrepant information. Jervis demonstrates a number of ways in which a belief may be untestable (1976: 310–15). The most vulnerable beliefs are those predicting definite, observable, short-run consequences. If, on the other hand, anything can be taken to be compatible with a belief, this belief is invulnerable; Jervis's chief example is the well-known "inherent bad faith model," which is presumably a significant stabilizer of hostile policies. In an intermediate category can be found beliefs that, even though testable in principle, can be checked only against evidence that is rarely accessible or against events that rarely occur. Hence, the testability of a belief is a function of (1) the extent to which it can be falsified in principle, and (2) the extent to which relevant evidence is available in practice.

Swedish beliefs about arms exports vary in their degree of testability. The belief that the production of weapons for export provides a significant number of jobs is relatively easy to test and is therefore relatively vulnerable. It may be more difficult to determine the contribution made by the weapons industry to technological development. And the belief that the export of arms undermines Sweden's diplomatic efforts in disarmament is likely to lead a sheltered life (it is difficult to isolate the contribution of single factors to complex social outcomes).

Testability is a difficult concept, and it is different in an important respect from consistency and centrality. Assuming that we know a person's beliefs, nothing prevents us from mapping their degree of consistency and specifying the centrality of single beliefs. Testability, in contrast, is not an objectively observable feature of the belief system's structure but a genuinely subjective matter of how large an impact empirical evidence would have on the believer. This is a reason for excluding the concept of testability from the theoretical sketch.

Testability does seem to be important for understanding policy change and stability, however. As we shall see in Part Two, Soviet détente policy was based in part on the belief that détente would bring rapid and substantial economic gains, and U.S. détente policy was based in part on the belief that détente would imply global Soviet restraint. These beliefs proved to be sufficiently testable to render détente vulnerable to negative feedback on both sides—more vulnerable than if détente had merely been expected to contribute to improved relations and a peaceful development in the long term. It would be questionable to exclude this phenomenon from consideration. Including it in the theoretical sketch suggests that it be put on the agenda of the analyst concerned with a problem of foreign policy stability, even though judgments about the testability of the beliefs on which a policy is based cannot be but relatively speculative.

2.3. POLITICAL STABILIZERS

The possibility that a foreign policy is protected against pressure for change by domestic politics will now be considered. It is common to assume domestic politics to be important in accounting for stability and change in foreign policy. The failure to adapt or to learn is due, analysts often feel, to domestic politics. Conversely, overreaction and vacillation often seem to be due to domestic politics. The object of this section is to make these notions more precise.

Recall that the factors usually called "domestic" in foreign policy analysis comprise more than what is meant by "domestic politics" in this study. The "domestic" factors are generally taken to include the beliefs on which foreign policies are based as well as the governmental apparatus by which they are implemented, monitored, and revised. In the present study, domestic politics refers to neither of these. It is used in the narrow sense of competition for power and leadership, and the present section is concerned with the effects of this competition on the stability of foreign policies.

At one extreme, a foreign policy has developed into a national dogma; heresy would be a heavy burden in the competition for leadership and power and is, therefore, unlikely to occur. At the other extreme, a policy has just been adopted over major opposition; it is not too late for change, and the opposition exploits every new piece of evidence, every sign of negative feedback, as a weapon in the power struggle. The objective, in essence, is to make a more careful comparison between these two situations.

It is necessary to start almost from scratch. The complaint about a lack of systematic research on the domestic politics of foreign policy is common. Cohen talks of a disciplinary failure of political science (1973: 24), and other authors appear to agree (Hughes 1978: xi; Wallace 1971: 40; Rosenau 1967: 3, 1969: 4). Wallace's small book *Foreign Policy and the Political Process* (1971) uncommonly gives the problem a reasonably extensive treatment at the theoretical level; it is a survey of the field rather than theory proper, however. With the exception of the CREON publication quoted above (section 1.2), no work on the theory of foreign policy has been found in which the role of domestic politics in the narrow sense is given more than cursory attention.

Can suggestions for such a theory be found in the literature about individual countries? We will briefly consider a small part of the works on the domestic "context" or "sources" of the foreign policy of the three countries with which Part Two is concerned: the United States, West Germany, and the Soviet Union.

The United States   The classic is Almond's *American People and Foreign Policy* (1950). Almond sees foreign policy primarily as the result of the views held by different foreign policy elites and of their debate before the "attentive public." There are four types of elite: political, administrative or bureaucratic, interest, and communication. Almond is concerned in particular with the degree of consensus among the elites and with the existence of competing foreign policies (pp. 136–43).

It is common for studies of the domestic politics of U.S. foreign policy to focus on the attitudes held or the policies advocated by bearers or segments of public opinion, the degree of consensus among them, and their actual impact on foreign policy. For example, Cohen (1973) has studied perceptions of public opinion in the State Department, Rosenau (1963) the role of "national leaders," and Hughes (1978) the factors accounting for the variability in the influence of mass opinions, parties, and interest groups on foreign policy. The oft-quoted volume *Domestic Sources of Foreign Policy* (Rosenau 1967), although theoretical in intent, is primarily devoted to the United States; the table of contents reveals that the volume follows the convention of focusing on foreign policy attitudes, mass communication, interest groups, and the like (see also Rosenau 1961).

One author explicitly relates domestic politics to the problem of foreign policy change. In an essay on "Domestic Constraints on Regime Change in U.S. Foreign Policy" (1980b), George stresses the need for "policy legitimacy." To be able to conduct a coherent, consistent, and reasonably effective long-range policy, the president must achieve a "fundamental and stable national consensus," he argues. His main concern is with the difficulty of achieving this kind of legitimacy. One difficulty is the need to change previous policy: "Once a foreign policy is established and achieves a degree of policy legitimacy . . . it is difficult for policymakers to contemplate replacing that policy with one that is radically different."

In the vast literature about the making of U.S. foreign policy, there is no lack of examples of the use of foreign issues for purposes of domestic politics (see Hallenberg 1986 for a recent survey). However, it appears uncommon to theorize about the way in which the stability of American foreign policies is affected by their being used as tools in the struggle for power and leadership, which is our present concern. Cohen has published an essay considering, among other things, the use of the Cold War and other international issues "as a technique of power manipulation—i.e., as a means of mobilizing or organizing support for the acquisition and the exercise of political power" (1969: 127–28). He emphasizes the preliminary nature of the effort.

West Germany   In a work published in the 1950s, Deutsch and Edinger set out to study "some of the main background conditions of West German foreign policy making." They focus on the interplay of mass opinion and elites with an emphasis on the prevailing consensus and its limits and on the distribution of influence among the elites (1959, esp. pp. vii, 8). The approach is similar to Almond's, and some of Almond's concepts are used.

Hanrieder, in his extensive writings on West German foreign policy, is especially concerned with the interaction between foreign policy and domestic politics. His reason for considering domestic factors is his interest in motivation rather than in the political process, however. Consensus is one of his key concepts; he sees a minimum degree of consensus as a prerequisite for action. The degree of consensus can be ascertained approximately on the basis of "the expressed attitudes and conduct of political parties and relevant pressure groups," he writes. In practice, Hanrieder devotes most of his analyses to party politics, with merely occasional references to industry and labor (1967: esp. 2, 9, 1970: chap. 4).

Verwaltete Aussenpolitik, a collection of articles published in 1978, devotes considerable attention to the factors that are here called administrative. It also considers the role of politics in the narrow sense, however. As in Hanrieder, politics is equated with party politics. A contribution by Kuper starts out with the notion of "foreign policy conception" (*Aussenpolitische Konzeption*), defined as a hierarchical system of goals and strategies giving a relatively consistent structure to a foreign policy. This conception has two functions: an internal function of aggregating a multitude of interests into "a system of goals that can be legitimized as broadly as possible," and an external function of reducing the complexity of the message directed to the environment. A foreign policy conception may change but may also freeze and "finally become a doctrine" (Kuper 1978: 242). The suggestion that a government may have to construct a conception in order to put together a domestic coalition and the notion that this conception may freeze into a doctrine is reminiscent of George's argument about policy legitimacy.

The Soviet Union   Standard contributions to the literature about the domestic politics of Soviet foreign policy include an essay originally published in 1966 by Aspaturian (1971), and one originally published in 1969 by Dallin (1980). In a more recent volume, *The Domestic Context of Soviet Foreign Policy* (1981), the contributions by Dallin and the volume's editor, Bialer, are particularly helpful.

The extent to which Soviet politics is sui generis and needs a theory of its own is debatable (Dallin 1981: 340–44). Some Western analysts assume that in the Soviet Union, just as in the West, different elites advocate different foreign policies. In fact, a feature of the Western literature about the USSR was for a time a tendency to take conflict for granted and not to pursue a question commonly considered in the literature on the United States and West Germany: the extent of the national consensus.

One line of thought starts with the observation that a foreign policy may affect different groups differently. Aspaturian (1971, esp. 530–47) takes into consideration the following "social and institutional groups": the party apparatus, the state bureaucracy, heavy industry, light industry, the armed forces, the cultural-professional-scientific groups, and the consumers. The groups will disagree over the policy because of its differential impact, and the special interests are in turn exploited by the participants in the power struggle within the Kremlin. This, in Aspaturian's view, is how foreign policy is drawn into the domestic politics of the Soviet Union. The model leaves little room for consensus.

Dallin (1980) stresses the extent to which cleavages over foreign policy have been congruent with cleavages over other matters; it is possible to talk of a left and a right, and Dallin emphasizes their continuity. He cautions us that what looks like consensus often conceals bitter debates; "it is certainly a safer course to assume the existence at all times of significant disagreements in the Soviet elites over objectives and policies" (p. 47). A central issue is whether the left-right cleavage reflects group interests, as proposed by Aspaturian, or whether it cuts across social and institutional lines; Dallin has failed to arrive at a definite conclusion on this point, which is controversial among Sovietologists (1981: 375–79).[6]

Bialer (1981: 414–15) suggests that some differences over foreign policy can be traced back to particularistic interests and some to orientations that cut across organizational lines. He is, however, more concerned than Aspaturian and Dallin with the possibility of a consensus over foreign policy. And Adomeit (1981: 76–78), in contrast to Aspaturian and Dallin, suggests that decision making in the Soviet system, at least in crises, is "shaped much more by consensus on political issues and operational principles than by domestic conflict." This is due to three reasons: ideology, common background and experience among leaders, and a constant reassessment of the validity and effectiveness of the Politburo's modus operandi. In the 1980s Western Sovietologists have tended to turn from a "conflict approach" to a "revised totalitarian approach," in which foreign policy is assumed to be under the full control of a basically consensual Politburo (Nygren 1986).

Still, a difference between the literature on the USSR and that on the other two countries appears to be the greater emphasis of the former on the role of foreign policy as a tool in the domestic competition for power. Aspaturian stresses this aspect, as does Armstrong (1980). Dallin suggests the importance of considering cleavages in the elite due to power struggles, factionalism, and personality conflicts (1980: 39). Bialer maintains that foreign policy and its successes are nowadays "used to an increased degree and probably play a greater role in the legitimation of the position of the leader and leadership among the elites and legitimation of the regime in society at large" (1981: 414). There is to my knowledge no major work going beyond case studies and very general observations; there seems indeed to be a need for more elaborate theory about this aspect of politics, both in the Soviet Union and generally.

WE ARE CONCERNED in the present study with merely one aspect of the domestic politics of foreign policy—the possibility that a foreign policy may be protected against pressures for change by being embedded in domestic politics. Three dimensions of this "embedment" are rather obvious and are reflected in the literature on individual countries:

---

[6] For a brief survey of the interest group controversy among Sovietologists, see Hoffmann and Fleron 1980: 33–34. See also section 7.3.3 of the present book.

1. The degree of institutionalization, or roughly the extent to which the government has become committed to pursue the policy.
2. The degree of support, or roughly the extent to which the various actors in domestic politics support, are indifferent to, or oppose the policy.
3. The degree of salience, or roughly the significance of the issue in the domestic power struggle.

If a foreign policy has become an institution, if there is national consensus over it, and if the issue is highly significant in domestic politics, then the pressure for change needs to be substantial in order to bring about a deviation from previous policy. Institutionalization, support, salience—these are the dimensions of the domestic politics of foreign policy with which the present study is concerned.

Note that institutionalization and support are considered to be separate phenomena: it is possible for an institution to be controversial and for consensus to exist over a policy that is not (yet) an institution. The relationship between institutionalization and support may be complex: institutionalization seems likely to increase support (there is, hypothetically, an increasing acceptance of the policy as inevitable or natural), but active opposition can conceivably increase rather than decrease institutionalization—strengthen rather than weaken the government's commitment to the policy. Hence, opposition to a policy may be counterproductive.

Salience is similarly regarded as separate from both institutionalization and support. That a policy is highly institutionalized does not necessarily mean that the issue is politically salient. Moreover, both consensus and controversy may exist over both salient and nonsalient issues. Salience is unlikely to have a direct effect on policy stability, but it is likely to reinforce the effects of institutionalization and support. See Figure 2.4!

The concept of salience forms a bridge between the present notion of political stabilization and the CREON proposition cited previously (section 1.2) and that suggests in effect that major policy change is more likely to be initiated by unified than by fragmented regimes. A unified regime, virtually by definition, is one in which single issues are insignificant for the domestic power struggle. Hence, the CREON proposition may be taken to imply that the degree of institutionalization and support have a larger impact if the regime is fragmented than if it is unified.

Recall the university professor who is now editing a newspaper

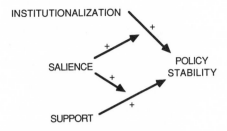

Figure 2.4. The political stabilizers.

advocating, among other things, the use of nuclear power. The likelihood that the newspaper will continue to do this depends, it is now suggested, on whether a pronuclear policy has become institutionalized as part of the paper's political profile. It depends on whether this policy is supported not just by the editor but generally among owners and staff. And it depends on whether there is an ongoing power struggle within the newspaper building in which the nuclear power issue is salient.

Institutionalization   The notion that policies may be more or less institutionalized assumes not only that the members of a political system expect consistency from their governments but also that these expectations are stronger and more widespread with regard to some policies than with regard to others. If a policy exists on an issue, the government is expected not to act ad hoc but to pursue this line of action unless there are good reasons to do otherwise, and the more institutionalized the policy is, the better the reasons for deviation have to be. In other words, the more widespread and the stronger the expectation that a policy will continue to be pursued, the more institutionalized this policy. A minimum degree of institutionalization is implied in the very concept of policy; at the other extreme there is the unshakeable institution to which the government is expected to adhere, come what may.[7]

Institutionalization, like international and cognitive stabilizers, is assumed to affect policy stability in two ways, one direct and the other indirect. The direct effect is to increase the political cost of deviating

[7] It has been pointed out to me that the term *institutionalization* may suggest the establishment of organizations and that this is peculiar, since the workings of the government apparatus is here seen as a matter of administrative rather than political stabilization. My intention, however, has been to use the term *institution* not in the narrow sense of an organization but in the broad sense of an established practice or custom.

from previous policy. Obviously, the larger this cost, the more pressure needed to bring about a deviation, other things being equal. The indirect effect is to reduce the likelihood that alternative policies are considered in advance, that is, the likelihood of contingency planning. The higher the political cost, the more likely the presumption that contingency planning is a waste of time.

The effects of institutionalization are inherent in its definition: policies imply obligations, institutionalization strengthens obligations, and obligations are not violated without cost. The causes of institutionalization are less self-evident. What factors tend to institutionalize a policy?

Three ways in which a policy may be institutionalized will be suggested here: by policy declarations, by custom, and by investment. These are three plausible indicators of institutionalization, so to speak. The ways in which they may influence policy stability is shown in Figure 2.5.

Policy declarations are commitments. Commitments reduce one's freedom of action. Why do governments make policy declarations?

There may be several reasons. Commitment improves credibility, and this is important when a policy can succeed only to the extent that others are convinced of its stability (for example, policies of deterrence, alliance, and neutrality). Moreover, a policy declaration may be necessary as a directive to one's foreign policy apparatus. It may be a response to a demand for action. It may be a method for consensus building, for legitimation, as suggested by Kuper's notion of "foreign policy conceptions." A government may even be compelled to commit itself more strongly than it would have preferred because of being under attack from the opposition; this is one reason why opposition may be counterproductive.

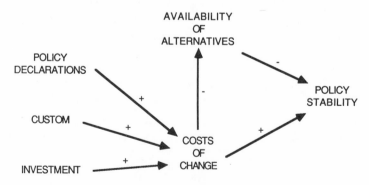

Figure 2.5. A model of policy institutionalization.

The degree of commitment likely varies with the authority of the official making the declaration (the president or an anonymous spokesperson?), the frequency of such declarations (time after time, year after year, or on a single occasion?), and the context in which the declaration is made (the state of the union address or an aside at a news conference?).

Suppose, however, that the policy satisfies some minimum requirement for commitment in terms of authority, frequency, and context. Then a fourth aspect becomes important: the very wording of the declarations. A policy declaration may be anything from a self-imposed categorical imperative to the mentioning of a mere possibility. To specify the scale from one to the other is an important task for research on the verbal aspect of politics (see Graber 1976 for a survey of this field).

One question is overdue at this stage: Can differences between political systems really be ignored? Whereas it seems obvious that it is costly to violate a commitment in democracies, this may not be the case in nondemocracies, where continued office-holding may be less dependent on consistency and no open opposition stands ready to exploit any inconsistency. The difference is not absolute; there is no certainty of punishment in democracies, and punishment may occur in nondemocracies. The difference in degree may be substantial, however. Institutionalization by policy declaration may be easier to avoid and—the other side of the coin—more difficult to bring about in nondemocracies than in democracies. Commitment may be a less effective stabilizer in nondemocracies than in democracies. However, since its effectiveness is unlikely to be nil even in a nondemocracy, it is probably worthwhile to consider the extent to which, say, the Soviet government has committed itself to détente, world revolution, or whatever.

So much for policy declarations. It is assumed here that not only declarations but also behavior patterns may create expectations of consistency and continuity. By this assumption, an action is more costly, and therefore less likely, if it contradicts a well-established custom than if it does not. Institutionalization by custom is the mechanism that makes policies self-reinforcing: the mere fact that a policy is being pursued increases the likelihood that it will continue to be pursued. Such stabilization of a policy may or may not be intentional. The actor may be faced with a dilemma common in politics: a trade-off may be necessary between the short-term advantages of a line of action and the long-term disadvantages of becoming increasingly tied to this line of action. Institutionalization by custom may even be inadvertent:

the actor may find himself gradually tied to a policy he had never intended to pursue in the first place.

Identifying institutionalization by custom carries a problem of validity. Behavior patterns are interesting because deviations may lead to sanctions. However, it may be uncertain whether that which is a pattern to us observers is also perceived as a pattern by actors and sanctioners. A way out may be to study justifications of actions rather than the actions themselves.[8]

Some policies require the investment of resources into physical capabilities or administrative agencies for their implementation. This is a third way of institutionalizing a policy. It too may create expectations of consistency and continuity. Moreover, investment implies that policy changes will carry the cost of not using an existing asset, which may in turn increase the political cost.

A major example of this kind of policy stabilization is military strategy: weapons systems tend to stabilize strategic doctrines. An example of stabilization by organization is the creation of an agency to administer a new welfare system. Generally speaking, policy stabilization by investment may play a smaller role in foreign policy than in defense and social policy.

Institutionalization has hitherto been regarded as a matter merely of domestic politics. Declarations, custom, and investment may create expectations abroad as well as at home, however. The potential sanctioners may be foreign as well as domestic. The institutionalization of a foreign policy may be seen as unilateral international regulation (section 2.1). So-called foreign policy doctrines, for example, may commit a country internationally as well as domestically. The phenomenon we call institutionalization stands on the border between international and domestic stabilizers of foreign policy. It is not always possible to keep the international and domestic aspects apart. Institutionalization, in addition to being a dimension of domestic politics, may also be seen as a special type of international regulation.

Support   Perfect consensus over a foreign policy—an unrealistic ideal type—means that everybody actively supports this policy. The student of foreign policy stability is concerned with deviations from this ideal type. There are several dimensions to consider.

1. Amount of support and opposition: At the individual level we may conceive of a scale from active positive support via indifference to

[8] See Goldmann 1971 for the logic of identifying custom by justifications and for an example of such an investigation.

active negative support, that is, to active opposition. It is misleading to apply this scale at the aggregate level and to regard the net support for a policy as the amount of support minus the amount of opposition. Zero on this scale would represent two radically different situations— two quite different deviations from perfect consensus: indifference on the one hand and polarization on the other. These two situations may have different implications for policy stability. Therefore positive and negative support will be regarded as separate variables—as two different scales along which reality may differ from the ideal type of perfect consensus.

2. The substantive distance between government and opposition: There is greater consensus if opponents advocate marginal change in government policy than if they propose a radically different course. It goes without saying that it is difficult to "measure" the substantive distance between policy proposals, but this aspect of the lack of consensus is vital and must be included in the study of domestic politics as a stabilizer of foreign policy.

3. The weight of supporters and opponents: Even very enthusiastic support or very radical opposition by a small number of marginal activists may lack significance. The crucial question concerns the main forces in domestic politics: key actors like the chief political parties and interest organizations, perhaps the leading media, maybe public opinion. When considering deviations from perfect consensus, the political weight of those who deviate must be taken into account.

This brings us to a definition according to which the amount of support for a foreign policy is a function of the amount of positive support and opposition from each of the political forces in society, the contribution of each being weighted in terms of both political importance and substantive distance. No quantitative index can be developed on the basis of this definition. The definition is nevertheless useful in setting priorities for the student of foreign policy support: the most important thing to do is to study the policies advocated by the chief political actors and perhaps to examine public opinion; if they oppose government policy, it is important to consider the extent to which their alternatives deviate from it. The question of who the "chief political actors" are will soon be considered.

The extent of positive support and opposition may affect policy stability in more than one way (Figure 2.6). The most obvious suggestion is: The more positive support for a policy, the greater the political cost of not pursuing it and, consequently, the more stable the policy. Another obvious suggestion is: If opposition to a policy exists, there likely exists at least one preplanned alternative, and this, other things being equal, helps to reduce policy stability; the larger the substantive distance between the lines of action advocated by the government and the opposition, presumably, the larger the scope of plausible policy change. In less abstract terms: the existence of strong, active opposition to a policy implies that a shift in government, or in the domestic balance of power, is more likely to lead to a shift in policy than would otherwise have been the case.

A third suggestion can be added: opposition implies that there are some who have an interest in taking note of, and spreading information about, changes in the conditions for the policy as well as negative feedback, and this increased sensitivity to the environment in turn implies a decrease in policy stability. The stability inherent in very selective perception of the environment is less likely to obtain if there is opposition than if everybody supports the policy or is indifferent.

This last suggestion needs to be qualified in one respect, however. The relationship between the amount of opposition and the sensitivity to the environment may not be linear. In the complete absence of opposition, a policy is never questioned. Now, if the underlying ideas never need to be made explicit and defended against criticism, the policy may be more vulnerable to new information than if its supporters have been vaccinated by intermittent challenges. Major opposition against a policy is certainly likely to be destabilizing, but perfect consensus may

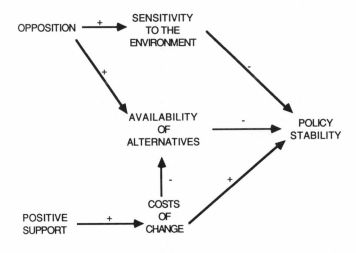

Figure 2.6. The effects of support and opposition.

not be the most stabilizing condition; a modest amount of opposition may be more stabilizing than perfect consensus.[9]

As can be seen in Figure 2.6, opposition is suggested to affect policy stability only by its effects on the sensitivity to the environment and on the availability of alternatives. It is not suggested to reduce the cost of policy change. To be sure, the more opposition, the less positive support; the two are necessarily negatively correlated. From this point of view opposition does reduce the cost of change. However, every participant in and observer of politics knows that the very fact of opposition may increase the cost of giving in; strong opposition may freeze government policy. This is one more way in which opposition may be counterproductive, in addition to its effect on institutionalization suggested previously. A further complication is that if opposition exists from both the left and the right to a center policy, the two may cancel each other out; French policy in Algeria during the Fourth Republic would seem to be an example. No simple relationship can be postulated between the amount of opposition to a policy and the cost of deviating from it.

It is now necessary to comment on the difficulty of determining the relative weight of the actors in a political system and of public opinion. We may begin with Almond's typology of elites and distinguish between political, interest, and communication elites (Almond 1950: 139–41).[10] Such elites presumably exist in all political systems. However, their concrete manifestations and their relative significance for foreign policy may vary. There is, moreover, the problem of how to evaluate the significance of mass attitudes. The role of public opinion is clearly marginal in some political systems; in others it may or may not be important. Almond suggests, on the one hand, that the "moods, interests, and expectations" of the masses "set limits on the discretion of their representatives," including the interest organizations and the media, but, on the other hand, that the American foreign policy mood "will follow the lead of the policy elites if they demonstrate unity and resolution" (pp. 88, 139).

As pointed out, the obvious research strategy for the student of the stability of a particular foreign policy is to begin with the fundamentals: what positions do the chief political actors or forces take on this policy? An answer to this question is likely to improve considerably his

[9] I am indebted to Merrick Tabor for having reminded me of this possibility.

[10] Almond's scheme also includes administrative elites, but they will be considered in section 2.4.

ability to explain and predict what will happen to the policy in case of pressure for change. He may go on to include additional political forces in his study; this will permit more precise and detailed analysis, but the returns are likely to be diminishing. His key problem is how to identify the chief political forces and not how to include everything.

Suppose first that he is concerned with a parliamentary democracy like West Germany. Central features of this type of political system are strong and centralized political parties, a strict division between government and opposition, close links between parties and interest organizations, and consistent political relations between the parties and some of the media. In this case the study of the main political parties must be given the highest priority. The differences and similarities between their policies are likely to reflect prevailing trends in the country at large; it would not be grossly misleading to interpret bipartisanship as an indication of a national consensus. The next step, if it is possible and necessary to go deeper, may be to explore differences within the parties and the positions taken by the main interest organizations. Further down on the list would be the media as well as public opinion as reflected in polls, demonstrations, and ad hoc movements. However, the central focus should remain on the parties, as seems generally to be the case in the literature on the domestic politics of West German foreign policy.

The priorities are less clear as regards the more complex and loosely structured political system of the United States. The positions advocated by parties and candidates for office are probably less representative in this case. What can be done in a study limited to the most obvious aspects of politics is probably less informative with regard to the United States than with regard to a country like West Germany.

It is also difficult, although for other reasons, to explore the amount of consensus over foreign policies in the Soviet Union. Here the difficulty is due less to complexity and loose structure than to invisibility. The nonspecialist must remain content with taking note of the results reached by expert scholars wrestling with the analysis of the domestic politics of Soviet foreign policy.

Salience The stabilizing impact of institutionalization and support depends on the political salience of the issue, according to the present theoretical sketch. On this assumption, even a highly institutionalized and consensual policy is vulnerable to disturbances if the actors in domestic politics deem the issue to be politically trivial. If they consider the issue to be politically salient, it matters more the extent to which a policy has become institutionalized as well as whether it is consensual or controversial. To continue with Scandinavian examples, both the policy of neutrality and the policy of consulting with Nordic governments are highly institutionalized and consensual in Sweden; however, whereas everybody in Swedish politics takes it for granted that there would be major repercussions in domestic politics if a political party were to opt out of the consensus over neutrality, the implications of a change in position on Nordic consultations are certainly assumed to be less far-reaching. More is at stake in domestic politics with regard to neutrality than in the case of Nordic consultations.

As the examples make clear, salience is not here equated with prominence in political controversy. Issues like the Swedish policy of neutrality are holy cows—they are noncontroversial and yet politically significant. The salience of such issues is latent rather than manifest, so to speak, but the effect on policy stability may be the same. Conversely, all widely debated issues may not be equally important from the point of view of policy stability. Salience in the sense of amount of controversy is not what we are after.

Instead, political salience will be defined here in the following way. Coalition formation is determined not only by the distribution of power but also by positions on issues. As is sometimes suggested in the literature on Soviet foreign policy, issues may be used for building coalitions and creating cleavages. Conversely, positions on issues set limits to possible coalitions and cleavages. The more important an issue is for determining coalitions and cleavages, the greater its salience. Hence, the more a given pattern of coalitions and cleavages would be affected by an actor's changing his position on an issue, the more salient this issue. By this definition, issues may be debated without being salient; more important, issues may be salient without being debated.

Salience, according to this view, is a disposition, a potential, a conditional prediction. It is similar in this respect to the concept of power. Every student of political power knows the difficulty of operationalizing such a concept: there are grave problems with inferring power as a potential both from capabilities and from the actual exercise of power (Goldmann 1979b). The rough equivalents of these indicators in the study of salience are the allocation of attention on the one hand and actual changes in the pattern of coalitions and cleavages on the other; both have problems.

Attention may be measured by content analysis and by survey research. The problem, of course, is that attention is also a function of controversy. As has just been emphasized, controversy does not correspond to salience in the present sense. Attention is a risky indicator of salience because it may make us overestimate the salience of controversial issues and may in particular make us underestimate the salience of consensual issues.

A possible remedy in content analysis is to examine documents intended to give an overall view of everything important, regardless of whether there is controversy or not: the election platforms of Western political parties, or the secretary general's report to a congress of the Communist party of the Soviet Union (CPSU), for example. The proportion of such documents devoted to an issue does not reflect its salience precisely, of course, but the relationship may be closer than in other political texts. An additional possibility is to take into account the extent to which the issue is treated in a polemical or nonpolemical fashion: the more polemical the context, the more attention data may exaggerate the salience of the issue.

The other main approach to the empirical study of political salience is to examine changes in the pattern of coalitions and cleavages that have taken place, or debates about the possibility of such changes, and the role played in these events and debates by the issue with which one is concerned. It is obviously problematic to generalize about the salience, and particularly about the nonsalience, of an issue on such a basis. However, such research may be a useful complement to the conclusions drawn on the basis of attention data.

2.4. ADMINISTRATIVE STABILIZERS

The administration of a policy is here taken to encompass four tasks: intelligence, planning, decisionmaking, and implementation. Policy conditions and feedback need to be monitored; this is the object of intelligence. Options need to be prepared; this is the essence of planning. Decisions may have to be made about whether and how to modify the policy; the making of such decisions is here regarded as an aspect of the administration of the policy (but not the competition over their substance, which is politics). A policy, finally, needs to be implemented.

The suggestion that administrative phenomena may function as stabilizers rests on the assumption or observation that the tasks of intelligence, planning, decisionmaking, and implementation are sometimes carried out in a way that inhibits change. "Bureaucratic inertia"—this expression may be used as a synonym of administrative stabilization. Since bureaucratic inertia has pejorative overtones it may be necessary to repeat that policy stability is neither good nor bad in itself. Bureaucratic inertia may render rational adaptation and learning difficult, but it may also help to protect a policy against irrational or irrelevant change. Bureaucratic inertia may be a problem or an irritant but also an insurance against arbitrary vaccillation and irrational overreaction.

The absence of bureaucratic inertia would imply the following:

1. Changes in policy conditions and negative feedback are discovered immediately.
2. Alternatives have already been prepared or are promptly invented.
3. A decision to change policy can easily be made.
4. This decision is fully implemented without delay.

Administrative stabilization leads to deviations from this ideal type. The suggestions about to be made about the kind of administrative phenomena likely to produce this effect incorporate some insights from the literature about organization processes as well as the CREON proposition about decision structures (section 1.2). "Bureaucratization" will be suggested to imply an increasing organizational fragmentation, increasingly narrow standard operating procedures for what is critical when monitoring the environment, an increasingly limited response repertory, and an increasingly cumbersome decision process.

Consider again the conservative newspaper and its pronuclear policy. This policy, it is now suggested, will tend to be stable if there is a division of labor among the staff of the paper on energy-related matters (one member reports on science and technology, another on the economy, a third on environmental issues; one member specializes on foreign policy, another on national issues, a third on local matters). It will tend to be stable if there are standard operating procedures to the effect that, say, information from antinuclear groups is systematically disregarded. It will tend to be stable if no consideration has been given to what a different policy might be like. And it will tend to be stable if a change in policy can be obtained only by means of bargaining between adherents of different views within the board and the staff, and only with the consent of all concerned.

Bureaucratization in this sense is not a necessary concomitant of administrative growth. Growth does necessitate fragmentation and standardization, and it does complicate planning and decisionmaking. At the same time, however, a large organization has a greater capacity for intelligence and planning than a small one. There is more reason to be concerned with the possibility of bureaucratic inertia in Washington and Moscow than in, say, Jerusalem or Stockholm; size is important. The relationship between size and inertia is complex, however; the tension between increased administrative capability and increased bureaucratization will be considered in this section.

In what follows, the focus is on intelligence, planning, and decision-making. Implementation will not be considered. This limitation results from our concern with foreign policies rather than policies in general. Implementation research has mostly been devoted to large programs in medicare, education, social welfare, and the like (Municio 1982 is a useful survey). Many of us seem to have taken for granted that implementation is less problematic in foreign policy and that a decision to modify previous policy is unlikely to be seriously distorted by foreign ministry officials.

This assumption is reflected in the fact that, in the present theoretical sketch, policy change is seen as an intendedly rational decision. The intervening variables—sensitivity to the environment, availability of alternatives, costs of change—represent conditions for decision-making. A phenomenon is assumed to function as a stabilizer by working on these variables. There is no simple way of incorporating implementation in this framework.

It is uncertain how serious a limitation this is. Empirical research on foreign policy implementation is needed. Implementation may be more important for explaining the outcome in some foreign policy issue areas than in others: quite important, perhaps, in matters of foreign economic policy; rather unimportant, perhaps, in "high politics." In the present study, the empirical focus is on tension and détente in recent East-West relations, and the question of implementation is probably less important for the analysis of this problem than in the case of health, education, or foreign aid policy.

Two of the four administrative stabilizers in the theoretical sketch are structural in the sense that they concern the structure of the administrative apparatus: fragmentation and decision structure. Two are substantive in the sense that they concern the substance of what the apparatus is doing: critical variables and response repertory. Both the structural and the substantive aspects of bureaucratization are difficult to examine empirically—more difficult, perhaps, than any other type of foreign policy stabilizer.

Fragmentation   One reason for administrative growth is the need to increase the intelligence and planning capability of the organization—to improve, in other words, the organization's ability to adapt and to learn. The argument about bureaucratic inertia is in effect that such efforts may fail. Fragmentation, by this argument, may hinder the discovery of new patterns. Growth increases the capability for data collection, but the correlation between the amount of available data and the visibility of important features may be negative. Moreover, organizational compartmentalization may inhibit the communication of important information and may render planning cumbersome. It also necessitates standard operating procedures, and the standardization of intelligence and planning cannot but inhibit the discovery of the unexpected as well as innovation and improvisation. Such problems as these may render administrative growth counterproductive from the point of view of adaptation and learning.[11] This is the case for regarding administrative fragmentation as a foreign policy stabilizer.

There are remedies, however, and the extent to which fragmentation does stabilize a foreign policy will be suggested to depend on them.

Thus, the stabilizing impact of fragmentation can be reduced by providing a mechanism for coordinating, integrating, or—a term that will be used here—synthesizing the efforts of the separate parts of the organization. This is important for overcoming the loss of perspective inherent in compartmentalization and for benefiting from the investment in increased capability.

A mechanism for providing a comprehensive estimate on the basis of fragmented intelligence may take a variety of forms. One possibility is to set up a system for collaboration or bargaining among subunits; the National Intelligence Estimates (NIES) of the United States perform such a function. A second possibility is to provide an outside official or agency with the task of overseeing and coordinating the work of the intelligence community; this can be one of the functions of the "custodian-manager" in what George terms the "multiple advocacy" model of American foreign policy management.[12] A third possibility may be to organize the very process of decisionmaking so as to stimulate the crossfertilization of conflicting perspectives among top-level policymakers; this is what George calls the "collegial model" (1980a: 157–58). It is natural for these examples to be American, since the U.S. foreign policy bureaucracy is exceptionally large and fragmented. However, it is meant to be a general proposition that the stabilizing impact of administrative fragmentation is reduced by such measures as these.

As should be obvious from the examples, the extent to which synthesizing is apt to protect against inertia may vary with the way in which it is set up. If there is a single "synthesizer"—a sole authoritative, integrated estimate—the analysis may remain overly standard-

[11] For an analysis of organizational behavior and bureaucratic politics as impediments to information processing, see George 1980a, esp. pp. 109–14.

[12] George (1980a: 195–96) is more concerned with guaranteeing a multisided examination of the issues than with the problem of synthesizing fragmented information and does not include the latter function among the tasks of the "custodian-manager."

ized. Competition between, or pluralism among, synthesizers—advanced multiple advocacy—is apt to reduce further the inertia following from fragmentation.

A system in which synthesizers compete can be made even more pluralistic by also using independent specialists. An "independent" specialist here means a person who is professionally active outside the administrative apparatus in an organization with different standard operating procedures. The archetype is the advisory academic.

Hence, fragmented systems for intelligence and planning can be of different types, only one of which would seem to be unambiguously stabilizing. The rank order between the main types, from the most to the least stabilizing, is:

1. fragmentation without remedies,
2. fragmentation with noncompetitive synthesizing,
3. fragmentation with competitive synthesizing,
4. fragmentation with competitive synthesizing and independent specialists.

Hence, if a policy is found to be administrated by a fragmented structure, it is important to consider the extent to which synthesizing is provided for, the extent to which competition between synthesizers exists, and the extent to which independent specialists are employed.

It may be useful to repeat again that policy stability in itself is neither desirable nor undesirable. This is not an attempt to model the most rational type of foreign policy administration. Our concern is with the propensity for change or lack of change in policy, regardless of whether change is desirable or undesirable. Competitive synthesizing, especially if combined with the use of independent specialists, is likely to facilitate adaptation and learning; it may at the same time fail to protect a policy against such disturbances as the coming into power of ignorant leaders with extreme views (if the administrative apparatus is sufficiently pluralistic, it stands ready to provide a professional justification for any policy).

The most obvious difficulty with putting these theoretical ideas into operational practice is to identify and delimit the administrative apparatus associated with a given policy. Full information about who does what in the bureaucracy may not be available, even though the scope of this difficulty is likely to vary from one polity to another as well as from one policy to another. To draw the line between those bureaucrats who are concerned with a specific policy and those who are not may also be difficult. Still, it may be possible to judge whether the apparatus is slightly or highly fragmented and, in the latter case, to assess to which of the above four types it is most similar.

Critical Variables   It can be taken for granted that administrative growth necessitates standard operating procedures. There will, among other things, emerge written or unwritten rules for what are the critical variables—that is, rules about what to take into account when monitoring the environment. Rules are also likely to emerge about tolerable ranges—that is, about the changes in the values of the critical variables that would justify reconsidering current policies.

Knowledge of critical variables and tolerable ranges is useful for the student of foreign policy stability in three ways.

First, the fewer the number of critical variables, the more stable the policy, other things being equal. In the extreme case, if no single variable is considered critical, there is no regular monitoring of the environment.

Second, the larger the tolerable ranges, the more stable the policy. The Swedish policy of neutrality cannot be unconditional; some variables must be assumed to be critical. However, the tolerable ranges on these variables are certainly very large; revolutionary change in the conditions for Swedish foreign policy would seem to be a prerequisite for a reappraisal of the policy of neutrality.

The main utility of knowledge about critical variables and tolerable ranges, however, lies in their telling us about the kind of stress to which the policy is vulnerable. The more we know about critical variables, the more we know about the factors that may trigger a change in policy as well as about the factors unlikely to do it. The more we know about tolerable ranges, the more precise these conclusions.

An important possibility is that the standard operating procedures facilitate change in one direction and inhibit change in another. A hypothetical example of such an administrative bias: the foreign aid bureaucracy of a nation may be designed to take note of almost anything that might justify increases in aid (such as economic needs) but almost nothing that might justify decreases in aid (mismanagement and corruption, for example). This bias may contribute to making foreign aid policy stable in the sense of inhibiting decreases but unstable in the sense of facilitating increases.

Can critical variables and tolerable ranges be identified empirically? We are concerned, to repeat, with the substantive content of standard operating procedures, with rules that have been decided on or have emerged informally in an administrative system. Content analysis of documents, the study of the flow of events within the bureaucracy, participant observation—these are among the methods that might be used, in principle. In practice the operational difficulties may be immense, particularly if we are concerned with a foreign government, which is the usual object of study for the analyst of foreign policy stability. Open documents will likely provide an incomplete view of what is considered to be critical and intolerable. Interviews with officials are also unlikely to give a complete picture—or at least unlikely to provide reasonable certainty that the picture is complete. Past history may no longer be relevant; there is no guarantee that the standard operating procedures of yesterday are also those of today. It is important for the student of foreign policy stability to consider the matter of critical variables and tolerable ranges, but it will likely be necessary to rest content with impressions.

Response Repertory   The assumption that the freedom of action of an organization is restricted to its repertory of programs is a central feature of the cybernetic paradigm (section 1.2). In terms of the present theoretical sketch, planned alternatives may be "available" in the form of opposition policy as well as of bureaucratic programs. We considered the former when discussing the stabilizer called support (section 2.3), and we will now limit ourselves to the latter.

Thus, the response repertory of a country is composed of those contingency plans that have been worked out by its bureaucracy. Hypothetically, a shift to a new policy is facilitated by the preexistence of this option in the repertory of responses. The complete absence of planned options need not be maximally stabilizing, however. If no contingency plans exist, a policy may break down completely under stress rather than be modified. The stability of a policy may benefit from the existence of planned moderate alternatives.

Knowledge of the response repertory would in particular provide a basis for forecasts about the kind of change that is likely and unlikely to occur in various contigencies. However, if this information would be useful, it is also unlikely to be accessible. Occasional insights will not suffice, since the absence of plans is as significant as their presence. There is a need for reasonably comprehensive information about matters governments are prone to keep secret. The main reason for putting the response repertory on the analyst's agenda is the usefulness of knowing what one would need to know but cannot know.

Decision Structure   Recall the CREON proposition about decision structures, which was cited in section 1.2. The proposition essentially contrasts rational decisionmaking with so-called bureaucratic politics.

"Leader-autonomous groups" engage in an uninhibited search for alternatives, and then the leader selects the best one; this kind of decisionmaking facilitates change, according to the proposition. If, on the other hand, decisionmaking consists in bargaining among the delegates of a variety of entities, each of whom has veto power, change is rendered difficult, and the policy is apt to be stable.

Suppose that the United States were to ask its allies to cut down their trade with the Soviet Union. If, say, the British response were to be decided by the prime minister after a many-sided discussion with her closest associates in the cabinet, this would approximate the former model. If instead the British response would have to be based on agreement among the representatives of several ministries as well as of business, labor, and perhaps other interests, this would approach the latter model. According to the proposition, change in British policy—adaptation to American demands in this example—would be less likely to occur in the latter case than in the former.

Now, what does it mean to say that a particular decision structure is associated with a policy? The student of the stability of a current foreign policy is concerned with decision structures for the same reason as he is concerned with stabilizers in general: he wants to improve his ability to predict what would happen to the policy, if there were to occur a pressure for change. Therefore, his concern is with the way in which decisions will likely be made about whether to deviate from the policy. If such a decision is likely to be made in a leader-autonomous group fashion, this helps to make the policy unstable; if it will probably be made by means of bargaining among delegates, this helps to make it stable. Thus, to associate a decision structure with a policy means to predict the process by which decisions about the policy will be made (or, in a historical study like the one in Part Two, to consider the process by which such decisions would have been or were made). An analyst concerned with the stability of British trade policy, to continue the example, would have to consider the likely decision process in the event of, say, an American demand for change.

On what basis can such judgments be made? Possible evidence includes the way in which decisions are normally made in the system with which we are concerned as well as previous decisionmaking about the issue. This is weak evidence, and conclusions about this kind of stablilizer seem bound to be uncertain (with the possible exception of the historical study of policy changes that have either taken place or have been seriously contemplated).

Especially since the publication of Allison's *Essence of Decision* (1971), it is common to regard American foreign policy as the result of bureaucratic politics. Similar trends are said to exist in Soviet foreign policymaking (Bialer 1981: 414–16). It may be important to distinguish between crisis and noncrisis, however. The literature suggests crisis decisionmaking to approach the destabilizing ideal type, regardless of noncrisis procedures (see chapter 10). Crisis management is "the way in which resistance against thorough-going changes can be eliminated"—this is a German comment about policymaking in Bonn (Krause and Wilker 1980: 165).

2.5. THE LIMITATIONS OF THE INVENTORY

The first task of an analyst concerned with what will likely happen to a foreign policy is to consider the probability of disturbances. Will conditions change? Will there be negative feedback? Will there be stress from other events (a shift in government, for example)? Of course, the less likely disturbances are, the less likely the policy is to change. However, since stress can rarely be ruled out, it is as important to consider stabilizers as it is to speculate about disturbances.

The inventory of foreign policy stabilizers made in the present chapter is summarized in Table 2.1. The quality of the definitions provided in the table is uneven; there is room for improvement by further reflection and research. However, the more important aspect of the table is the "empirical focus" of each concept. The empirical focuses form a checklist of questions to ask when an attempt is made to forecast the future of a policy. Some of the operational difficulties with following this advice are also indicated.

My contention is that it is better to employ this checklist than to use no conceptual tool at all in an attempt to analyze the stability of a foreign policy. The checklist is relatively explicit and systematic. Therefore it is open to systematic criticism and hence to improvement. The point about improvement is fundamental: this is not meant to be the final word on foreign policy stability but a mere step in the direction of theory proper.

The theoretical sketch in its present shape has four main limitations: (1) a number of conceptual deficiencies, (2) the weakness of its causal claims, (3) the limited extent to which these claims have a basis in research, and (4) its static nature. Conceptual improvement, strengthening of the causal assumptions, empirical testing, introducing dynamic hypotheses—these are essential for making strong theory out of the sketch.

The Concepts The chief conceptual problems are operational. A variety of operational difficulties will have to be faced by an analyst applying the checklist to a specific problem of foreign policy stability: the difficulty of measuring the degree to which inter-state relations are positive or negative as well as the relative weight of states, which are the key dimensions of third party stabilization; the problem of validity inherent in any attempt to identify foreign policy beliefs; the lack of precision in the observations that can be made about domestic politics; the difficulty of getting sufficient insight into administrative phenomena; in particular, the problem of measuring dependence, which may be among the most important items on the list.

Conceptual improvement is likely to come primarily from attempts at empirical application. One objective of the study reported in Part Two is to improve the conceptual tools by putting them to use. This experiment may be useful as a source of ideas for further applications. These in turn would undoubtedly contribute to further refining the inventory by making the theoretical concepts more realistic and at the same time making the operationalizations more sophisticated.

The Causal Claim The only causal claim made in the sketch is that a number of phenomena tend to block, delay, or reduce the scope of policy change, even in the presence of a pressure for change. Put differently, these phenomena are hypothesized to increase the amount of disturbance necessary to produce a change in policy. This claim is a modest one. It is limited to suggesting that a number of phenomena are sufficiently important determinants of foreign policy stability to be worthy of attention. As is often the case with political science theory, the sketch is limited to the mere listing of phenomena presumed to have an impact. This is weak theory.

Thus, the theoretical sketch does not suggest anything at all about the combined impact of all the stabilizers; the overall explanatory power of the model is not specified. Hence, even though it can be taken for granted that the inventory of stabilizers is incomplete, it is impossible to say anything about how large this deficiency is. By the same token, no assumption is made about the relative significance of each individual stabilizer. Nor is there a systematic consideration of third variables that may determine the impact of each of the stabilizers. Some stabilizers have been suggested to be more effective in some political systems than in others, and we have touched on the possibility that stabilizers may lose their effectiveness in crisis situations, but the sketch does not include any such refinements. Each stabilizer is likely to raise the disturbance threshold significantly and is therefore worth taking into account—this is all that is claimed.

The application of the sketch to specific empirical cases, as in Part Two, and to a specific policy problem, as in Part Three, may help to

Table 2.1. Checklist for the analysis of the stability of a foreign policy (P)

Stabilizer	Definition	Empirical focus	Operational note
Normative regulation	The degree to which international norms contain an obligation to pursue P.	Are there international norms prescribing P? What is their precise substance? What is the legal status of agreed norms? How strong is the evidence of the existence of customary norms? Is the obligation to pursue P contradicted by other norms? What problems of application are likely to occur?	It may be difficult to determine the existence and the precise substance of customary norms; the study of justifying statements may be useful for this purpose. The consideration of problems of application is necessarily subjective in part; the examination of controversies which have in fact occurred may be a means to reduce this difficulty.
Dependence	The extent to which the pursuit of P has led to a regular relationship between actor and environment which would be interrupted, if the actor ceased to pursue P; the degree of dependence is a function of the cost of goal-attainment if the relationship were to be interrupted in comparison with the cost of goal-attainment if the relationship had never been established.	How has the pursuit of P affected the actor's international relations? What would be the effects of a change in P on these relations? How costly would the effects be?	Since the concept is defined in terms of hypothetical situations, dependence cannot be precisely measured. Empirical data may provide clues, however. The availability of data and their reliability and validity vary with the substance of P. Economic indicators may be used if the pursuit of P has affected the actor's economic relations with the environment. Military data may be relevant if the pursuit of P has implied international cooperation about security matters.
Third parties	The degree to which there is structural balance in the triads formed by the actor, the object of P, and third parties.	What is the state of the relationship between the actor and third parties? What is the relationship between third parties and the object of P? What is the weight of each third party?	A variety of indicators may be used to measure the state of relationships (e.g., indicators of "tension") and the weight of third parties (e.g., indicators of "power"). There is a problem of

			validity with such measurements or observations, but precision may not be necessary for the limited purpose of examining the extent of third party stabilization.
Consistency	The extent to which the actor believes that P is not counter-productive and that it lacks negative side-effects.	What are the actor's assumptions about the causal paths from P to the intended outcome? Are any of the paths thought to be negative? Is the pursuit of P thought to have other unfavorable effects?	The available documentation may—but need not—be incomplete or invalid.
Centrality	The extent to which the actor believes the pursuit of P to be a prerequisite for the successful pursuit of other policies.	How, in the view of the actor, is the pursuit of P linked to the pursuit of other policies?	The available documentation may—but need not—be incomplete or invalid.
Testability	The extent to which the ideas upon which P is based can be refuted by empirical evidence.	Are the actor's causal beliefs testable in principle? How likely is evidence that the actor would regard as significant to be available in practice?	The documentation of the actor's beliefs may—but need not—be incomplete or invalid. The very concept of testability is subjective; only a tentative assessment is possible.
Institutionalization	The extent to which the members of the actor's polity expect P to continue to be pursued.	To what extent has the actor made declarations committing him to pursue P? How often, in how authoritative a way, in what context? Are the commitments worded in such a way as to strengthen or weaken them? Regardless of verbal commitment, to what extent is there evidence of a behavior pattern? To what extent has the pursuit of P implied investments in capabilities or administrative agencies?	There is insufficient theoretical basis for making strong inferences from the wording of commitments. It may also be difficult to determine the existence and the precise substance of a behavior pattern; the study of justifying statements may be useful in some cases.

Table 2.1. Checklist for the analysis of the stability of a foreign policy (P) (*cont.*).

Stabilizer	Definition	Empirical focus	Operational note
Support	The extent to which P is supported rather than opposed by the members of the actor's polity.	To what extent is there active support of P, and how important are the supporters? To what extent is there active opposition to P, and how important are the opponents? How large is the substantive difference between P and the policy advocated by the opponents?	It is impossible to be precise about the political importance of supporters and opponents; however, it may be sufficient to examine the position of what are evidently the dominating political actors of the polity. No systematic method exists for the "measurement" of substantive differences between policy proposals.
Salience	The extent to which the pattern of coalitions and cleavages in the actor's polity would be affected by the actor's changing his position on the issue with which P is concerned.	How much attention has been devoted to the issue? What has been the role of the issue in previous coalition formation?	Both attention and previous experience carry problems of validity when used as indicators of salience.
Fragmentation	The extent to which the administration of P is compartmentalized.	What is the structure of the apparatus administering P? To what extent is synthesis provided for? To what extent is there competition between synthesizers? To what extent are independent specialists employed?	It will probably be difficult to get detailed information about what the administrative apparatus is in fact like. However, it may in many cases be possible to make judgments sufficiently well-founded for the limited purpose of assessing the extent of administrative stabilization.

Critical variables	Those aspects of the environment that are regularly monitored by the apparatus administering P.	What are the standard operating procedures for monitoring the environment? What are the tolerable ranges on the critical variables? To what extent do the SOPs imply a bias facilitating change in one direction but inhibiting change in another?	Among the methods that might be used are the content analysis of documents circulating in the apparatus, the reconstruction of the flow of events within it, and participant observation. In practice the systematic study of critical variables is likely to be difficult in many cases, and weaker evidence will have to suffice.
Response repertory	P and those alternatives to P that have been identified and planned for by the administrative apparatus.	What is the substance of the contingency planning that has been carried out by the bureaucracy? What options have been developed?	The response repertory will likely be impossible to study, when it is a matter of a policy pursued in the present or the recent past.
Decision structure	The process by which decisions about whether and how to modify P will be made.	To what extent will decisions about P be made by leader-autonomous groups? To what extent will decisionmaking be of the delegate type?	One kind of evidence consists in the decisionmaking routines of the administrative apparatus with which we are concerned. Another consists in the experience from previous decisionmaking about P. The conclusions that can be drawn are necessarily tentative, however, since the concept is defined in terms of a hypothetical situation.

make it more comprehensive and sophisticated. In Part Two, U.S.-Soviet and West German-Soviet relations in the 1970s are compared. This is a device for exploring in a tentative fashion the relative significance of the various stabilizers as well as the impact of such an obviously relevant third variable as regime type. In Part Three, détente is considered as a general problem in international politics. Applying the sketch to this problem compels us to consider, among other things, the special case of policies in interaction: if feedback from state A is a disturbance for the policy of state B toward state A, and vice versa, the stability of B's policy toward A is in part a function of the stability of A's policy toward B, and vice versa, an intriguing possibility that we have not considered in the present chapter. The special features of crises will also be considered in Part Three.

The long-term objective is a theory good enough to make strong causal claims. All that is suggested here is a starting point. The reader is asked to contribute to improving the theory that I have merely been able to sketch.[13]

The Research Basis   No systematic evidence has been cited in support of the claim that the various phenomena are "important" as stabilizers of foreign policy. This does not mean that the theoretical sketch is taken out of the blue.

About half of the stabilizers are based on previously existing, reasonably strong theory. This is true in particular with regard to the cognitive stabilizers: this aspect of the theoretical sketch draws on standard notions in a relatively well developed field of study. The suggestions about administrative stabilizers are also inspired by—even though not strictly deduced from—relatively sophisticated theory. Moreover, the reasoning about third party stabilization is rooted in the strong device of structural balance theory.

With regard to all or most of the remaining stabilizers, the stabilizing impact is in large measure inherent in their definitions; these factors affect the costs of policy change by definition, or virtually by definition, and the claim that they are stabilizers therefore carries an inherent plausibility. This is the case not only with dependence but also with all the political stabilizers and perhaps even with international regulation. Rationalistic assumptions do not necessarily fit the reality of international politics, but as long as the claim is only that the vari-

---

[13] The theoretical sketch (or the preliminary version reported in Goldmann 1982) has been used in studies of American, Chinese, and Finnish foreign policy (Hallenberg 1984, Stubbe Østergaard 1983, and Väyrynen 1987, respectively).

ables tend to have a "significant" impact, the lack of empirical proof may not be all that serious. In my view, the chief limitation of the sketch is not the lack of confirmation but the modesty of its claims. The sketch does not represent bold, unconfirmed speculation but is a cautious synthesis of rather obvious ideas.

The Dynamics   The way in which the various stabilizers may develop over time and affect one another has been touched on only in passing. The theoretical sketch is static. It indicates only how the presence of a number of phenomena may affect policy stablility. The processes of stabilization and destabilization of policies remain to be considered. We will take up this matter in the next chapter.

CHAPTER 3

Policy Stabilization as a Process

ALTHOUGH it may be premature, what amounts to a model of the process of foreign policy stabilization will be sketched in this chapter. The order in which the stabilizers emerge and gain strength is unlikely to be random. Some stabilizers—such as normative regulation—are likely to become significant early in the life of a foreign policy. Others—such as "bureaucratic inertia"—are likely to come about only after a considerable time. Moreover, some stabilizers are likely to reinforce others; for example, an increase in economic dependence can conceivably reinforce both political support, cognitive centrality, and administrative fragmentation.

Almost anything can happen. It is probably possible to find historical incidents showing that the stabilization of foreign policies may take place in any order and that any stabilizer may have a positive or negative effect on any other. However, some such events seem more likely than others. It should be possible to specify the typical chain of events and hence to model the most plausible and significant links between the stabilizers.

Such a model will be outlined here as a postscript to the presentation of the stabilizers in the previous chapter. The model is concerned only with the stabilization of policies and not with their destabilization. This is so because a model of stabilization may not be reversible and may fail as a model of destabilization. Whether destabilization can also be modeled is considered in the latter part of the chapter.

3.1. THE PROCESS OF STABILIZATION

The first step in the construction of the model is shown in Table 3.1. A judgment has been made, for each pair of stabilizers, whether there is likely to be a significant direct relationship; if there is one, whether it is primarily symmetrical or asymmetrical; and if it is primarily asymmetrical, in what direction. A critical consideration of the model should start with the zeros in the table; they may be its most vulnerable aspect.

The speculative model shown in Figure 3.1 is based on the assumptions made in Table 3.1. It suggests the typical process of stabilization

Table 3.1. Hypotheses about links between stabilizers

	Regulation	Dependence	Third parties	Consistency	Centrality	Testability	Institutionalization	Support	Salience	Fragmentation	Critical variables	Response repertory
Dependence	←											
Third parties	↔	→										
Consistency	0	0	←									
Centrality	0	←	0	0								
Testability	0	0	0	0	0							
Institutionalization	←	←	0	↔	←	0						
Support	←	←	0	↔	←	0	0					
Salience	0	←	0	0	↔	0	←	←				
Fragmentation	0	←	0	0	0	0	0	0	0			
Critical variables	0	0	0	0	0	0	←	←	0	←		
Response repertory	0	0	0	←	0	0	←	←	0	←	0	
Decision structure	0	←	0	0	0	0	0	0	0	←	→	0

← Column variable tends to reinforce row variable.
→ Row variable tends to reinforce column variable.
↔ Column and row variables tend to reinforce each other.
0 No significant reinforcement.

to begin at the international level, whereas significant administrative stabilization is assumed to take place only toward the end of the process. From international agreements and third party relations via dependence, cognitions, and domestic politics to "bureaucratic inertia"—this is the essence of foreign policy stabilization, according to the model.

The process is not presumed to be deterministic. The model is meant to describe a series of events likely to occur under favorable circumstances. It indicates a scenario as it will probably develop in the absence of disturbances. However, disturbances are likely and may

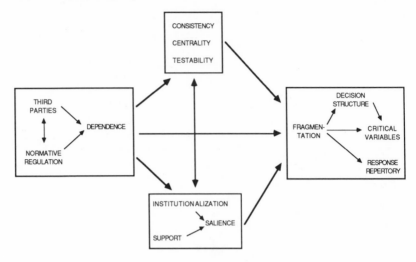

Figure 3.1. A speculative model of the process of foreign policy stabilization.

slow down, stop, or even reverse the stabilization process. Hence, foreign policy stabilization is a race between the gradual buildup of stabilizers and the incidence of stress. This theme is pursued in Part Three.

Brief comments will now be made about the main causal links suggested in Figure 3.1. They will be illustrated with notes about developments in Chinese foreign policy, which have been studied with the help of the present theoretical sketch by Stubbe Østergaard (1983). The notes are intended merely to help the reader follow a condensed theoretical argument and are by no means meant as empirical evidence.

From International to Cognitive Stabilization   In the model, the international stabilization of a foreign policy is a process by which the actor's international relations are increasingly colored by his pursuit of this policy. The main path from international to domestic stabilization goes through dependence. In fact, dependence is suggested as the most important variable in the stabilization process (Table 3.1).

In the 1970s China shifted to a policy of improved relations with the West and Japan. By the early 1980s this policy encompassed a rapid buildup of economic relations. There is little question that the Chinese economy became increasingly dependent on the continuation of a foreign policy of this kind. That in turn served to stimulate the stabilization of the new foreign policy in a number of other ways, according to the model.

We must pause here to consider whether the continued pursuit of any foreign policy implies an increased dependence on the environment. The answer seems to be yes, with one exception. The pursuit of a foreign policy implies some sort of interaction with the environment, and continuing interaction of this sort will increase the cost of breaking it off; you cannot pursue one option and at the same time keep all other options as open as they were originally. Of course, different policies imply different types and degrees of dependence. The model suggests that policies leading to strong dependence are particularly likely to become stabilized in other ways.

The type of foreign policy that cannot lead to dependence as defined here is the avoidance of interaction. Interaction is a prerequisite for dependence in the present sense. Of course, policies of isolationism may nevertheless be stable; dependence is not a prerequisite of stabilization.

Among other things, dependence is presumed to reinforce the cognitive centrality of a policy, as shown in Table 3.1. As dependence increases—this is the hypothesis—the continued pursuit of the policy will be perceived as increasingly important for the attainment of an increasing variety of objectives. In effect this is to suggest that perceptions tend to be correct: the more structural adaptation, the more far-reaching the consequences of a change in policy.

In China the new foreign policy became associated with a shift in priorities in the direction of modernization; the Third Plenum of the Eleventh Central Committee in December 1978 is generally considered to have been the watershed. This shift in priorities entailed a demand for foreign technology and capital (Stubbe Østergaard 1983: 253). Hence, the new foreign policy became cognitively central in the sense of being considered essential for the attainment of major domestic objectives. The suggestion made in the theoretical sketch is that an increasing dependence on foreign technology and capital would be apt to strengthen even further the perceived links between the new foreign policy and success in modernization.

The other path from international to cognitive stabilization goes from third party stabilization to cognitive consistency. This, too, is a hypothesis to the effect that perceptions tend to be correct. Structural balance in inter-state relations tends to produce structural balance in foreign policy beliefs, according to the hypothesis (see Goldmann 1981 on this link between international politics and attitudes). If third parties adapt to your pursuit of a given policy, you will likely have fewer questions and contradictions in your thoughts about the virtues of this policy.

The improvement in Sino-Western relations went together with a deterioration in Soviet-U.S. relations. This, according to what has been suggested previously, would serve to stabilize the new Chinese foreign policy. We now add the suggestion that structural balance in the U.S.-Chinese-Soviet triangle would also help to render Chinese foreign policy thinking more consistent and hence cognitively less problematical. It appears, however, that this process was disturbed by American policy on Taiwan as well as by developments thought to indicate a reduced Soviet threat (Stubbe Østergaard 1983: 250–51).

From International to Political Stabilization   It can be seen in Table 3.1 that dependence is suggested to have an impact on all three aspects of domestic politics. The idea is simple: as the policy becomes increasingly consequential, the issue gains in political salience. At the same time, the government has an increasing propensity to reinforce its commitment to the policy while support for the policy increases and opposition to it decreases. That some such mechanism is operating is the core of the idea that economic interdependence breeds peace, a notion to which we will return.

The hypothesis, applied to China's new foreign policy, goes like this: the more dependent China became on economic relations with the West and Japan, the more consequential the continued pursuit of the new foreign policy would be for conditions inside China and, therefore, the greater its political salience and the stronger its institutionalization, the more numerous its supporters and the fewer its opponents. Opposition to the new directions in Chinese foreign and domestic policy surfaced by the early 1980s (Stubbe Østergaard 1983: 254–55), but it was too early to conclude that the new foreign policy would fail to gain a firm foundation in domestic politics.[1]

The suggestion made in Table 3.1 that political stabilization may benefit not just from dependence but also from international regulation is based on the assumption that if an international agreement is made to pursue a policy this adds an incentive for institutionalizing it while also adding some strength to its supporters and detracting some from its opponents.

[1] During a visit to China in September–October 1985 I was repeatedly told that even though China had gone through several drastic swings in policy after 1949, this was unlikely to happen again. The reason most frequently given was the great changes that had taken place in domestic politics.

In the Chinese case the new directions in foreign policy were normatively regulated, inter alia, by the establishment of diplomatic relations with a large number of states, by bilateral treaties like the Sino-Japanese treaty of peace and friendship in 1978, by diplomatic communiqués in connection with high-level visits, and also by China's entering the network of international conventions and organizations on a large scale.[2] The hypothesis is that this strengthened the position of the new foreign policy in domestic politics to at least some extent by stimulating its institutionalization and by strengthening the hand of its supporters.

From International to Administrative Stabilization   The pursuit of some foreign policies may lead to a situation of the type Keohane and Nye (1977) call complex interdependence. One implication may be an increase in various forms of "bureaucratic inertia." The vast increase in the number and complexity of China's international ties will help to stabilize the new foreign policy by "bureaucratizing" its conduct, according to this argument.[3]

From Cognitive to Political Stabilization, and Vice Versa   Included in Table 3.1 is the hypothesis that there is mutual reinforcement between cognitive consistency on the one hand and institutionalization and support on the other. Cognitive centrality, moreover, is hypothesized to stimulate further institutionalization and support. You are particularly likely to commit yourself strongly to a policy if the policy is based on consistent reasoning and if it is perceived to be central, according to this line of thought. It is also easier to mobilize support in this case. Conversely, strong commitment and weak opposition would seem to render it easier to get rid of contradictions and questions in the beliefs underlying a policy.

Cognitive centrality and political salience are also suggested to reinforce each other. Centrality increases the likelihood that the issue will be salient. Increasing salience may in turn make the policy more cognitively central.

A number of ways in which the development of thinking and of domestic politics may go hand in hand are suggested here. In the case of China, according to this argument, the firmer the foundation of the

---

[2] For data about diplomatic relations, treaties, and accession to international conventions and organizations, see *Politics* 1985: 175–209.

[3] Stubbe Østergaard (1983: 262) suggests, however, the existence of several destabilizing features in the administration of Chinese foreign policy in the early 1980s.

new foreign policy would become in Chinese thinking, the stronger its domestic politics base would be, and vice versa.

From Cognitive to Administrative Stabilization   The suggestion here is simply that the more consistent the beliefs on which a policy is based, the poorer the response repertory. Uncertainties and contradictions increase the demand for planned options, according to this hypothesis. Since Chinese thinking appears to have been relatively complex— sophisticated may be a better expression—the latter rather than the former should have been the case with regard to the new foreign policy.

From Political to Administrative Stabilization   The basic suggestion on this point is that opposition tends to increase the number of critical variables and to decrease the tolerable ranges and that it tends to broaden the response repertory. Conversely, political consensus is suggested to facilitate the emergence of "bureaucratic inertia." We add the hypothesis that institutionalization may have similar effects: strong governmental commitment tends to reduce the bureaucracy's sensitivity to the environment and to deprive it of the incentives for keeping the option of policy change alive. If in fact the new foreign policy of China were to become increasingly institutionalized and consensual, foreign policy intelligence and planning would be apt to be constrained in the long term, according to the hypothesis.

3.2. THE PROCESS OF DESTABILIZATION

The process of stabilization may be hastened—an obvious point not made previously—by "favorable" changes in policy conditions, positive feedback, and residual events such as those precipitating the coming into power of the policy's most wholehearted supporters. According to the above model, the stabilization process also has a dynamic of its own, however: the very pursuit of a policy tends to make it increasingly stable. Destabilization may be seen as a result of disturbances that are insufficiently severe to bring about a change in policy and yet sufficiently severe to have an impact on the stabilizers and hence to counteract the ongoing, self-reinforcing process of stabilization.

The occurrence of such a disturbance—a change in conditions, negative feedback, some residual event—may have various consequences for a policy. One possibility is that nothing happens: neither the policy itself nor its stabilizers are affected by the disturbance. The more advanced the process of stabilization, the larger a disturbance must be in order to have an impact. On the other hand, if the disturbance is sufficiently severe, the actor will deviate from a previous line of action. The deviation may be a definite change in policy, or it may prove to be temporary. This may depend on the degree of stabilization: the more stabilized a policy, the more likely deviations are to be temporary rather than definite, it would appear.

Between the extremes of a lack of impact and a change in policy there is the possibility of destabilization. The actor may continue to pursue a previous line of action in spite of the disturbance, but the stabilizers have been weakened, and therefore the policy has become more vulnerable to future disturbances. Destabilization, in other words, is the weakening of stabilizers under the impact of disturbances.

Different disturbances have different destabilizing effects. Negative feedback, for example, may lead to cognitive inconsistency as well as to increased opposition. Substantively irrelevant events may bring about political and administrative changes. A change in conditions may have a direct impact on international as well as on cognitive and political stabilizers. Since disturbances may come from such a variety of sources, it does not seem meaningful to try to model the destabilization process. Destabilization seems less likely than stabilization to follow a typical pattern that can be described in the form of a model.

Moreover, whereas stabilization seems bound to be a gradual process, destabilization may take the form of a sudden event. The most obvious example is a shift in government. If the architects of a policy are replaced at the top by the opponents of this policy, the result will at a minimum be a decrease in cognitive consistency and centrality, rendering the policy more vulnerable to stress. This may have happened in Bonn in 1982, when the Christian Democratic Union (CDU) replaced the Social Democratic party (SPD) as the main government party: the Ostpolitik continued but apparently with less conviction (more about this in Part Two).

The suggestion that destabilization is unpredictable and that it may take the form of a sudden event need not mean that anything can happen to any policy. Rather, the more stabilized a policy, the less destabilizing the impact of disturbances. On this assumption, the more we know about the extent to which a policy has in fact been stabilized, the more we know not only about how likely it is to change but also about how likely it is to be undermined.

A house must be built step by step in a relatively predictable order, but it can collapse in a variety of ways. The stabilization of foreign policies can be modeled, but destabilization cannot. However, the more stable a building, the less likely are disturbances—a flood, an earthquake, insects, whatever—to make it so fragile that it will collapse for nothing. The more stabilized a policy, the more it takes to destabilize it.

PART TWO

Détente: Evaluation of an Experiment

CHAPTER 4

The 1970s as an Experiment

"DÉTENTE" is the label commonly used for the improvement in East-West relations that began in the 1960s and peaked in the early 1970s. It was a contradictory phenomenon. Both sides emphasized the necessity of preventing a nuclear war, and yet one of the chief post-1945 crises occurred at the height of "détente"—the Yom Kippur war of 1973, which is one of the few occasions when U.S. nuclear forces have been placed on a higher state of command readiness during an international crisis (Sagan 1985). Agreements were made about strategic arms control, moreover, and yet the arms race continued, albeit in a partly regulated form. "Détente" did not put an end to the East-West cleavage. It was a new way of managing a relationship that remained one between adversaries. It was peaceful coexistence in the sense of a continuation of conflict by means other than war. It was amity between enemies.

"Détente" can be considered as an experiment. Would this combination of cooperation and conflict endure? Can such a relationship be maintained between the major powers in an anarchical system?

This is one evaluation of the experiment:

1. The détente construction subject to test was maximally advanced.
2. The stress to which it was exposed was normal and neither unusual nor extreme.
3. The construction broke down under the impact of this stress.

Hence, the 1970s confirmed that the idea of stable détente is unrealistic.

Is this skeptical, or "realist," view justified? Did in fact the 1970s confirm that stable détente is impossible—between the East and the West, or even generally between adversaries in international politics? Or is there room for a different conclusion?

The question will be approached with the help of the theoretical sketch introduced in Part One. "Détente" will be regarded as a set of policies that (1) was exposed to pressure for change from various sources, (2) was protected to some extent by stabilizers, and (3) was modified to an extent determined by the confrontation between the

pressures for change and the stabilizers. The above evaluation, refor-
mulated in these terms, is:

1. Policies of détente were first pursued and then given up.
2. The pressures for giving up détente were of a kind that cannot be
   avoided in international politics.
3. The stabilization that took place represented the maximum possible.

Are these observations correct?

4.1. The Détente Crisis

It is necessary now to consider the notion of a policy of détente more
carefully. The term *international tension* can be defined as the degree
of mutual threat perception (Goldmann 1974: 17–23). The term
détente can be used to denote a process of decreasing tension. A *policy
of détente* can be defined, roughly, as one calculated to reduce the
threat perceptions of an adversary or as a policy toward an adversary
in which there is a high ratio of friendly to hostile elements. Specifically, what became known as a policy of détente in the 1970s had three
main dimensions, which may, however, be typical of policies of détente
more generally:

1. The avoidance of actions that might increase the risk of war (the
   restraint dimension).
2. Efforts to control and limit the deployment and use of arms (the
   arms control dimension).
3. Efforts to increase cooperation, contacts, and communication (the
   cooperation dimension).

This is the way in which the term *détente* is used in the present study.
It is not suggested that this usage is the only proper one. No stand is
taken on the meaning of "true" détente. This is a scholar's attempt to
make the concept of détente analytically useful without departing radically from common usage.

Governmental usage of the concept of détente has been systematically examined by Frei and Ruloff. Their content analysis of declarations made at meetings of the Conference on Security and Cooperation
in Europe (CSCE) revealed the existence of five "master dimensions" of
détente—namely, (1) disarmament and security, (2) peace and conflict,
(3) economic cooperation, (4) human rights and contacts, and (5) sov-
ereignty and independence (1983, 1: 46). The concept of détente used
in the present study is more narrow, particularly in excluding most of

"master dimensions" (4) and (5). The concept is here limited to three dimensions—restraint, arms control, and cooperation—which are universally relevant for adversary inter-state relationships, while leaving out some matters that were specific to East-West diplomacy in the 1970s. Hence, détente in this sense does not include everything that was put into the Helsinki package. In the terminology adopted here, agreement on détente became possible in Helsinki because some other issues (human rights in particular) were added to the bargain. It must be emphasized that this is a matter of terminology and not one of policy evaluation or preference.

There is no question that both the East and the West had begun to pursue policies of the type here called détente by the early 1970s. Skeptics may argue that "détente" was superficial, a mere cover for continuing aggression or conflict. This, however, is an objection merely against the way in which the terms *policy* and *détente* are used in the present study. As made clear in chapter 1, *policy* here implies publicly declared programs as well as actual patterns of behavior, but it does not necessarily imply intentions. It is irrelevant for the issue of whether the United States or the Soviet Union pursued a policy of détente whether Nixon or Kissinger, Brezhnev or Ustinov were serious. As regards the term *détente*, it has been made clear that it implies neither the resolution of fundamental differences, disarmament, nor any other basic transformation of the adversary nature of the relationship. Given the terminology used here, it is clear beyond doubt that policies of détente were adopted by both sides. All three dimensions were present in East-West diplomacy: restraint (for example, the U.S.-Soviet agreement about Basic Principles), arms control (for example, SALT I), and cooperation (for example, trade). The Helsinki Final Act confirmed the commitment of both the East and the West to pursue policies of this type.

According to the above evaluation, all of this had vanished by the early 1980s. When Georgiy A. Arbatov, the leading Americanist of the USSR, said in April 1983 that there had occurred a "tremendous deterioration" in U.S.-Soviet relations, that the situation was worse "than at any time since the Cuban Missile Crisis," and that "the danger of confrontation and conflict" had become "much more real," he expressed what had become the standard view (*International Herald Tribune*, April 11, 1983).

Whether détente was fully abandoned in U.S.-Soviet relations may be debatable. On the one hand, arms control got stuck on the issue of land-based intermediate range missiles and were suspended altogether when NATO began to deploy these missiles in December 1983. Trade and other forms of cooperation and contact, moreover, were reduced. On the other hand, the parties appeared more anxious to exercise restraint in the 1980s than they had been in the 1950s and early 1960s; there was no return to the kind of relationship that had existed at the time of the Korean War, the building of the Berlin Wall, and the Cuban Missile Crisis.

More importantly, however, détente was by no means abandoned in the relationship between the Soviet Union and Western Europe, and particularly not between the Soviet Union and West Germany. A peculiar combination of increasing conflict and continued cooperation emerged in Europe. Trade and other contacts went on, and in arms control some Western European countries came to play the role of a pressure group for talks and concessions.

It is instructive to compare the way in which East-West relations were described in Washington, Bonn, and Moscow at the beginning of the 1980s. President Reagan devoted only a small part of his inaugural address to foreign policy. Almost all of this section of the address was concerned with the need for sufficient strength to prevail and with the determination to act; this would provide "the best chance of never having to use that strength" (*DSB* 81, no. 2047 [1981]: special supp., pp. a–c). Deterrence was emphasized, not détente.

As regards East-West cooperation, a new policy was introduced by the Reagan administration. To quote from a statement by the new administration's undersecretary of state for economic affairs, Myer Rashish, economic policy "must support our key objectives of deterring Soviet adventurism, redressing the military balance ... and strengthening the Western Alliance." Trade must not enhance Soviet capabilities and must not increase Western vulnerabilities. There had to be restraint as regards the transfer of technology. Even in the area of nonstrategic trade, the United States was "not prepared to foreswear the use of controls as part of an overall response to future Soviet aggressive action."[1]

Contemporary statements in Bonn differed. An authoritative presentation of West German foreign policy was made in the governmental declaration about the state of the nation on April 10, 1981. It was necessary, according to the declaration, to preserve the confidence of everybody, including the Soviet Union, that no increase in tension would be brought about by developments in Germany. The military balance must be preserved, but there was no striving for superiority. It was a basic principle to combine military security with arms control

---

[1] Telex copy obtained from the American Embassy, Stockholm, September 1981.

and cooperation; there was an "imperative interaction" between balance of power and cooperation. Peace was a condition that must always be reestablished by a balance of power at the lowest possible level, by negotiation and treaties, by the creation of mutual confidence, by cooperation. A balance of power was insufficient. It was also necessary to talk to one another, to listen to one another, and to compromise (*Bulletin* [1981], No. 36/S).

About a month after President Reagan delivered his inaugural address, Leonid Brezhnev spoke to the Twenty-sixth Congress of the Communist party of the Soviet Union (CPSU). The speech, which is considered in more detail in chapter 7, reaffirmed the commitment to détente, emphasized that the Soviet Union did not seek superiority, and confirmed Soviet interest in treaties and agreements, in "an active dialogue at all levels," and in peaceful "ties," particularly trade. There was no counterpart to West German formulations about an obligation not to increase tension, to create mutual confidence, and to compromise, however. Moreover, whereas the importance of cooperation in Europe was stressed, the objective in regard to the United States was described merely as "normal relations" (*CDSP* 33, no. 8 [1981]: 3–21, 9 [1981]: 4–15).

These documents exemplify how, in the early 1980s, much of détente had disappeared from U.S. foreign policy; they show that much of it remained in West German foreign policy; and they suggest that Soviet foreign policy was in between. This difference between Soviet-U.S. and Soviet-West German relations is fundamental. The skeptical evaluation appears to be merely exaggerated with regard to the former but quite incorrect with regard to the latter.

It would be desirable to be able to check this impression by the use of systematic data. To my knowledge, no fully satisfactory data exist. There are clues, however. One set of events data confirms that there was less conflict in Soviet-West European relations than in Soviet-U.S. relations throughout the period 1974–79, and a smaller increase in conflict from 1974–76 to 1977–79 in the former case than in the latter (Hopmann 1981). It can be shown on the basis of another data set that the ratio of the number of cooperative actions to the number of cooperative plus conflictive actions was consistently lower in the relationship between the United States and the Soviet Union than in the relationship between the Soviet Union and West Germany throughout the period 1971–78; moreover, the decrease after 1975 was very much larger in the former than in the latter.[2] Trade data, it may be added, show a

---

[2] This is based on COPDAB data taken from Frei and Ruloff 1983, 2: 232–41.

similar pattern: in the period 1974–81, Soviet imports from West Germany were, on the average, 1.4 times larger than its imports from the United States, and its exports to West Germany were 12 times larger than its exports to the United States; trade with the United States, moreover, dropped about 50 percent after 1979, whereas no such decrease occurred in trade with West Germany.[3]

Why this difference between Soviet-West German and Soviet-U.S. relations? Why did détente survive more fully in the former case than in the latter? Two possibilities exist in the present framework of analysis: a difference in stress, and a difference in stabilization. It will be argued below that the former difference does not suffice to explain the difference in outcome. Rather, the two relations appear to have been exposed to reasonably similar pressures for change, and therefore a comparison between U.S., West German, and Soviet détente policy is apt to shed light on the problems and possibilities of détente stabilization.

4.2. The Pressures for Change

There are at least four common, obvious ways of explaining why détente failed or, rather, why the détente crisis occurred.

1. Shifts in the balance of power. Détente had been a response to— or had been made possible by—a particular strategic situation among the Great Powers, and this situation changed in the course of the 1970s. In particular, the balance of military capability shifted to the advantage of the USSR. The United States, on the other hand, had been in a peculiarly weak position in the early 1970s because of the war in Vietnam; the healing of the wounds could not but strengthen the inclination to meet the challenge posed by Soviet rearmament.

2. Disappointments. The United States had expected the Soviet Union to be more restrained in the Third World. The Soviet Union had expected the United States to be more forthcoming on trade and on China and, generally, to be awarded the status of an equal by the United States (Blacker 1983).

3. A series of international crises, from the Yom Kippur war and Angola to Afghanistan and Poland (this aspect is considered in detail in George 1983).

4. Substantively irrelevant events with big consequences like Watergate, which drove a leading proponent of détente from power.

[3] Data from the 1979 and 1981 editions of the United Nations *Yearbook of International Trade Statistics*.

According to the first explanation, the détente crisis resulted from a change in conditions—that is, from pressure for adaptation (see chapter 1). According to the second explanation, the crisis was the result of negative feedback—that is, of pressure for learning. The remaining explanations refer to two kinds of residual factors. Détente, in other words, had come about under the impact of a certain state of the balance of power; it was associated with certain expectations regarding the adversary; and it was brought about by certain political leaders. As long as the balance of power remained the same, the adversary behaved as expected, the same men remained in power, and no unforeseen, dramatic event occurred, détente could be expected to continue. It received stress when the balance of power changed, when expectations were baffled, when shifts in government took place, and when it was exposed to international crises.

It is not necessary for our present purposes to consider the various explanations of the détente crisis more closely. What needs to be emphasized is that they are trivial. These are not exceptional events but everyday occurrences in international politics. It can be taken for granted that the balance of power will change; at the very least, economic and technological developments will keep producing long-term shifts in the distribution of advantages and disadvantages, opportunities and vulnerabilities (Gilpin 1981). Disappointments are equally difficult to avoid: assumptions about the adversary sufficiently optimistic to produce a policy of détente are unlikely to be fully realistic. Shifts in government are unavoidable, even though the particular circumstances of Watergate were exceptional, and crises are commonplace in international politics.

It cannot be maintained, then, that the 1970s were uncommonly hostile to détente. The skeptical evaluation seems to be essentially correct on this point. The test was not unrealistically difficult.

But was it reasonably similar in the Soviet-American and Soviet-West German cases? As pointed out previously, it is assumed in this study that the difference in outcome cannot be fully explained in terms of a difference in stress; this is the rationale for maintaining that a comparison between the two cases is apt to shed light on the impact of stabilizers.

One disturbance, first of all, was unique to the United States: Watergate. We cannot know what would have happened to West Germany's Ostpolitik if its chief architects had been driven from power under equally humiliating circumstances. It also seems obvious that Moscow had more reason to be disappointed with Washington than with Bonn. The point usually made in the West, however, is that there was a difference in stress in the sense that Soviet provocations were directed primarily against its companion superpower and not against a smaller power like West Germany. This is the critical objection to the claim that the cases are reasonably comparable.

The argument is plausible so far as Soviet activities in Africa are concerned as well as with regard to the increase in Soviet intercontinental ballistic missile (ICBM) capability. It is less plausible in the case of Afghanistan: if the Soviet invasion implied a threat to its neighbors and to Western oil supplies, this threat was at least as significant for Western Europe as for the United States. And the argument is quite implausible in the case of the Polish crisis and the buildup of Soviet intermediate range missiles. Hence, it cannot be considered self-evident, to say the least, that all of the difference between Bonn's and Washington's policy toward Moscow was due to a difference in stress from Soviet behavior (unless it is assumed that any unfriendly Soviet act is necessarily a greater challenge to the companion superpower than to anybody else).

The assumption that the difference in stress was insufficient to bring about the difference in outcome would seem to be justified. Reasonable similarity in stress does not suffice to establish comparability, however. John Stuart Mill is credited with having been the first to formulate the comparative method in a strict way. What he calls the "method of difference" consists of "comparing instances in which [a] phenomenon does occur, with instances in other respects similar in which it does not" (quoted from Lijphart 1971: 687). To guarantee similarity "in other respects" is the crucial difficulty, and Mill himself thought the method inapplicable to the social sciences.

Lijphart has suggested a number of ways to ameliorate the problem, but none of them could have been used here (pp. 688–89). There is no getting away from the fact that the comparability of the two cases cannot be satisfactorily established. For example, it appears that there is a difference in political culture—Americans seem more apt than Europeans to assume political problems to be solvable. Such a difference would render changes in conditions and negative feedback more likely to provoke a change of policy in the United States than in Western Europe, even if the previous policy had been equally stabilized on both sides of the Atlantic. There is no way of controlling for this possibility in the present study.

Therefore, the conclusions that will be drawn are bound to be tentative. This, however, raises the question whether definite proof is necessary in order for the results to be useful. The method employed here is reminiscent of what Alexander George calls the method of "focused comparison," which in essence is to develop theory by making systematic intensive studies of a number of cases on the basis of a common set of questions. His advocacy of this method is linked to his view of the role of theory in policymaking. Focused comparison is considered to be a means for developing theory that is specific enough to be relevant for policy. Such theory is presumed to be useful even if the degree of verification is less than is generally considered necessary for scientific generalizations. The criterion for the plausibility of an assumption is suggested to be that it does not contradict established facts and is supported by some facts, at least (George and Smoke 1974: 94–97, 616–39; George 1979).

The comparison to follow between American-Soviet and West German-Soviet relations is based on a similar view of the utility of making comparisons. Even though the cases are not perfectly comparable, comparing them is apt to provide insights into the problems and possibilities of détente stabilization that are plausible enough to be useful and that could not have been obtained by mere theorizing or by the study of a single case.

The use of the comparative method in the present study is further discussed in the Appendix.

4.3. The Détente Construction

One element remains in the skeptical evaluation of the 1970s: the "détente construction." Did the construction represent a maximum? What was it like? To what extent did the difference in outcome between Soviet-American and Soviet-West German détente result from a stronger "détente construction" in the latter case than in the former? What would such a difference imply for future attempts at détente?

Détente construction—this notion will be explored with the help of the concept of the foreign policy stabilizer. We will examine the extent to which each of the stabilizers in the checklist presented in chapter 2 did in fact emerge, compare the Soviet-American case to the Soviet-West German one, and consider whether a difference in stabilization can account for the difference in outcome. The two will also be compared to what a maximally stabilized détente relationship—a maximally advanced détente construction—would be like.

It is because of its focus on stabilizers that this study of détente can hope to make a contribution. In the literature on the theme of "why détente failed," much has already been said about the pressures for abandoning this policy, whereas there seems to have been less interest in a comprehensive consideration of the factors that might have protected détente but failed to do it. There is obviously much to learn from, say, the misperceptions and provocations of the parties. However, there may also be something to learn from a study of the other aspect—the weaknesses of the détente construction itself and its consequent vulnerability to misunderstandings, provocations, and other disturbances.

It has not been possible to make a full-scale empirical study of the détente construction, however. To examine in detail each of the thirteen stabilizers with regard to three different countries was a task beyond the means of the present project. The extent of détente stabilization in the United States, West Germany, and the Soviet Union will be considered in broad outline only. Comprehensiveness entails a cost in thoroughness.

The limitations imposed on me by necessity are from one point of view a virtue, however. I hope that the concepts proposed in Part One may prove useful as practical tools for the analysis of immediate issues. What follows can in part be regarded as an exploration of what such a less ambitious use of the concepts may be like—a consideration, if you wish, of the utility of that empirical information about foreign policy stabilizers that can be obtained with a relatively limited effort.

CHAPTER 5

The International Stabilization of Détente

5.1. NORMATIVE REGULATION

THE EAST AND THE WEST pursued policies of détente toward each other for a time. This fact by definition implies that there occurred a minimum degree of regulation in the form of customary norms. The extent to which détente was also regulated by explicit agreement is striking, however. The several agreements can be regarded as deliberate attempts at détente stabilization. The objective of this section is to assess how far the attempts went.

We will consider first the Helsinki Final Act of 1975 and then some of the bilateral Soviet-American and Soviet-West German agreements. Our concern is with the legal status of the rules, the occurrence of contradictory regulation, and the problems of application associated with the rules (these concerns were explained in section 2.1).

The Helsinki Final Act The Helsinki Final Act is an extremely detailed document covering everything from the nonuse of force to the use of containers. All three dimensions of détente—restraint, arms control, and cooperation—are treated in this document at both a very general and a very specific level.

The legal status of the act may have a bearing on its efficiency as a stabilizer. If the act were binding under international law, violations would legally justify reprisals as well as claims for compensation. It might also be more costly politically to break a binding obligation than to violate a weaker form of commitment. International lawyers appear to agree that the act is not legally binding (Kühne 1977: 138; McWhinney 1978: 164–66; Schütz 1977: 158–59). It is pointed out, among other things, that several participants in the Helsinki process made it clear that they did not intend to create a binding treaty.

On the other hand, the Helsinki Final Act is considered to be more than merely a nonbinding declaration of intentions. One author suggests that the act may in practice have the juridical status and quality of a treaty (McWhinney 1978: 165). Another author emphasizes that, even though not legally binding, the act is "not irrelevant" from the point of view of international law (Schütz 1977: 165). The act appears to be located in a gray area between law and nonlaw; it is similar to unanimous United Nations resolutions, according to an official evaluation of Sweden's Foreign Ministry (UD 1975: 9) and is *rechtsähnlich*, as a German commentator puts it (Kühne 1977: 138).

The incompatibility or inconsistency most often ascribed to the act is the one between the principle of nonintervention on the one hand and the protection of human rights on the other (Schütz 1977: 169–70). It resulted from the fact that the West made a Soviet commitment to human rights a condition for accepting the status quo in Europe. Hence, the act is not just a detailed codification of the principles of détente in the relatively narrow sense of the present study (see section 4.1) but also includes Guiding Principle VII: "respect for human rights and fundamental freedoms, including the freedom of thought, conscience, religion or belief." Guiding Principle VII is special in its concern with the domestic affairs of the parties rather than with the relations between them.

The act maintains that there is no incompatibility: respect for "human rights and fundamental freedoms," it says, "is an essential factor for the peace, justice and well-being necessary to ensure the development of friendly relations and co-operation." Still, a trade-off may be difficult to avoid between restraint and cooperation, on the one hand, and concern with the human rights situation of the adversary, on the other. It can be taken for granted that a government accused of violating Guiding Principle VII will reply that the accusation does not only violate Guiding Principle VI about nonintervention but also the "Helsinki spirit" and hence that it is a threat to détente.

It is important to note that Guiding Principle VII has been considered in the West to have changed the rules of the game. Sweden's Foreign Ministry, for example, has officially maintained that the act has made human rights a proper object of negotiation and that this represents "essential progress" (UD 1975: 9). A legal analyst argues that the act rules out the use of the principle of nonintervention in the human rights area (Schütz 1977: 170). This is precisely the reason why the act may be problematic from the point of view of regulating détente in the narrow sense. The reality of the problem became apparent during the follow-up meeting held in Belgrade in 1977 (UD 1978: 18). Western comments on human rights in the Eastern countries contributed to putting détente under stress. The Helsinki Final Act may be considered to have established not just a right but even an obligation to put forward this sort of criticism. Hence, the act may have served not just to stabilize but also to destabilize détente.

It goes without saying that the act is associated with problems of application. This is pointed out, for example, in an evaluation published by Sweden's Foreign Ministry: "Many of the prescriptions of the document are so vague that they may be interpreted in different ways without its being possible to maintain that a given signatory has violated them" (UD 1975: 9).

The very method of interpretation is uncertain. This is considered to follow from the act's ambiguous legal status. A common view appears to be that it is irrelevant to apply ordinary rules of legal interpretation and in particular to refer to the "spirit" of the document for guidance. Rather, it has been argued, interpretation must proceed from the political, military, and social circumstances surrounding the act (Kühne 1977: 142–46). This would seem to imply that the risk of indisputably violating the document is limited.

The act also carries another fundamental problem of application: distinguishing between unjustified violations and justifiable retaliation. This problem stands out even more clearly in the U.S.-Soviet Basic Principles agreement and will be considered below.

U.S.-Soviet Relations   A large number of treaties and agreements were made between the United States and the Soviet Union in the early 1970s (Nygren and Lavery 1981: 23). Most were concerned with such specific matters as trade. Their sum, however, amounted to a bilateral Helsinki act, with one exception and one addition. The exception: human rights were not included in this package. The addition: substantial agreements were made about arms control, including SALT I. The relationship between the superpowers was so close for a time that a rule of the game seemed to be emerging that their respective national security was an issue for common consideration, economic cooperation a matter for continuing expansion by agreement, and governmental contact at the highest level a regular feature.

Two agreements were especially important in the sense of formally establishing general rules of conduct. One was the remarkable Basic Principles agreement (BPA), which was signed by Leonid Brezhnev and Richard Nixon in Moscow in May 1972. This was followed by the Agreement on the Prevention of Nuclear War (APNW), which they signed in Washington in June 1973.[1]

The BPA constituted a "charter defining the basis for the further development of détente" (George 1983: 107). According to its first article, the parties would "proceed from the common determination that in the nuclear age there is no alternative to conducting their

---

[1] The texts can be found, for example, in *Keesing's Contemporary Archives (KCA)* 1972: 25313–14; 1973: 25999.

mutual relations on the basis of peaceful coexistence." The second article amounted to a mutual commitment to the restraint dimension of détente: the United States and the Soviet Union attached "major importance to preventing the development of situations capable of causing a dangerous exacerbation of their relations"; they would "do their utmost to avoid military confrontations and to prevent the outbreak of nuclear war"; they would "always exercise restraint in their mutual relations" and would be "prepared to negotiate and settle differences by peaceful means"; they recogized that "efforts to obtain unilateral advantages at the expense of the other, directly or indirectly," were "inconsistent with these objectives." According to the third article, the parties had a "special responsibility . . . to do everything in their power so that conflicts or situations will not arise which would serve to increase international tensions." Other parts of the document dealt with arms control and cooperation.

The APNW elaborated on the undertaking to exercise restraint. The parties agreed to "act in such a manner as to prevent the development of situations capable of causing a dangerous exacerbation of their relations" and to exclude the outbreak of nuclear war. They agreed, moreover, "to proceed from the premise" that each party would refrain from the threat or use of force "in circumstances which may endanger international peace and security." If a risk of nuclear war were to arise, the United States and the Soviet Union should "immediately enter into urgent consultations with each other and make every effort to avert this risk."

The validity of the détente principles, and specifically of the BPA, was further confirmed at the summits Brezhnev held with American presidents: with Nixon in 1973 (KCA 1973: 26001–3), with Ford in 1974 (1974: 26869), and with Carter in 1979 (1980: 30123–25). Hence, we are dealing here with a set of rules that, even though not contained in a binding treaty, were agreed on at the highest level and were repeatedly reaffirmed, also at the highest level, over a period of seven years.

One contradiction in the BPA is often pointed out, however. The document included, in Articles 1 and 2, respectively, an acceptance of "peaceful coexistence" and a commitment to restraint. Much has been said to the effect that there was a mutual misunderstanding on this point and that this is why détente failed later on. More likely, both sides were aware that "peaceful coexistence" might imply Soviet actions in third areas of the type Article 2 might appear to rule out.[2]

[2] See George 1983: 107–10. For a detailed study of the Soviet concept of peaceful coexistence, see Nygren 1984.

Soviet-American disagreement over what détente ought to mean was resolved by including both views in the BPA, thereby making the regulation of détente inconsistent in this respect.

Among the several problems of application associated with the BPA and the APNW four may be mentioned. They reflect more general difficulties with limiting international violence by making rules.

First, some of the verbs used in the BPA were only weakly committing. The parties "will proceed from the common determination that"; "attach major importance to"; "will do their utmost to avoid"; "will be prepared to"; "have a special responsibility to do everything in their power so that"; "will seek to promote"; "intend to"; "reaffirm their readiness to"; and so on. It can always be discussed whether rules expressed in such terms have been violated or not.

Second, the principles were in large measure formulated as obligations to prevent particular situations from occurring—situations that were not defined in precise terms. It may not be self-evident whether a situation is "capable of causing a dangerous exacerbation" of a relationship or whether, under the circumstances, an action amounts to an "effort to obtain unilateral advantage at the expense of" the other party. The controversy over whether Soviet activities in the Third World "violated" détente showed this problem of application to be far from hypothetical (George 1983: 114–15).

Third, several rules prescribed that the parties do something in common: negotiate, exchange views, attempt to limit armaments, agree on trade, and so on. It is rarely difficult to put the blame on the adversary if negotiations do not take place, views are not exchanged, armaments are not limited, and so forth.

Finally, the BPA, the APNW, and all the other documents regulating U.S.-Soviet détente may be assumed to have implied a right, perhaps even a duty, to reply in kind to violations. When this is the case with a set of norms—when, as in the United Nations Charter, aggression is prohibited but defense is permitted—distinguishing between the offense and the defense is a central problem of application. Who began? Which act was an unjustified deviation from détente, and which act was justifiable retaliation? In ambiguous situations—and many situations are ambiguous—both parties may be able to argue that they are obliged by the rules to punish the adversary. Then the rules encourage rather than inhibit escalation. This problem cannot be fully solved by prescribing proportionality. The difficulty of determining in actual situations what is proportional and what is not tends to render this prescription ineffective, which is one more experience of the attempts of generations to outlaw war.

In the Soviet view, the accusation that Soviet involvement in Angola contravened détente testified to "a false understanding of the meaning of détente, which never implied and cannot imply giving a free hand to aggressors" (*New Times*, quoted in Nogee and Donaldson 1981: 274). There can be no better illustration of the parallel between the problem that Nixon and Brezhnev purported to solve—that is, the stabilization of détente by the making of rules—and the classical problem of proscribing war and at the same time permitting defense against aggression.

Soviet-West German Relations   Between the Soviet Union and West Germany détente was formalized by treaty. The so-called Eastern treaties, which played such an important part in the shift from Cold War to détente, were not only concerned with regulating some of the problems left unresolved since 1945. In Article 1 of the Soviet-West German treaty of 1970, the parties also stated that they considered it "an important objective of their policies to maintain international peace and achieve détente." They affirmed their endeavor "to further the normalization of the situation in Europe and the development of peaceful relations among all European States." The preamble made it clear that this included the expansion of economic, scientific, technological, and cultural cooperation and contacts. The so-called Bahr Paper associated with the treaty confirmed that the two parties would "continue to develop" such relations.[3]

Cooperation and contacts were the main themes in the joint documents that emanated from Soviet-West German summits in the 1970s. Brezhnev and Willy Brandt agreed in 1971 that there existed "extensive possibilities" for cooperation "in the most diverse fields" and that "the practice of exchanging views and of consultation at various levels" was "useful and should be continued" (*KCA* 1971: 24857). In 1973 they expressed their joint determination to develop their relations on the basis of the treaty of 1970; "meetings and exchanges of views between political leaders" would play "a special role," and the development of economic and industrial relations was "a major aim of both countries' policies" (1973: 25977). Annual foreign ministers' meetings were institutionalized in 1974 (1975: 26896). When Brezhnev visited West Germany in 1978, he and Helmut Schmidt issued a joint declaration reaffirming the treaty of 1970 and containing a strong commitment to further détente: "Détente is necessary, pos-

[3] On the Eastern treaties, see Birnbaum 1973: chap. 1. The texts cited here can be found on pp. 109–16.

sible and useful. . . . [There is] no reasonable alternative to peaceful cooperation between states. . . . [We] wish to expand and deepen the process of détente and to make it progressive and stable" (1978: 29093–94).

DÉTENTE, in summary, became extensively regulated. All three dimensions—restraint, arms control, and cooperation—were prescribed in agreements of various kinds. The two first-mentioned dimensions were more prominent in Soviet-American than in Soviet-West German relations, but this difference may not have been significant; all three dimensions were present in the Helsinki Final Act, which was valid for both bilateral relations.

The regulations had three weaknesses from the point of view of détente stabilization, however. First, with the exception of the Soviet-West German treaty, the legal status of the détente agreements was less than that of a formal treaty. Second, the regulation of détente as defined in the present study was combined with agreements on norms that were to some extent inconsistent with détente in this sense—such as the inclusion of human rights in the Helsinki Final Act and of "peaceful coexistence" in the BPA. Third, détente regulation was associated with fundamental problems of application—not just because of oversight or because difficulties were papered over but also because of problems that may be inherent in attempts to prescribe détente between sovereign states.

5.2. DEPENDENCE

Dependence here refers to the structural adaptation of a state to the continued pursuit of a foreign policy (see section 2.1). In the case of a policy of détente, this is generally thought to be mainly a matter of adaptation to economic interaction with the adversary. It has long been controversial whether economic relations help to preserve peace; Blainey (1973) is often quoted in support of the view that it is a liberal prejudice that the two are connected. This has also been a much-discussed aspect of East-West détente. Other kinds of dependence have hardly been mentioned in this context, and only the economic aspect is considered in this study.

Dependence on economic interaction is necessarily mutual. The terms *mutual dependence* and *interdependence* will be used interchangeably. This is not meant to suggest that interdependence is necessarily symmetrical. The opposite is more likely the case. As will be shown in this section, the interdependence that appears to have developed between the East and the West during détente was quite asymmetrical.

Interdependence helps to stabilize détente—this hypothesis was part not only of Henry Kissinger's thinking (see, for example, Starr 1984) but also of that of the West German government (Kreile 1980: 138) as well as of the Soviet leadership (Nygren 1984: 176–80). The hypothesis, as mentioned already, has not gone unchallenged. The effects of East-West cooperation, in the words of one of the several authors considering the matter, "is one of the most controversial problems in the contemporary discussion of détente." At the end of the 1970s, she writes, it remained impossible to determine which tendency was the stronger one, since intersystemic cooperation had proven to have both stabilizing and conflict-generating aspects (Fritsch-Bournazel 1980: 47, 49).

A prerequisite for considering whether the evidence from the 1970s supports the hypothesis that economic interdependence functions as a stabilizer of détente is an assessment of the extent to which the parties became dependent on each other. This is not easy to do (some of the difficulties with such a study are considered in Dunér 1977). As emphasized in section 2.1, structural dependence cannot be precisely measured. The use of simple economic indicators is worthwhile but insufficient. A detailed economic analysis of each of the parties to the détente process would be needed; the objective would be to consider in as much detail as possible the economic effects of their mutual economic relations so as to be able to make as good an assessment as possible of what it would imply for each of them if this relationship were interrupted. Such a detailed analysis could not be made within the framework of the present study. The objective here, as pointed out previously, is limited to exploring what can be obtained by simpler means. We will have to rest content with some basic data about East-West trade plus some of the assessments economists have published about its significance.

In the 1970s, the link between economic interaction and political détente was commonly discussed as a matter of "leverage." It was assumed that economic relations could be used to induce the adversary to continue to pursue a policy of détente. Since economic dependence is mutual, the link between economic "leverage" and détente is an intricate one, however. The mutuality of economic interdependence poses a problem for the analysis of its role as a stabilizer of détente that is reminiscent of the logic of mutual nuclear deterrence. This matter is considered in chapter 10.

Soviet foreign trade multiplied in the 1970s. The trade turnover in current prices increased from about 22 billion rubles in 1970 to about 63 billion rubles in 1977 or from about $25 billion in 1970 to about $86 billion in 1977. In volume, this represented an increase in Soviet exports of 66 percent and in imports of 88 percent (Dohan 1979: 369; Caldwell and Diebold 1981: 53; for detailed data about Soviet export values, 1955–76, see Treml 1980: 187).

Trade with the West increased even more. The Soviet Union "realized a dramatic shift in the geographic direction of its trade away from socialist countries and toward capitalist countries" (Hewett 1983: 274). Different authors define "capitalist countries" and "the West" differently, and therefore their data on East-West trade differ. However, the shift from Eastern Europe to the West is obvious. Cooper reports that Soviet exports to the West increased from 19 percent of total exports in 1970 to 32 percent in 1980 and that imports from the West increased from 24 percent of total imports in 1970 to 35 percent in 1980. At the same time, exports to Eastern Europe decreased from 53 percent of total exports (1970) to 42 percent (1980) and imports from 57 percent (1970) to 43 percent (1980) (Cooper 1982: 460; for similar data, see Caldwell and Diebold 1981: 53). Using an index employed by Hewett that set 1970 as 100, the quantity of total Soviet exports was 148 in 1974 and 190 in 1978, whereas exports to capitalist countries increased to 170 and 242, respectively. Similarly, whereas total imports were 160 in 1974 and 236 in 1978, imports from capitalist countries increased to 189 and 293, respectively (Hewett 1983: 272). The nominal annual growth rate in trade with the West, which in the period 1966–70 had been 10.7 percent for exports and 12.3 percent for imports, increased to 22.5 percent and 30.5 percent, respectively, in the period 1971–75 (Antal 1980: 221).

By the mid-1970s, however, "the momentum for expanding East-West economic relations . . . declined markedly" (Bornstein 1979: 299), and the "expansionary phase" was replaced by a "period of consolidation" (Kreile 1980: 139). The loss of momentum was primarily a matter of a declining growth rate in Soviet exports (Stankovsky 1981: 48). The further expansion of East-West trade was inhibited by recession in the West in combination with growing debts in the East (Bornstein 1979: 299).

When assessing the significance of the rapid increase in East-West economic relations during the first half of the 1970s, it is necessary first to emphasize that East-West trade remained a small proportion of world trade. According to GATT statistics, exports from the "Eastern trading area" (CMEA plus Mongolia, Vietnam, Cuba, China, and North Korea) to "industrial areas" (the rest of the world minus OPEC and "other developing countries") composed a mere 2.6 percent of world trade turnover in 1978, whereas trade in the reverse direction composed 3.2 percent of world trade. This was only slightly more than fifteen years earlier: the percentage in 1963 had been 2.3 for both exports and imports. In contrast, trade within the category of countries called "industrial areas" amounted to 45 percent of world trade in both 1963 and 1978 (GATT 1979: 5). The amount of intra-Western trade, in other words, remained about eight times that of East-West trade.

Another feature of the trade expansion in the 1970s was the striking difference between the Soviet-American relationship and Soviet-West German relations. The difference is illustrated by the following data about mean annual exports and imports (U.S.$ billion) during the period 1977–79, that is, during the "period of consolidation":[4]

	United States	West Germany
exports to Soviet Union	2.495	3.182
imports from Soviet Union	.286	2.741

Whereas the United States was somewhat less important than West Germany as an exporter to the Soviet Union, there was a radical difference with regard to imports. Exports and imports were approximately balanced between the Soviet Union and West Germany, whereas Soviet exports to the United States were miniscule. Interdependence was more asymmetrical in the Soviet-American than in the Soviet-West German dyad.

The difference can be further illuminated by the use of data published by Stankovsky (1981: 76–81). In 1978, 46 percent of OECD exports to the Soviet Union came from the European Community and 20 percent from West Germany alone, whereas 14 percent came from the United States. Ranking OECD countries according to the Eastern share of their total exports in 1978 (of which roughly half went to the Soviet Union), gives these results:

1. Finland 21%
6. West Germany 5%
   Sweden 5%
   Switzerland 5%
13. United States 3%

[4] The data are computed on the basis of export and import values reported for the United States and West Germany in the United Nations *Yearbook of International Trade Statistics* for 1981.

Similarly, 57 percent of total OECD imports from the Soviet Union in 1978 went to the European Community and 19 percent to West Germany alone but only 4 percent to the United States. Ranking OECD members in terms of the Eastern share of their total imports (half of which came from the USSR) gives this result:

1. Finland 23%
6. Sweden 5%
   West Germany 5%
   Italy 5%
   Denmark 5%
20. United States 1%

Bearing in mind the smaller size of the West German economy, these data suggest a rather clear ranking of the four "dependencies" considered here: West Germany on the Soviet Union, the Soviet Union on West Germany, the Soviet Union on the United States, and the United States on the Soviet Union. These dependencies will now be considered in more detail.

West Germany   Opinions differ about the extent to which Western Europe in general and West Germany in particular became dependent on trade with the Soviet Union during the "period of expansion."

One author suggested in 1979 that exports to the Soviet Union had become an important counter-cyclical force in several West German industrial branches and that "many West Europeans probably live with the fear" that their trade "could be adversely affected by a fundamental deterioration in United States-Soviet relations" (Wolf 1979: 320, 324). It was also pointed out that much trade with the USSR was conducted through long-term agreements and that they would be difficult to renegotiate if trade were interrupted (Hardt and Tomlinson 1983: 186). Italian industrialist Giovanni Agnelli thought that even though Western Europe was insufficiently dependent on East-West trade to be "forced to sacrifice any vital interest . . . just to maintain trade with the East," there was reason for concern over the possibility of reducing or cutting off East-West trade, since 300,000 jobs in Europe directly—and many more indirectly—depended on it and since the cut would be concentrated in particular segments of the mechanical industry (1980: 1030). This emphasis on the need of the Western Europeans to continue their exports to the Soviet Union was replaced to some extent in the early 1980s by concern with their energy imports.

Other observers emphasized instead the relative unimportance of Soviet-West German trade. Kreile recalled that West German industry was an early supporter of the Ostpolitik; still, he suggested the "overall significance" of West Germany's trade with the East to have remained "relatively modest" (1980: 138). Stent, in her oft-quoted work about the economic aspects of the Ostpolitik, concluded that "one should not exaggerate the dependence of either economy on the other." Even though "dependency figures" for certain sectors were "not insignificant," they "do not represent a substantial dependency for either economy" (1981: 214–15). A study of Soviet-West German interdependence published in 1982 by the Deutsches Institut für Wirtschaftsforschung (DIW), from which we will quote extensively (Bethkenhagen and Machowski 1982), also reached this conclusion.

Those who share this view start out by emphasizing that, even though it grew rapidly, Soviet-West German trade remained limited. At the end of the 1970s, trade between the two countries did not amount to more than about 1 percent of West Germany's GNP (p. 11; see also Cooper 1982: 464). The total trade of West Germany, by contrast, corresponded to almost half of its GNP. It was pointed out in the DIW report that West German imports from the Soviet Union was merely DM 120 per capita, as compared with total imports of DM 5,560 per capita. This, according to the report, was too little to create significant dependence (p. 12).

The composition of Soviet-West German trade was asymmetrical. It was basically a matter of exchanging Soviet raw materials, particularly energy, for West German industrial goods. By 1980, about three-fourths of West German imports from the Soviet Union consisted of fuels. The figure for 1981 was 77 percent. An additional tenth consisted of other raw materials, whereas the import of manufactures amounted to less than 9 percent. On the other hand, no less than 86 percent of West Germany's exports to the USSR in 1981 consisted of manufactures, of which 34 percent was machinery, 35 percent semifinished tools, and 13 percent chemicals (Cooper 1982: 464; for additional data, see Stent 1981: 211). According to the DIW study, a trade war would be more expensive for West Germany than for the Soviet Union in the short run, but in the long run it would be the other way around. The West German economy would suffer in particular from disturbances in the supply of energy, but this could be repaired; the Soviet Union would, however, suffer a decrease in long term economic growth (Bethkenhagen and Machowski 1982: 11).

West Germany's economic dependence on the Soviet Union, then, had two aspects: its export of manufactures and its import of raw materials. As regards the former, the DIW study rejected a Soviet claim that West German-Soviet cooperation had secured as many as 500,000

German jobs. A more correct figure, according to the report, was that in 1979 about 90,000 people were engaged, directly or indirectly, in producing goods for export to the USSR. This amounted to about .4 percent of those employed; the figure had been .5 percent in 1976 (p. 13; for a slightly higher estimate, see Cooper 1982: 464). The proportion, however, exceeded 1 percent in two sectors: metal products (2.7 percent in both 1976 and 1979) and machinery, including computers (2.5 percent in 1976, 1.8 percent in 1979). This corresponded to about 22,000 jobs in the former sector and about 31,000 (1976) or 21,000 (1979) jobs in the latter. Almost every second person producing exports to the Soviet Union could be found in these two sectors. The DIW study concluded that even though a noticeable dependence might obtain for some enterprises and some regions, the effect on the economy as a whole was too small to provide the USSR with political leverage (pp. 15–18).

As regards imports, the main dependency problem was related to energy. The share of West Germany's energy consumption that was imported from the Soviet Union increased from 2.4 percent in 1970 to 4.1 percent in 1975 to 5.5 percent in 1980. The essence of the detailed argument in the DIW study was that this did not amount to signficant dependence. A sizeable proportion of West German imports of certain important metals also came from the USSR, including nickel (75 percent in 1980), palladium (48 percent), and titanium (22 percent). However, according to the DIW study, these and some other products, which were also bought from the USSR, could be stockpiled and could be bought elsewhere without serious difficulty (pp. 21–27; on West Germany's dependence on raw materials from the USSR see also Cooper 1982: 464).

More than marginal but less than vital—this may be a reasonable summary characterization of the importance of Soviet trade for West Germany.

United States   Soviet-U.S. trade in the 1970s consisted mainly of American grain sales. About two-thirds of U.S. exports to the Soviet Union were agricultural (Heiss, Lenz, and Brougher 1979: 191). The far smaller U.S. imports from the Soviet Union consisted primarily of such raw materials as platinum, palladium, chrome, and petroleum (Goldman 1982: 118).

Wolf (1979), in an analysis of the distribution of costs and benefits in U.S.-Soviet trade, made a distinction between dependence on the adversary as a supplier of raw materials and intermediate products and as a market. Neither type of dependence was likely to become significant for the United States "even with greatly expanded trade with the Soviet Union." The only possible exceptions were certain metals (in 1976, about one-fourth of American imports of platinum came from the Soviet Union). Wolf also suggested, however, that the need of the U.S. government to respond to the demand of American farmers for access to the Soviet grain market might be greater than that of the Soviet government to satisfy the demands of Soviet consumers (pp. 322–24).

The first major grain sales were negotiated in 1972. The value of U.S. agricultural exports to the USSR in that year was about $460 million. This figure increased considerably during the 1970s and peaked in 1979 at a level of about $3 billion (Byrne et al. 1982: 74). American farmers adapted to this expansion of their market. In the words of Marshall Goldman, "excited by the prospects, the farmers expanded their crop potential to take advantage of the opportunity. The general prosperity such large sales seemed to promise set off an expansion of farming activity and an increase in land values" (1982: 124). Hence the controversy over the partial embargo imposed by the Carter administration after the Soviet invasion of Afghanistan. The embargo was lifted by the Reagan administration, and in March 1982 Reagan reaffirmed that farm exports would not be used as a foreign policy instrument except in extreme situations, and then only as part of a general embargo (Byrne et al. 1982: 66).

The cost of the embargo to the United States was difficult to assess. Commodity prices returned to pre-embargo levels after only a few weeks. This, however, was due to such government actions as storing embargoed grain in reserves and buying up canceled contracts at a cost of more than $2 billion. The embargoed grain, moreover, dampened market prices. There was also the long-term difficulty of regaining the previous share of the Soviet market; because of the embargo, Argentina had replaced the United States as the largest grain supplier to the Soviet Union (Roney 1982: 135–36).

The American grain sales to the Soviet Union illustrate the mechanism of détente stabilization by economic dependence with great clarity. The sales began as an aspect of détente and led to structural adaptation on the part of American farmers. This made it more costly for the American government to deviate from détente than it would otherwise have been. The cost prevented the embargo from enduring and caused the Reagan administration to commit itself against future embargos. In other words, U.S. export dependence visibly protected an aspect of the détente policy. At the same time, this dependence was limited to a single sector, and so was its stabilizing effect; it had little visible impact on détente in general.

The Soviet Union   One of the issues in the Western controversy over détente has been the question of Soviet dependence on East-West trade. No measure of the importance of foreign trade for the Soviet economy is generally accepted. Hence assessments differ.

Treml (1980), for example, reports Soviet trade turnover to have increased from 11 percent of national income in 1960 to 15 percent in 1970 and to 21 percent in 1976. The last-mentioned figure, according to Treml, equals 16 percent of the GDP of the Soviet Union. This, Treml explains, is less than the world average but "in the category of such countries as the United States, Brazil, Argentina, and Turkey" (pp. 187–89).

Treml's data and interpretations have been questioned by Bergson, who suggests that Soviet trade turnover in 1976 was merely between 4.5 percent and 5.9 percent of GDP (see Rosefielde 1980: 153; Bergson 1980: 207–11). A third analyst, Turpin, estimates total Soviet trade to have composed about 10 percent of the GNP in 1975 (1977: 31).

On the basis of the last-mentioned estimate, trade with West Germany amounted to about .6 percent and trade with the United States to about .4 percent of the GNP of the Soviet Union by the mid-1970s. These data are very uncertain; the DIW study quoted above found trade with West Germany in 1979 to compose only about .4 percent of the Soviet GNP (Bethkenhagen and Machowski 1982: 38). It is clear, however, that not even toward the end of the "period of expansion" in East-West trade did either country play a significant part for the overall Soviet economy.

Dohan in 1979 reported a study examining in detail the extent to which foreign trade had led to export specialization and import dependence (his terms) on the part of the Soviet Union. The former was defined as exports relative to production and the latter as imports relative to consumption. Some of his findings are summarized here (Dohan 1979: 350–60).

First, Dohan found Soviet net exports of many raw materials to have increased more slowly than output in the first half of the 1970s. "Overall, the U.S.S.R.'s minerals, metals, and energy sectors appear to have become less export-oriented in the mid-1970's." For example, the export of chromite ore decreased from 74 percent of production in 1970 to 61 percent in 1975; the export of aluminum decreased from 44 percent to 40 percent; and the export of crude oil from 28 percent to 26 percent. There was practically no evidence of an increase in export specialization.

Second, the Soviet Union relied less rather than more on imports for its chemicals. For example, the import ratio for artificial fiber decreased from 14 percent in 1970 to 4 percent in 1975, and the ratio for synthetic fiber decreased from 18 percent to 13 percent.

Third, both imports and exports of machinery increased during the first half of the 1970s, but imports increased more rapidly than exports. Moreover, whereas in 1975 a mere 5 percent of the exports went to the West, 40 percent of the imports were from the West. If a distinction is made between factory equipment and mass produced items (automobiles, trucks, farm machinery, tractors, construction equipment, pumps, electric motors, and ships) almost all imports in the latter category came from Eastern Europe, whereas a significant proportion of the former, especially high technology products, came from the West; "the modernization of Soviet production facilities . . . depends on imports from the West" (p. 358).

Fourth, "the most outstanding development in the 1970s" was "the conversion of the U.S.S.R. to a regular large net importer of grain" (p. 353). The import ratio was 9 percent in 1972 and as high as 13 percent in 1975.

Fifth, intrabranch specialization became increasingly important during the 1970s. One pattern consisted of Soviet importation of advanced equipment from the West and exportation of standardized equipment to Eastern Europe and developing countries. This was true, for example, with regard to traditional high-priority industries such as metalworking, iron, and steel.

It should be added to Dohan's findings that a negative balance of merchandise trade was counterbalanced by gold sales, military sales, and net services (Hewett 1983).

Four analyses from the 1970s suggest the points at issue in the controversy over what these developments implied. Would the Soviet Union become increasingly dependent on the West as East-West economic relations multiplied? Turpin (1977) was one of those who replied in the negative. He argued that the Soviet objective in trading with the West, in addition to making up for temporary shortfalls, was to "import capital goods in large quantities followed by increasing reliance on domestic production." Hence, Soviet trade was "directed toward minimizing dependence on foreign sources" (p. 29)—imports to promote autarchy, in other words. In attempting this, the Soviet Union had the advantage of oligopolist-oligopsonist power (p. 84). Through the concentration "in the hands of its state apparatus . . . of all its external economic dealings," the USSR "is in a position to divide and conquer the outside trading world by playing both nation against nation and company against company" (p. 131).

Wolf held a different view of Soviet market power: even though it might be significant in some products, "in general it is likely to remain negligible for the foreseeable future" (1979: 337).

Marshall Goldman (1976) put forth an analysis that differed from Turpin's in a more fundamental way. He agreed that a "return to autarchy" remained possible. There was historical evidence of first Russia's and later the Soviet Union's ability to manage in spite of the interruption of its economic relations. "Moods" in the Soviet Union favored independence from the world capitalist economy. Soviet factories had a tradition of striving to be self-supporting. A decision to break off relations could be implemented more rapidly and completely than in a pluralist society.

Still, three factors pointed in a different direction, according to Goldman. First, the decision to increase meat consumption committed the USSR to import livestock feed from the United States, which was "the only country that could provide the large quantities needed by the Soviet Union" (pp. 77–78). Second, the Soviet Union had invested in exports that could not easily be converted to production for domestic use—in banking and marketing, in a merchant fleet, in the Baikal-Amur railroad, in pipelines, and in electrical grid projects. Third, the importation of technology was self-reinforcing: "If the Soviet Union is to keep abreast, it must constantly upgrade existing procedures and factories. . . . [It] will prove to be increasingly difficult to terminate interchanges of technologies and technicians once started" (pp. 93–94). Goldman concluded that by the mid-1970s the Soviet Union would still be able to extract itself from its economic relations with the West without too much trouble. However, if these relations continued to intensify, "the cost of severing ties with the West will mount rapidly" (p. 95).

Turpin's view may be labeled pessimistic and Goldman's optimistic. Müller (1977) represented an intermediate position, arguing that the West was confronted with a dilemma, an *Ambivalenzproblematik*. On the one hand, trade structures and instruments might be "stabilizing" (Müller's usage of this term is similar to mine): the West and the East would have a common interest in a long-term, stable, and predictable division of labor, and this could counterbalance "the antagonism between the systems." On the other hand, the trade structure held a potential for conflict—in the complementarity of the trade, in increasing Eastern debts, and in the risk that Western technology would serve the purposes of Soviet arms policy. Technology transfers were particularly likely to be stabilizing in the long run. However, the Soviet Union could increase its importation of technology only by exporting raw materials to the West. This was where the dilemma must be faced: in the event of a crisis, dependence on raw materials could not be compensated for by the other side's dependence on technology.[5]

The debate in the 1970s was concerned with the long-term implications of increasing East-West trade rather than with existing developments. Turpin, Goldman, and Müller all seemed to assume that the "expansionary phase" in the first half of the decade had been insufficient to make a significant difference. This, essentially, was also the conclusion drawn by Dohan on the basis of his massive data about Soviet import dependence and export specialization (1979: 366–68). Similarly, Rosefielde maintained that "no persuasive evidence has yet appeared in print supporting the contention that the Soviets are highly dependent on foreign trade" (1980: 157).

We will now consider more closely the two relationships with which we are primarily concerned: those with West Germany and the United States.

The DIW study, which concluded that Soviet-West German trade was indecisive for West Germany, found it to be even less important for the USSR, despite West Germany's having become the Soviet Union's leading Western trade partner in the 1970s. Their trade, as we have seen, consisted primarily in Soviet exportation of fuels and importation of machinery and equipment. The role of fuels in Soviet exports to West Germany increased from 35 percent in 1970 to 67 percent in 1975 and no less than 83 percent in 1980. Still, only about 1 percent of the Soviet production of oil and gas went to West Germany. Fuel exports were significant for obtaining foreign currency, however; by the mid-1970s about 10 percent of all Soviet income of convertible currency was obtained by selling oil to West Germany (Bethkenhagen and Machowski 1982: 39–40).

By the mid-1970s about half of the Soviet imports from West Germany consisted of machinery and equipment, and more than 10 percent of all such Soviet imports came from West Germany. According to the DIW study, this corresponded to about 3 percent of Soviet capital investment in 1975. It was pointed out in the DIW study that such data as this might underestimate the degree of Soviet dependence, since more than one-fifth of Soviet imports from West Germany consisted of high technology products; no other country was equally important for

[5] For another author stressing the *Ambivalenz*, see Fritsch-Bournazel 1980.

the Soviet Union from this point of view (pp. 41– 46). However, high technology imports were not crucial for Soviet economic growth; "the U.S.S.R. will not be a second Japan" (p. 55). Cessation of the importation of West German high technology would have marginal impact (p. 81). An OECD study of East-West technology transfers published in 1984 (OECD 1984) drew a similar conclusion. Other analysts emphasized that trade with West Germany was significant for the Soviet Union only in certain sectors (Cooper 1982: 465; Stent 1981: 215).

Even before the invasion of Afghanistan, American analysts were prone to downplay Soviet dependence on trade with the United States. For example, in an analysis of U.S.-Soviet commercial relations published in 1979, Heiss et al. emphasized the dominant role of agricultural products and concluded that there were "few items or technologies" that the Soviet Union could not obtain from non-U.S. sources "in quantity and/or state of the art acceptable to Soviet needs" (p. 206). Wolf (1979: 322–23) similarly argued that the benefits that the Soviet Union derived from trade with the United States had been overstated, and hence also the potential for "leverage." Even the USSR's dependence on U.S. grain might have been exaggerated: the Soviet leadership might not need to be responsive to public demands and might be relatively invulnerable to grain shortages.

When the Carter administration considered the possibility of an embargo at the beginning of 1980, there was confusion regarding the expected impact on the Soviet Union. The eventual outcome was a 3 percent decline in meat and milk production during 1980. A key factor in reducing the impact of the embargo was the availability of other grain suppliers. The embargo's defenders emphasized the reduction in Soviet grain stocks, the record meat imports, the delay of increases in meat consumption, and the higher price of Argentinian grain (Roney 1982: 128, 135). Still, the embargo seemed to confirm to what a limited extent the Soviet Union had in fact become economically dependent on détente with the United States.

EVEN THOUGH it is impossible to be precise, it is clear that the degree of East-West economic interdependence did not become very high during the 1970s. Soviet-West German trade did become significant for the West German economy; still, if it had ceased, inconvenience rather than catastrophe would have resulted. This was equally true with regard to its role for the Soviet economy. United States-Soviet trade was even less vital for both parties. In fact, the hypothesis that economic ties help to stabilize a relationship of détente was not seriously tested.

5.3. THIRD PARTIES

A variety of third parties may have had an impact on East-West relations in the 1970s. Only the two most obvious possibilities will be considered here. China might have been a stabilizer of East-West détente
by virtue of the maxim "My enemy's enemy is my friend," which refers
to the stabilizing effect of a common enemy. The United States and
Western Europe, by contrast, might have helped to stabilize European-
Soviet and U.S.-Soviet détente, respectively, by virtue of the maxim
"My friend's friend is my friend," which refers to the stabilizing effect
of a common friend. (On the maxims and generally on the theoretical
argument about third party stabilization, see section 2.1.) From the
point of view of stabilizing East-West détente, the structure of Great
Power relations should ideally be that shown in Figure 5.1.

We must pause here to consider an ambiguity in the theoretical
sketch. It has already been pointed out that it may occasionally be
debatable whether to regard a particular phenomenon as a condition
for a particular policy or as a stabilizer of it (see the early part of
chapter 2). The question of the third party stabilization of détente is a
case in point. Détente is assumed in the present analysis to have been
a response to a particular state of the balance of power, and a change
in this balance is assumed to have been one of the disturbances of the
1970s. This, in terms of the framework of analysis, was a change in
the conditions for détente that created a pressure for adaptation. It can
be argued that third party relations—the pattern of friendships and
enmities—formed part of that balance of power to which détente was
a response and hence of the conditions for this policy. In that case,
however, they cannot also be regarded as stabilizers. Third party reasoning is concerned with the role of coalition formation in international politics, and the question facing us here is whether it is reasonable to regard the demands of coalition policy as stabilizers of foreign
policies rather than as conditions for them.

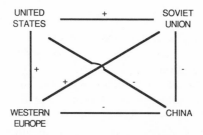

Figure 5.1. A Great Power system tending to stabilize East-West détente.

When the framework of analysis was introduced in chapter 1, it was emphasized that whether to regard a phenomenon as a condition for a policy or as something else is largely a matter of analytical preference. We have a choice between regarding détente as a response to the demands of coalition politics or as a policy that was a response to other factors but may have been stabilized by the coalition structure. My preference has been the latter—to regard third parties like China as potential stabilizers of East-West détente rather than as conditions for it. Notions similar to the concept of third party stabilization have been prevalent in the discussion about East-West relations, especially with reference to China, which is one reason for also considering this possibility in the present analysis. Moreover, the object of the study is not only to analyze détente but also to test the concepts, and I have wanted to take the opportunity of gaining practical experience with applying the notion of third party stabilization to a specific problem. Still, the somewhat arbitrary character of the choice is disturbing. This conceptual problem may need to be considered further in an attempt to improve the theoretical sketch.

A "theory" of the third party stabilization of a détente relation can be put in the form of a three-step argument. First, when tension is decreasing in a dyad, the relations others have with each of the two parties tend to change accordingly. Second, these changes tend to go in the direction of structural balance. Third, when a balanced structure has emerged, it tends to be stable, including the relation of détente with which the argument began.

A previous study of variations in bilateral tension among Great Powers cast some doubt on this "theory." At least during the period 1950–75, the Great Power dyads seemed to be weakly interconnected; changes were not always in the direction of structural balance; and situations of structural balance did not seem to be highly stable (Goldmann 1979a). Some aspects of the problem will now be considered more closely.

THE ROLE of China as a stabilizer of East-West détente, according to the theoretical sketch, is a function of (1) the state of Sino-Soviet relations, (2) the state of Sino-Western relations, and (3) China's weight (see section 2.1). I now suggest that, at most, only the first-mentioned aspect fit the my enemy's enemy argument and therefore that China's role as a stabilizer of détente is unlikely to have been important.

Chinese-Soviet Relations   In a world of change, the conflict between China and the Soviet Union remained an island of stability—or so it seemed to several observers at the end of the 1970s (see, for example, Levine 1979: 649; Robinson 1979: 624). There had been ups and downs, however. The clashes on the Ussuri River in March 1969 were followed by a period of reduced Chinese hostility, a sort of détente beginning in October 1969. Tension returned to a higher level toward the end of 1971 (Garver 1980). The Soviet Union deployed a large military force in the area at this time and "panicked Beijing into thinking that war was around the corner" (Robinson 1979: 624).

Mao Ze-dong's death was followed by another attempt at détente (Dittmer 1981: 501; Gelman 1979: 63–64), but tension reached a new peak during the war between China and Vietnam in early 1979. Just as in the aftermath of the Ussuri clashes, this crisis was followed by conciliatory measures on the part of China (Levine 1979: 662), and Chinese-Soviet talks took place in October and November of 1979. They were suspended by the Chinese after the Soviet Union invaded Afghanistan (*KCA* 1980: 30240).

This description is not based on systematic data, and one close student of Chinese politics has arrived at a different periodization and interpretation (Hart 1983). What is important for our present purposes, however, is that even though the relationship remained tense, it was not static.

According to Hart (1983: 79), "foreign policy specialists and academic scholars specializing in Chinese and Soviet affairs are probably in greater agreement concerning the central issues in Sino-Soviet relations than they are regarding any comparable area of international politics today." They did disagree in the late 1970s and early 1980s about the future of Soviet-Chinese relations, however. Some authors believed in the possibility of a rapprochement. One author went so far as to suggest that "Moscow and Peking might manage to restore the close collaboration that marked their relationship during the early 1950s" (Albright 1977: 227). Another found a rapprochement to be not only possible but "even surprising in its absence since 1976" (Wilson 1980: 78). Other observers emphasized the likelihood of continued conflict. In the words of one author, "the probability of significant progress soon toward the normalization of Sino-Soviet bilateral relations" was "modest at best," and "large and important steps toward rapprochement" appeared "highly improbable for a long time" (Gelman 1979: 66). Adherents to the former school of thought tended to argue, among other things, that the ideological dispute was vanishing (Levine 1979: 663), that China was no longer dramatically inferior to the Soviet Union (Albright 1977: 223–24), that the Chinese urge for modernization would contribute to Soviet-Chinese détente (Robinson 1979), and that the progressive bureaucratization of both countries tended to reduce the conflict between them (Bianco 1976: 16; Robinson 1979: 641). Counterarguments were made, among other things, in terms of geopolitics (Bianco 1979: 10–11; Carrère d'Encausse 1979: 26; Gelman 1979: 52–53), China's nuclear inferiority (Bianco 1979: 15), its bitter memories (Gelman 1979: 53), the striving of both countries for autarky (Robinson 1979: 638–39), and Chinese fears of Soviet hegemony (Gelman 1979: 62–63). It is beyond the scope of this study to go deeper into the literature about the subject (a relatively recent book is Jacobsen 1981). What has been mentioned may suffice to illustrate that even though the Sino-Soviet cleavage was an island of stability in a sea of change, there was not only some movement but also a measure of uncertainty about the future.

Chinese-Western Relations   Structural balance was never attained in the U.S.-Sino-Soviet triangle during the 1960s and 1970s. The Sino-Soviet rift led first to a situation in which all three bilateral relations were tense; this, according to structural balance theory, is an imbalanced situation. In the 1960s, the first steps were taken toward Soviet-American détente while Sino-American relations remained enimical, and this did point to a situation of the my enemy's enemy type. When Soviet-American détente became pronounced, however, a shift in U.S. policy toward China was already underway. The first Chinese-American Ping-Pong balls were played in 1971—the year before SALT I and the Basic Principles agreement. The process of normalization continued throughout the 1970s, even though the rate of change was slower than might have been expected. Hence, the common enemy became less and less common. Structural balance was not attained until after the Soviet invasion of Afghanistan—and then it was a matter of stabilizing a U.S.-Soviet relationship of tension rather than one of détente, with the Soviet Union and not China playing the role of the common enemy.

Hence, one condition for China's functioning as a stabilizer of U.S.-Soviet détente never obtained.[6] However, it may be worth noting that West Germany pursued a more cautious policy toward China than the United States. This made the structural imbalance somewhat less pronounced in the West German-Soviet-Chinese triangle than in the American-Soviet-Chinese one.

[6] For a description of these developments on the basis of quantitative data, see Goldmann 1979a.

China's Weight A rapid reinforcement of Soviet forces on the Chinese border began in 1966; it has been pointed out that this occurred in response to Chinese provocations and that the Soviet defensive position in the Far East was tenuous (Hart 1983: 89). The scope of the Soviet buildup is indicated by the increase, in the three years after the Ussuri River clashes, in the number of Soviet divisions in the area from twenty-one to forty-five (Albright 1977: 209). After 1973 the readiness status of Soviet forces in the Far East was reduced, but the Soviet force level in the area remained stable throughout the 1970s, and equipment was continually modernized (Hart 1983: 89). Moreover, the Soviet nuclear threat increased during the decade; among other things, about forty SS-20s had been deployed in the Far East by 1980. At the same time, the Soviet Pacific fleet expanded (Jacobsen 1981, chap. 1). What could China put up against such an opponent?

A buildup also took place on the Chinese side in the years around 1970, when war was widely expected (Hart 1983: 89). It did not make China a major military power, however. Judging from the Western literature about China's defense after Mao,[7] two events in the 1970s were indicative of Chinese military weakness: the modernization campaign and the war against Vietnam.

The "four modernizations" were launched at the Fourth People's Congress in January 1975. The objective was to accomplish a "comprehensive modernization of agriculture, industry, national defense and science and technology so that our national economy will be marching in the front ranks of the world" (quoted from Fraser 1979: 36). The program was delayed until Deng Xiaoping had defeated the Gang of Four. Of particular importance were four major conferences held in Beijing in 1977 with delegates from the People's Liberation Army (PLA) as well as from the weapons industry and research (p. 37). The modernization campaign showed that the Chinese leaders agreed with Western observers that the equipment of the PLA had grown increasingly obsolete during two decades of negligence. Strong measures were thought to be necessary to prevent a further increase in backwardness. A Chinese deputy chief of staff told a visiting French delegation in 1979 that the PLA was fifteen years behind Western armed forces (Joffe 1979: 575–77, 1981: 318–19). After an economic reassessment had been made in 1978, however, Deng told an American

---

[7] Fraser 1979; Guillermaz 1980; Jacobsen 1981; Joffe 1979, 1981; Problèmes politiques et sociaux 1978, Saint-Vincent 1977, Tan Eng Bok 1978, Tow and Stuart 1981. For a more recent Chinese account, see the pamphlet *China's Army—Ready for Modernization* (1985).

delegation that defense modernization had a lower priority than the other three modernizations (Fraser 1979: 38). A Central Intelligence Agency (CIA) assessment concluded that defense modernization would take decades to achieve (Tow and Stuart 1981: 287).

In the war against Vietnam in 1979, the PLA's performance was hampered by a shortage of armored personnel carriers, trucks, transport planes, and surface-to-air missiles. A document reportedly circulated among Chinese officials stated that the PLA had been unable to "conduct a modern war" (Joffe 1981: 321–23). One observer concluded in 1980 that the Soviet Union was now so superior in the air and on the seas that it could crush China's industrial infrastructure in a matter of weeks or months. The Soviet Union, moreover, could easily conquer the border areas and cut off Manchuria. For the PLA, on the other hand, offensives beyond Manchuria and Xinjiang were out of the question. The Chinese strategy necessarily was to prevent the enemy from permanently occupying large areas in the hope that assistance would be obtained from abroad and that the Soviet Union would be able to deploy a mere part of its military power in the East against China (Guillermaz 1980).

The nuclear sector appeared less harmed by the Cultural Revolution than other aspects of China's defense. Still, only two ICBMs were deployed by 1980. China was thought to be able to inflict punishment only on targets in the Far East, southern Siberia, and the Soviet central Asian republics. The Soviet Union, moreover, had anticipated a Chinese ICBM threat by deploying an ABM system around Moscow (Jacobsen 1981, chap. 1; see also Treverton 1980). Some analysts emphasized that China's nuclear capability might constitute a credible second-strike deterrent against the Soviet Union, especially since it was combined with a passive defense program (Segal 1981; Treverton 1980). China hardly posed an offensive threat, however.

A recurrent theme in the China-after-Mao literature is that China's military posture was defensive and that the PLA continued to obsolesce throughout the 1970s. The "Chinese factor" can be assumed to have played a part in Soviet thinking about détente with the West; among other things, as long as the Soviet leaders thought that they could count on East-West détente, they "could and did tend to ignore China" (Hart 1983: 93). Still, there is reason to believe that China's weight as a third party to Soviet-Western détente was relatively limited and that it decreased even further in the period from SALT I to Afghanistan. "In military terms it is hard to see what the Soviet Union has to fear from China," as a Western nuclear weapons analyst put it in 1980 (Treverton 1980: 42).

EXTENSIVE RESEARCH is hardly needed to assess the extent to which the Ostpolitiks of the Western countries might have functioned as stabilizers of one another. They ran roughly parallel during the first half of the 1970s, but then a more complex situation ensued as U.S.-Soviet relations deteriorated. The difference between American and Western European Ostpolitik became obvious after the Soviet invasion of Afghanistan and took the appearance of a regular feature of world politics in the 1980s.

By the early 1980s, then, it was clear that Western European détente policy had essentially failed to stabilize the détente policy of the United States, even though it may have played some part in softening the American retreat from détente. At the same time, U.S. policy toward the Soviet Union had become a source of stress on, rather than a stabilizer of, Western European détente policy, which nevertheless continued in its essentials. Both observations support the conclusion suggested already by the argument about China: third party stabilizers were relatively unimportant aspects of the détente construction put to the test in the 1970s—détente failed in spite of them or survived without them.

CHAPTER 6

The Cognitive Stabilization of Détente

WHEN CONSIDERING the cognitive stabilization of détente, or any foreign policy, we are not concerned with the beliefs of specific individuals, not even a Richard Nixon or a Henry Kissinger. Our concern is with those beliefs about a policy that are widely shared within the policymaking system. According to the theoretical sketch, a policy is more likely to be stable if those beliefs are consistent rather than inconsistent, if the policy is cognitively central rather than peripheral, and if the beliefs about the policy are untestable rather than testable.

The examination of officially adopted beliefs may be as close as we can get to the study of widely shared foreign policy beliefs (section 1.1). There is undoubtedly a correspondence between the two in many cases. However, official beliefs may cause us to exaggerate the consistency of widely shared beliefs, since they may be designed to play down trade-offs, uncertainties, and disagreements. Official beliefs may also cause us to underestimate the centrality of widely shared beliefs, since they may be designed to emphasize some considerations to the exclusion of others and hence to omit some of the benefits expected from the policy. These are serious problems in the present study, as they are likely to be in most similar studies. What follows is based on the assumption that it is better to study official beliefs than to speculate about widely shared beliefs on some other basis or to exclude cognitive factors from consideration. The problem appears to be particularly serious with regard to the consistency of the elaborate Soviet thinking about peaceful coexistence; more about this in section 6.3.

A study of declared United States policy toward the Soviet Union as well as toward China has been made by Jan Hallenberg (1984) in cooperation with me. Hallenberg has devised a method for the content analysis of policy declarations that refines so-called cognitive mapping (see Axelrod 1976). The method is designed to facilitate the consideration of whether a set of causal beliefs is consistent as well as of the centrality of single beliefs in relation to the whole set. Hallenberg applied the method to statements made by the presidents and secretaries of state in the years 1961, 1968, 1972, 1976, and 1980. The chief results were reported literally in the form of cognitive maps. Hallenberg then considered, among other things, what the maps had to say about consistency, centrality, and testability. His formalized approach is apt to minimize the risk of the analyst's reading too imaginatively between the lines, at the possible cost of increasing the problem of validity inherent in inferring beliefs from declarations. Politicians design their statements to minimize the cognitive problems of pursuing the policies they advocate, and when put in the form of cognitive maps, their reasoning may appear even smoother. This possibility must be taken into account when interpreting the maps, but it is a great advantage to be able to base one's interpretation on a systematic representation of the material rather than on a more intuitive reading of it.

As regards the Soviet Union we can draw on a study by Bertil Nygren (1984) of what he calls the Soviet "détente doctrine." Nygren has examined a vast amount of Soviet material, including authoritative pronouncements as well as scholarly writings. In contrast to Hallenberg he has not used a formal method for content analysis and has therefore been less constrained by the need to limit himself to codable assertions. On the other hand, conclusions about centrality and consistency cannot be drawn on an equally systematic and reliable basis.

There is no similar study of West Germany's Ostpolitik to depart from. However, the election programs of the Social Democratic party (SPD) in 1972, 1976, and 1980 outlined the beliefs behind this policy in their reasonably comprehensive consideration of its several objectives and results. This comes nowhere near the detailed studies by Hallenberg and Nygren and obviously is an insufficient basis for the analysis of West German thinking. It may suffice, however, for the limited purpose of making a rough comparison with American and Soviet beliefs in terms merely of consistency, centrality, and testability.

6.1. THE UNITED STATES

Consistency   According to the definition employed in the present study, the ideas on which a policy is based are consistent if all causal paths from policy to intended outcome are believed to be positive and if no negative side effects are thought to exist (section 2.2). Hallenberg reports his several cognitive maps to contain no single inconsistency in this literal sense (1984: 145–47). As he himself points out, this is probably because the maps represent policy justifications; presidents and secretaries of state are likely to stress the pros and not the cons of their policies in their public statements.

Still, Hallenberg shows official U.S. policy toward the Soviet Union during the first half of the 1970s to have been Janus-faced. What was often called a search for improved relations—détente—was one aspect. The other was the traditional policy of deterrence and of remaining prepared to resist aggression. Such a "dual track" policy is cognitively problematic if, as seems natural, the pursuit of a policy of deterrence-and-resistance is thought to counteract the improvement of relations and if the pursuit of a policy aiming at improved relations is thought to constrain a policy of deterrence-and-resistance. It can be argued that this cognitive problem is inherent in the very notion of détente, or peaceful coexistence, or amity between enemies.

Figure 6.1 is intended to focus attention on this feature of American thinking about the Soviet Union (cf. Hallenberg 1984: 136–39). The figure and subsequent illustrations use the symbols of cognitive mapping: the arrows represent positive or negative links between concepts; circles represent goal concepts, and rectangles, policy concepts.

The positive arrows in the figure stand for the most obvious aspect of American beliefs: both aspects of the "dual track" policy were presumed to improve the conditions for peace. The negative arrows stand for the belief that the pursuit of one "track" may have a negative impact on the pursuit of the other—the belief, in other words, that the two features of U.S. policy toward the other superpower might not be fully compatible.

Such an inconsistency would seem to be rooted in the different images deterrence and détente presume of the adversary; the rationale of one cannot be fully compatible with the rationale of the other. As Hallenberg puts it, "to seek a permanent improvement in relations

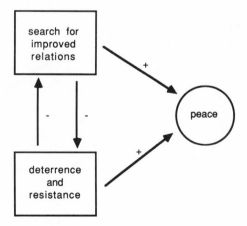

Figure 6.1. The "dual track" quality of American beliefs about détente.

with a country that one is, in principle, ready to annihilate at any moment is something of a contradiction in terms" (p. 147). More generally, deterrence assumes the adversary to be inherently aggressive and intent on going on the offensive unless kept in check by your ability and determination to defend yourself or to retaliate; détente assumes him to be intent on reciprocating your behavior toward him. A policy of deterrence would seem to assume that the game is essentially one of Chicken, whereas a policy of détente assumes that it is a matter of a series of Prisoners' Dilemma games, in which the adversary can be induced to cooperate by your own pursuing a cooperative strategy (Jervis 1976: 58–67).[1] If, however, the adversary is inherently aggressive, an attempt at détente will fail, and if the adversary is intent on responding in kind, deterrence cannot but hinder the improvement of relations. The pursuit of a dual track policy implies that the adversary is both. Hence the cognitive structure shown in Figure 6.2.

An ambivalent view of the adversary need not be erroneous, of course. Rather, it may be realistic to ascribe both aggressive and cooperative impulses to nations. It is not suggested here that a dual track policy is irrational for being inconsistent but that one potential stabilizer is likely to be weak or absent when it is a matter of such a policy.

Now, judging from Hallenberg's analysis, even though U.S. declarations did not explicitly acknowledge the inconsistency, the official view of the Soviet Union in the early 1970s was ambivalent. The American cognitive map of 1972, as drawn by Hallenberg (1984: 111–12), included a relatively complex theory of the adversary. According to the map, the Soviet Union was likely to seek a relaxation of tensions for several reasons, but other factors might push it in a different direction

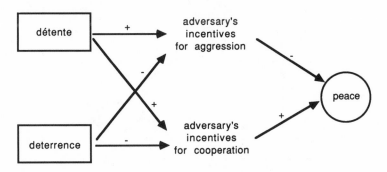

Figure 6.2. The cognitive inconsistency of a "dual track" policy.

[1] Zagare (1985) argues that deterrence is in fact more properly interpreted as a game of Prisoners' Dilemma.

and cause it to seek a "dominant position." It was U.S. policy to encourage the former tendency. However, if the increasing military power of the Soviet Union would in fact lead it to attempt to gain a "dominant position," the United States would act to "redress the balance," and this in turn would inhibit the "expansion of bilateral cooperation." Similarly, if the Soviet Union were to extend its strategic buildup beyond U.S.-Soviet parity, the United States would undertake compensating strategic programs, and this would restrain the improvement of their relations. Thus, it might prove problematic to pursue détente and deterrence-and-resistance at the same time, even though the problem was described as potential rather than actual.

It is common to consider the careful balancing between positive inducement and firm response to be a characteristic feature of Henry Kissinger's operational code (Starr 1984: 68–71), and Kissinger is often thought of as a statesman uncommonly capable of perceiving the world in complex and contradictory—and hence perhaps sophisticated—terms. He was, in other words, well suited for the cognitively difficult combination of détente and deterrence. However, even though a degree of cognitive inconsistency may be difficult to avoid when both are attempted at the same time, the Soviet doctrine of peaceful coexistence suggests a way of avoiding it; more about this in section 6.3.

Another seemingly obvious consistency problem was conspicuous by its absence even in American beliefs, as represented in Hallenberg's maps, and that is the problem of doing business with one's ideological enemy. The lack of moralism has been characterized as a peculiarly un-American feature of the Nixon-Kissinger foreign policy (Gaddis 1982: 336–43). When Jimmy Carter became president and human rights became a chief foreign policy concern, this changed to some extent, but at that time détente was about to become a less prominent feature of U.S. foreign policy anyway.

Centrality   A policy of détente may be intended to serve a variety of purposes in addition to peace and security. It may be considered economically advantageous by providing for trade and other exchanges and by reducing defense expenditures. It may be regarded as a means to promote one's political ideals abroad. It may be expected to facilitate the solution of some immediate problem.

A feature of U.S. declarations about détente, however, was the virtual absence of any objectives other than peace and security.[2] In this

---

[2] Hallenberg 1984, esp. pp. 147–49. The only exception registered by Hallenberg was the elaboration of the objectives of a European security conference made in 1972; see p. 111.

sense détente did not occupy a central position in American thinking. Détente was obviously thought to be "central" in another sense: peace, security, and U.S.-Soviet relations are "central" issues for any government in Washington in the sense of being important. But if the centrality of a policy is defined in terms of links to other policies, détente did not stand out as central in American declarations.

On this point officially adopted and widely shared beliefs may differ. Surely some Americans thought that détente would be economically beneficial or that it would further democratic ideals in the East. Surely such views were voiced also in the White House. Still, their absence in the official declarations may validly reflect the fact that at least the Nixon and Ford administrations thought of détente primarily in terms of peace and security and that the economic and ideological aspects were considered to be secondary.

Testability   The overall structure of American thoughts about détente is shown in Figure 6.3 (Hallenberg 1984: 111, 119). There was first a theory of Soviet behavior, second a theory about the immediate effects of U.S. policy, and third a theory about its long-term effects, which, as we have just seen, were almost exclusively thought of as a matter of peace and security. For example, in 1972 a variety of factors were thought to produce a Soviet desire for a relaxation of tensions; given this, American policy was to strengthen the "positive tendencies" in Soviet policy; this would increase bilateral cooperation in the short run, and cooperation would in turn contribute to a more stable international order.

Beliefs about long-term goal attainment ("a more stable international order") may be regarded as inherently untestable, except perhaps for the historians of a later age. Beliefs about short-term goal attainment ("increased bilateral cooperation"), on the other hand, may be quite testable.

The testability of theories about an adversary is a less obvious matter. A classical example of an untestable theory—this was pointed out in section 2.2—is the so-called inherent bad faith model by which whatever happens is taken to confirm the enimical or aggressive nature of the adversary. The relatively complex reasoning about the USSR in American declarations from the early 1970s was, as Hallenberg points out, quite different from this model (p. 150). It also differed from its opposite, the inherent good faith model, which can conceivably form the basis of a policy of détente. Rather, as we have seen, two parallel models of the Soviet Union were suggested: the Soviet Union might desire to seek a relaxation of tensions but might also be intent on

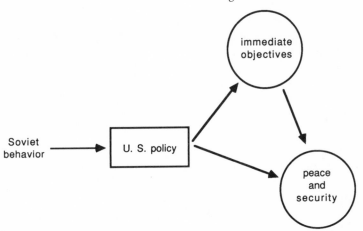

Figure 6.3. The overall structure of American beliefs about U.S. policy toward the Soviet Union.

gaining a dominant position. The former was thought to be more likely—hence the U.S. policy of strengthening the "positive tendencies." However, whether one model or the other was the more correct one was presumably thought to become revealed by Soviet behavior during the American experiment with détente (pp. 150–51). This was hardly an untestable matter.

WE HAVE FOUND the ideas behind the détente policy of the United States to have been neither fully consistent, nor central, nor untestable. This must have been a relatively vulnerable set of beliefs. Hallenberg suggests that American beliefs about normalization with China were both more consistent and less testable and that this may help to account for the difference in survivability (p. 241). The next task here is to consider whether there was a similar cognitive difference between the American policy of détente and West Germany's Ostpolitik.

6.2. WEST GERMANY

Consistency Two sources of cognitive inconsistency in a policy of détente were suggested above: the parallel pursuit of a policy of deterrence, and ideological considerations. The former seemed to obtain in American beliefs, but the latter was conspicuously absent during the Nixon and Ford administrations. Was this true also with regard to West German thinking?

The Ostpolitik was considered at length in all three election programs of the SPD—in 1972, 1976, and 1980. Less attention was devoted to defense in the 1972 program. The need for a military contribution to NATO was pointed out but was not justified in terms of deterrence. Rather, the capability of the Federal Republic as a negotiator and an ally—its *Verhandlungsfähigkeit und Bündnisfähigkeit*—was said to rest on its military contribution (SPD 1972). Not a word was said about the Soviet Union in this context.

However, Willy Brandt made the dual nature of West Germany's policy toward the Soviet Union clear on several occasions in the late 1960s and early 1970s. For example, in June 1971 he explained before an audience in New York that he had no illusions: détente was a matter not of a single decision but of a process that would take time. He continued: "Confrontation and cooperation exclude each other only in theory. In practice they will exist for a long time between the East and the West, in the world and in Germany." The political and ideological differences would continue to determine European and German politics. "We can only do our duty for Europe and for peace within the framework of our alliance" (Brandt 1972: 294).[3] In his Nobel Prize lecture given in December 1971, he recalled his experience as mayor of Berlin of the importance of standing firm, and he made it the first principle of a realistic policy for peace that "the equilibrium between states and groups of states" was preserved (pp. 355–59, 367). The argument can be traced back to the decision of NATO's ministerial council in 1967 about the Harmel Report, which, in the words of a West German author, bridged the latent conflict between military defense and political détente by making them the two pillars of the common security policy of the alliance (Haftendorn 1983: 720). We will soon consider whether the conflict was in fact bridged.

The SPD's election program of 1976 was more explicit than the 1972 program about the need for a defense against the East and for a military East-West equilibrium. Now a "convincing" West German defense policy was said to contribute to that military equilibrium that was "fundamental" for peace (SPD 1976: 6). The need for equilibrium was repeated elsewhere in the program, along with the elaboration of the Ostpolitik. The new emphasis on this point no doubt reflected the shift from Willy Brandt to Helmut Schmidt. The concept of a strategy of equilibrium was fundamental to Schmidt's thinking. Peace, in the words of Helga Haftendorn, was no longer thought to result from a

---

[3] Unless cited from a source in English, I have translated the German texts.

change in the existing security structure but from its stabilization (Haftendorn 1983: 734).

The program of 1980 was similar and stated the need for equilibrium in strong terms: "A military equilibrium between East and West is a central task of the policy of security in alliance. A policy of détente is impossible without such a balance" (SPD 1980: 11).

Whether a difference between West German and American thinking existed on this point hinges on the significance ascribed to a single difference in wording. United States statements, as we have seen, emphasized the need to deter the adversary and to stand ready to resist aggression. West German statements were instead concerned with the necessity for equilibrium. This difference may be unimportant, or it may suggest a difference in perspective. It is inherent in a policy of equilibrium—a systemic concept—that the interests of the adversary are taken into account, whereas a policy of deterring an adversary does not have any such implication. This in turn may suggest a difference in the degree of aggressiveness or offensiveness ascribed to the adversary—and, therefore, a difference in the degree to which the dual track policy is cognitively problematic.

The cognitive inconsistency of such a policy, as suggested previously, is rooted in its dual image of the adversary: détente assumes the adversary to be intent on responding in kind, whereas deterrence assumes him to be inherently aggressive. This is true whether the non-détente aspect is thought to consist simply of deterring and resisting the adversary, as in the U.S. case (Figure 6.2), or whether it is regarded as a matter of maintaining an equilibrium between oneself and the adversary, as in the West German case (Figure 6.4). The difference, I would suggest, lies in the different strength ascribed to two causal relationships (this is indicated by putting one plus sign and one minus sign within brackets in Figure 6.4). First, in the case of a policy intent on equilibrium rather than deterrence, the adversary is thought to be only moderately aggressive; hence, the pursuit of a policy of détente toward him will affect his incentives for aggression only moderately. Second, the relatively moderate aggressiveness of the adversary makes it possible to pursue a relatively moderate policy toward him (equilibrium rather than deterrence-and-resistance), and this reduces the negative impact on the adversary's incentives for cooperation. West German thoughts about relations with the Soviet Union may have been a shade more consistent than American beliefs (whether they were more or less realistic is of course a different issue).

So much for the dual track problem. The cognitive problem of pursuing détente toward an ideological enemy was as absent in the

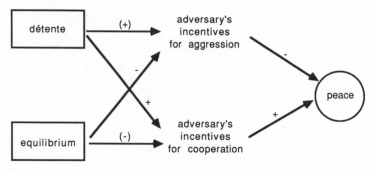

Figure 6.4. The cognitive inconsistency of a modified "dual track" policy.

present—admittedly limited—West German material as in the U.S. declarations of 1972 and 1976. It was mentioned only once in the election programs of the SPD, and then only to be minimized: according to the 1976 program, cooperation with the East was useful and could be increased "in spite of the necessarily enduring ideological differences" (SPD 1976: 48).

Centrality   In American thinking, détente was mainly a matter of peace and security and was only weakly linked to economic, ideological, and other concerns. In West Germany, the Ostpolitik was thought to have broader implications.

The economic aspect was emphasized in the SPD's program of 1976: the Ostpolitik was said to secure more than 300,000 jobs and to promote economic development generally (p. 46). A mildly ideological objective, moreover, was suggested in both 1976 and 1980: the Ostpolitik was asserted to be important in increasing peaceful contacts and human relations between the Europeans in the East and those in the West.

Two further themes were more prominent, however. All three election programs stressed that the Ostpolitik was essential for West Germany's international standing and for ameliorating the division of the country. The Ostpolitik was considered to increase the freedom of maneuver (*Spielraum*) of West German foreign policy, to make new friends for West Germany, and to strengthen old friendships; it was thought, in other words, to satisfy a peculiarly German need to be recognized as peaceful. As regards the division of Germany, the Ostpolitik was thought to be instrumental in two ways: it was a means to alleviate the situation of individual Germans, in the East and in Berlin as well as in the West, and, more generally, it was believed to counter the "estrangement of Germans" and to serve the "unity of the nation" (p. 9; SPD 1980: 12).

Testability   These ideas were not untestable. On the contrary, some of the advantages sought by means of the Ostpolitik were readily observable and quantitatively measurable: jobs, human contacts, even West Germany's international standing. However, the skeleton version of the belief system considered here contained nothing reminiscent of that theory of Soviet behavior that could be found in U.S. declarations about détente. If specific assumptions about the USSR did play a smaller role in West German than in American thinking, one source of instability in American beliefs was less important in the West German case.

THE ONLY clear difference between American and West German thoughts about détente was in terms of centrality: in Bonn the policy of détente was considered essential for a variety of vital objectives, but not in Washington. There was, on the other hand, no decisive difference in testability: détente seemed relatively vulnerable on this score in both countries, even though perhaps less so in West Germany than in the United States. As regards consistency, if there was any difference at all, American dual track thinking may have been somewhat less stabilizing than the West German version. Hence, to the limited extent that cognitive differences obtained, they contributed to explaining why West Germany's Ostpolitik fared better than the détente policy of the United States.

A note about the CDU-led government that succeeded the government of Helmut Schmidt may be added. The new government committed itself to continue, and did continue, the essentials of the Ostpolitik. Their beliefs about this policy may have differed somewhat from their predecessor's, however. It is instructive to compare the CDU/CSU's election program of 1983 with those of the SPD at the three previous Bundestag elections.

First, in the CDU/CSU program the nondétente aspect of the policy toward the Soviet Union was presented as a matter of maintaining a defense against an enemy and not of preserving a systemic equilibrium. The Soviet Union was said to be intent on world revolution and imperialism. The West had a "moral right" and a "political duty" to defend itself against "this threat against peace, human rights, and basic values." The program was rather explicit in its rejection of the systemic view: a large part of the SPD had forgotten why a strong defense was needed, it said, and the SPD ought to avow its commitment to the goals of the Western alliance and to give up its "political neutrality," which was an expression of a "dangerous neutrality of values." Peace in Europe necessitated a defense capability and a psychological preparedness to prevent the Soviet Union from gaining military superiority (CDU 1983: 8–10).

Second, the existence of an ideological problem of consistency was at least hinted: the CDU/CSU wanted not only to continue a policy of disarmament and arms control as well as of "dialogue and cooperation" but also to bring about what may be termed ideological concessions by the Soviet Union. The cause of tension was said to be the Soviet imposition of a social system and a military alliance on Eastern Europe, neither of which would have been freely chosen by the peoples on the other side of the iron curtain (the program did use this term). The CDU/CSU demanded that the Soviet Union recognize the right of self-determination of peoples as well as the freedoms of individuals. Then military alliances and rearmament would no longer be necessary (pp. 9–10).

Third, little was said about the diverse benefits of the Ostpolitik— nothing about the economy, nor anything about West Germany's reputation or about improving human relations in Europe by détente. The CDU/CSU did devote considerable attention to the unity of Germany in their program (pp. 11–12). The division of the country had to be overcome "by peaceful means and in freedom." As long as it lasted, moreover, its human consequences must be reduced. However, nowhere in the program were these objectives explicitly linked to the pursuit of a policy of détente toward the Soviet Union.

Here as elsewhere, too much should not be read into differences in rhetoric and propaganda (the SPD also devoted less attention to the Ostpolitik in their program of 1982 than they had done in the three previous elections). Still, the cognitive vulnerability of the Ostpolitik appears to have increased to at least some extent in connection with the shift in government.

6.3. The Soviet Union

Consistency   As previously, the focus will be on two types of cognitive inconsistency that may be expected to be associated with a policy of détente. One is the dual track problem: how can a policy of détente be reconciled with a policy of deterrence? The other is ideological: how can restraint and cooperation be justified in relation to an ideological enemy? As a matter of fact, judging from Nygren's careful and vast reading of Soviet material, neither inconsistency obtained in Soviet thinking about peaceful coexistence.

This is particularly obvious with regard to the dual track problem. According to the Soviet analysis, the military capability of the USSR was a prerequisite for détente: Soviet rearmament had helped to bring about a favorable change in the "correlation of forces," and this change had caused the West to revise their approach to the USSR (Nygren 1984: chap. 7). Furthermore, détente would benefit even more if the correlation of forces were to become still more favorable to the Soviet Union. A trade-off between détente and deterrence was not needed.

A solution is outlined here to the cognitive problem of dual images of the adversary, which would otherwise seem inherent in the notion of détente between adversaries. The solution is to assume your adversary's incentives for cooperation to be due to your strength rather than to your actions. Then the adversary implied in a policy of détente is precisely the same as the adversary implied in a policy of deterrence. If you grow stronger, your adversary will be not only more effectively deterred from aggression but also more rather than less intent on cooperation (cf. Figure 6.5). There is no question of your policy of deterrence giving your adversary an incentive to give up his policy of détente. On the contrary, a policy of strength on your part will deter your adversary from both aggression and noncooperation.

During the first half of the 1970s there was agreement between Soviet and American beliefs that the growth in Soviet power had paved the way for détente in U.S.-Soviet relations (Hallenberg 1984: 111–12, 119). Their difference concerned what a further increase in Soviet strength would imply and seemed to be rooted in their different beliefs about inter-state action-reaction. According to Soviet beliefs, an increase in Soviet strength would make the West even more intent on détente. According to American beliefs, the United States would on the

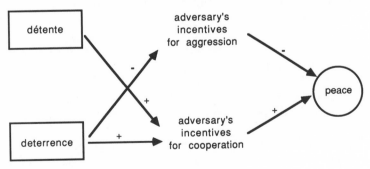

Figure 6.5. A cognitively consistent "dual track" policy.

contrary be compelled to meet the challenge, and this would impair the conditions for détente. The Soviet doctrine appears to have been more consistent—that is, less complex, and perhaps less sophisticated and realistic—than American thinking in this respect. (The rationale of the Reagan administration's approach to the Soviet Union appeared to have more in common with the Soviet belief that your own deterrence serves to make the adversary more rather than less cooperative.)

As regards the ideological problem of détente, which was found to be virtually absent from both U.S. and West German statements, the Soviet doctrine was more complex. Whereas Americans and West Germans tended to avoid the issue, it was a major one in Soviet declarations and analyses. In Nygren's interpretation, peaceful coexistence was for the USSR an integral part of the international class struggle. Indeed, in the Soviet view, peaceful coexistence was "a kind of class struggle" (1984: 70). Since this appears to many in the West to be a contradiction, it is necesary to consider the notion in more detail. The problem has two aspects: the compatibility of détente with the so-called ideological struggle, on the one hand, and with support of revolutions, on the other.

The question of the relationship between the ideological struggle and détente in Soviet thinking is confused by Soviet insistence that the ideological struggle ought to be separated from international relations, since it should not be fought by states (Nygren 1984: 107). Nevertheless, Soviet texts at length attempt to show how détente has transformed the conditions for the ideological struggle. Détente, according to the Soviet argument, has intensified the ideological struggle and has made it the main form of the class struggle by compelling the West to use this method and by offering new ideological opportunities to the Soviet Union (pp. 89–94). Hence, from the point of view of the ideological struggle, détente is both a risk and a chance: contacts with the West may increase Western influence in the East but are at the same time an opportunity to spread socialism in the West (p. 107). The reverse question about the impact of the ideological struggle on détente—Is it possible that the pursuit of the ideological struggle may render the West disinclined to participate in a détente process?—does not seem to be meaningful from a Soviet point of view. Rather, the continuation of the class struggle is conceived as a deterministic necessity and the West's interest in détente as a function of the correlation of forces.

The problem of combining détente with the support of revolutions is related to the larger issue of the role of military forms of the class struggle under détente. Peaceful coexistence, first of all, is assumed to exclude war between the "systems." The class struggle will inevitably continue in various forms: ideologically, economically, politically. However, to quote Brezhnev, "we shall strive to shift this historically inevitable struggle onto a path free from the perils of war, of dangerous conflicts and an uncontrolled arms race." It is also emphasized in Soviet statements that revolution cannot be spread by war and that the Soviet Union does not advocate the "export of revolutions."

However, what cannot be exported is the revolutionary situation rather than the revolution itself. Once a revolution is underway, it is the "international duty" of a socialist state to support it against the "export of counter-revolution" by imperialism (pp. 139–45). It similarly remains an "international duty" to assist in the national liberation of oppressed peoples. Peaceful coexistence, according to Soviet statements, is inapplicable to the relationship between "oppressors and oppressed" (p. 223).

It is a key element in the Soviet doctrine of peaceful coexistence that détente and national liberation reinforce rather than counteract one another. National liberation is presumed to improve the correlation of forces, which helps to strengthen the conditions for détente, which in turn improves the conditions for national liberation by reducing the freedom of action of the imperialists (pp. 223–46). Hence, in the Soviet doctrine there is incompatibility neither between détente and deterrence nor between détente and class struggle.

This is the point where the question of the relationship between officially adopted and widely shared beliefs is especially urgent. Must it not have been obvious to Soviet policymakers that the continuation of their rearmament program and their interventions in the third world might reduce the West's inclination to pursue a policy of détente? Can they really have been unaware of the conditional nature of American beliefs? Could they really escape the problem of making trade-offs between détente and deterrence and between ideology and security— the latter presumably a more serious problem for them than for the West, since the ideological objectives were more pronounced in their foreign policy than in that of the West? We cannot know.

Centrality   Nygren (1984: chap. 6) suggests the Soviet doctrine of détente and peaceful coexistence to be three-dimensional: there is a political dimension concerned with war and peace, an ideological dimension concerned with the class struggle, and an economic dimension concerned with economic competition and cooperation. The ways in which the three dimensions of détente were thought to be interrelated in the 1970s is shown schematically in Figure 6.6.

Economic cooperation with the West was considered to be an integral part of détente, and therefore détente was considered essential for economic policy. It was argued in particular that the so-called scientific-technical revolution had made an international division of labor essential (Nygren 1984: chap. 5). One Western analyst has gone so far as to maintain that Brezhnev's peace policy was first of all economic policy (Volten 1982). At the same time, economic cooperation was believed to create ties that would strengthen peace and security; this is represented by the arrow from economic policy to peace and security in Figure 6.6. Economic cooperation with the West was also thought to further the international class struggle, since Soviet economic progress would have a favorable effect on the correlation of forces as well as strengthen the "force of the [Soviet] example" (Nygren 1984: 167–76); this belief is represented by the arrow from economic progress to world revolution in the figure.

The class struggle was also expected to benefit from détente in a more direct way: by "pacifying" the imperialists. The ties thought to follow from détente were apparently believed to have a greater impact on the imperialists than on the socialists.

Testability   Two elements in Soviet thinking about détente seem to have been relatively testable. One was the belief that détente would

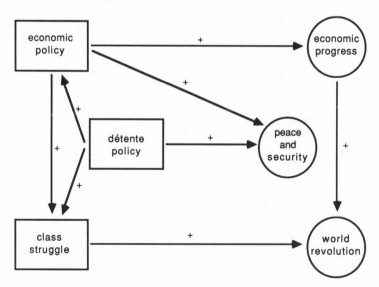

Figure 6.6. The cognitive centrality of Soviet détente policy.

bring about mutually advantageous economic cooperation, as it was put in Soviet statements. The other was the notion that the international class struggle would be helped along by détente, which could be operationalized in terms of domestic trends in the West and developments in the third world. The beliefs about long term implications for peace, economic progress, and world revolution were obviously more difficult to test, but Soviet détente policy was not fully protected by a lack of testability.

THE OVERALL IMPRESSION of the cognitive stabilization of Soviet détente policy is similar to that of West Germany's Ostpolitik. It was in both cases a matter of a relatively central but also a relatively testable policy. The consistency of the underlying set of ideas was in both cases difficult to assess but—at least if you read on the lines rather than between them—there seemed in both cases to be less inconsistency than in the case of American thinking about détente.

CHAPTER 7

The Political Stabilization of Détente

7.1. SALIENCE

THE SALIENCE of an issue, or, roughly, its significance in the domestic power struggle, has been defined in this study as the extent to which the pattern of domestic coalitions and cleavages would be affected by an actor's changing his position on it (section 2.3). Salience is presumed to be a stabilizer of policies by reinforcing the stabilizing impact of institutionalization and support (see Figure 2.3). Two principal methods for assessing the salience of an issue have been suggested: the measurement of attention it receives, and the examination of changes in coalitions and cleavages that have occurred or of debates about their eventuality.

The data used here are of the former type. The consideration of the political stabilization of détente—not just its salience but also institutionalization and support—in the United States and West Germany is based mainly on candidate statements and party programs in the elections of 1972, 1976, and 1980; it is a useful coincidence that presidential and Bundestag elections took place at the same time throughout the decade. In other words, the role of the Soviet Union as an issue in six Western elections will be examined in the hope that this is the best way of assessing, by a limited effort, its more general salience in the domestic politics of the two countries during the early, middle, and late days of détente. As regards the USSR, the focus will be on 1971, 1976, and 1981—that is, on the years in which the Twenty-fourth, Twenty-fifth, and Twenty-sixth party congresses were held.

The general problem of validity with using attention as an indicator of salience has already been considered (section 2.3). We must ask here whether the limited material used in this study (even though supplemented with U.S. and West German opinion polls) is sufficient for drawing any conclusions about the political salience of détente. For example, not just presidents and presidential candidates but also the Congress participate in the domestic politics of American foreign policy; the 1970s were in fact a period of congressional reassertiveness. Moreover, the salience of détente may have varied in the course of the 1970s in a way that cannot be ascertained on the basis of data limited to a few points in time.

There is no question that broader material would have been desirable. A full-scale study of the salience of an issue in American politics should probably include, among other things, a content analysis of the mass media and a perusal of congressional material. It is clear that precise, detailed conclusions cannot be drawn on the basis of the sources used in the present study. All we are after, however, is a basis for judging whether the political salience of détente was sufficiently high for significantly reinforcing the impact of institutionalization and support, whether large changes occurred in this regard between the early 1970s and the beginning of the 1980s, and whether there were large differences between the three countries in this respect. The data should suffice for this limited purpose.

There is reason to believe that candidate statements and party programs are more representative of politics in general in West Germany than in the more complex political system of the United States, however. Therefore, West Germany will be considered first.

7.1.1. West Germany

The Ostpolitik was born amid major political controversy. Under such circumstances policies may develop in different directions. The controversy may continue, with the losers doing their best to become winners and to change course. Or the losers may decide to live with the decision and choose not to challenge the winners on this issue again; the policy may in time develop into a national dogma. Or the issue may turn out to have little political salience once the matter has been settled. In content analysis data, continuing controversy would be reflected in the issue's retaining its prominence in both debates and programs. Dogmatization would be reflected in the issue's remaining prominent in programs but not in debates. Depoliticization would be reflected in the issue's disappearing from both debates and programs. We would run some risk, however, in the first case of overestimating salience, and in the third case of underestimating it.

To illustrate the idea and to get an impression of the salience of the Ostpolitik, we may examine how large a role concern with the Soviet Union played in the West German elections of 1972, 1976, and 1980 (see Tables 7.1 and 7.2). The data are based on simple coding: the texts have been divided into portions dealing with the USSR and with other foreign and defense matters; there is also a residual category.[1] Conclu-

---

[1] The content analysis has been made by Bo Björsson in cooperation with me. Björsson is due to report on his work in a separate paper. His coding unit is the paragraph. A paragraph is considered to deal with the Soviet Union as soon as it contains a reference to the USSR or to West Germany's relations with the USSR; hence, the data may exag-

Table 7.1. Contents of West German election programs (percent)

Year	USSR	Other foreign and defense matters	Domestic and miscellaneous	Sum
SPD				
1972	4	14	82	100
1976	4	17	78	99
1980	10	16	74	100
FDP				
1972	11	0	89	100
1976	3	12	85	100
1980	5	16	79	100
CDU/CSU				
1972	1	25	74	100
1976	5	16	80	101
1980	10	13	77	100

sions may be drawn about the approximate order of magnitude and the overall direction of trends, but no significance should be attached to the precise figures.

The data suggest continuing, or even increasing, controversy over a moderately salient issue and neither dogmatization nor depoliticization. In 1976, when the Soviet Union played a relatively small role as an issue in the television debate between the party leaders (14 percent), between 3 and 5 percent of the election programs were concerned with

gerate somewhat the proportion of the texts devoted to this matter (this is the case in particular with regard to the television debates in Table 7.2).

The chief coding problem is to determine what precisely should be regarded as reference to the Soviet Union; the borderline problems between the remaining categories are unimportant for our present purposes. Several ambiguous situations have had to be decided on the basis of relatively arbitrary rules, and this is the chief reason why the exact size of the figures should not be considered significant. However, the coding rules—to be reported by Björsson—have been applied consistently; comparisons across time and party can be made, and probably even with similar data on American election campaigns reported later in the chapter.

It should be pointed out that relations between East and West Germany have been coded as "other foreign matters" here in order to improve comparability with U.S. data.

The texts analyzed are the election programs supplied to us by the parties via the Swedish embassy in Bonn, mostly in the form of the original pamphlets, and photocopies of the original transcripts of the television debates.

Table 7.2. Contents of final television debates in West German election campaigns (percent)

Year	USSR	Other foreign and defense matters	Domestic and miscellaneous	Sum
SPD				
1972	31	21	48	100
1976	24	3	73	100
1980	53	9	38	100
FDP				
1972	19	26	55	100
1976	15	13	71	99
1980	33	16	52	101
CDU				
1972	32	11	57	100
1976	13	13	75	101
1980	17	33	51	101
CSU				
1972	32	11	57	100
1976	1	11	88	100
1980	43	17	40	100
All parties				
1972	25	22	53	100
1976	14	10	76	100
1980	37	19	44	100

this matter. In 1980 no less than 10 percent of the election programs of both main parties dealt with the Soviet Union, but this reflected the fact that policy toward the USSR had become a central issue in the polemics between the main candidates—Helmut Schmidt and Franz Josef Strauss used about half of their time in the television debate on this one issue, and the transcript shows how difficult it was for the moderators to make the candidates talk about other matters. More-over, no less than 84 percent of the references to the Soviet Union in the 1980 debate were made in the context of criticism of other West German parties, as against 63 percent in 1972 and a mere 38 percent in 1976. In precisely this kind of situation attention data are likely to give an inflated indication of salience. The Soviet issue did seem to become more salient toward the end of the 1970s, but the data probably exaggerate the increase.

Public opinion data give a mixed impression, it may be added. On the one hand, in answers to open-ended questions about good and bad aspects of the SPD and the CDU/CSU, relations with the East were mentioned by 10 percent in 1972, far more frequently than any other issue, foreign or domestic; in 1976 relations with the East, at 6 percent, were still the most frequently mentioned issue, together with economic policy and social policy. On the other hand, when voters were asked to rank issues in importance, relations with the Soviet Union scored lower than price stability, old age security, and law and order, in both 1972 and 1976 (Klingemann and Taylor 1978: 110–11, 129).

We seem to be dealing, therefore, with an issue that was neither overwhelmingly salient nor unimportant in West German politics— with what was neither the chief issue in the competition for power nor peripheral to it. This in turn may suggest that the progressive institutionalization of the policy of détente (see below) contributed significantly but not decisively to making it stable and that the continuing controversy over the Ostpolitik (visible in Table 7.2 and considered in more detail in section 7.3.1) contributed significantly but not decisively to making it unstable.

7.1.2. The United States

Data on the U.S campaigns of 1972, 1976, and 1980, which are roughly comparable to the data on the West German elections, can be found in Tables 7.3 through 7.5.[2] The platforms (Table 7.3) indicate the same trend and even roughly the same magnitudes as the election programs of the two main West German parties (Table 7.1): in 1976 a

---

[2] On the content analysis see note 1, above. Björsson has taken the texts of the 1972 platforms from Johnson and Potter 1973 and those of the 1976 platforms from *Historic Documents of 1976*. The text of the 1980 Democratic platform has been taken from the *Congressional Quarterly Almanac, 1980*, and that of the 1980 Republican platform from *Historic Documents of 1980*. The texts of the television debates were found in the *New York Times*, Sept. 9, Oct. 7, and Oct. 23, 1976, and Oct. 29, 1980. Those of 1976 can also be found in *The Presidential Campaign 1976*, vol. 3: *The Debates* (1979).

Table 7.5 is based on an analysis of the debates plus all other statements, speeches, news conferences, etc., found in the *New York Times* from January to election day (in one case—a speech by Carter on Aug. 21, 1980—the text as printed in the *Department of State Bulletin* (DSB) has been used, and the frequencies have been reduced by 20 percent to compensate for the difference in layout between the DSB and the *New York Times*).

little more than 5 percent of the platforms were devoted to the Soviet Union, as against an average of a little more than 10 percent in 1980.

The candidates held no television debates in 1972, but Ford and Carter debated three times in 1976 (once on foreign policy, once on domestic policy, and once on general issues) and Carter and Reagan debated once in 1980. The format of the U.S. debates may have given the candidates less control over the agenda than in West Germany, and this is one reason why comparisons are hazardous. A coding problem tends further to exaggerate the role of the Soviet issue in the West German debates (see note 1). It seems clear, however, that the increase in attention to the Soviet Union was smaller in the U.S. debates than in the West German ones (cf. Tables 7.4 and 7.2): from 8 to 13 percent in the United States, from 14 to 37 percent in West Germany. The smaller size of the U.S. increase was not due to a lack of increase in controversy: much as in West Germany, whereas only about 5 percent of the references to the Soviet Union in the Carter-Ford debates were polemical, this was the case with no less than about 80 percent in the Carter-Reagan debate.

Table 7.5 is based on a broader sample of candidate statements. It confirms a tendency on the part of presidential candidates to devote about 10 percent of their attention to the Soviet Union; there is no consistent difference between Democrats and Republicans, incumbents and challengers, or between 1972, 1976, and 1980.

Survey data show, in the words of two analysts, a "complete reversal" from concern with foreign and defense issues to concern with

Table 7.3. Contents of U.S. party platforms (percent)

Year	USSR	Other foreign and defense matters	Domestic and miscellaneous	Sum
Democrats				
1972	2	16	82	100
1976	6	23	71	100
1980	8	20	72	100
Republicans				
1972	5	20	75	100
1976	7	26	68	101
1980	16	19	65	100

Table 7.4. Contents of debates between the main candidates for president (percent)

	USSR	Other foreign and defense matters	Domestic and miscellaneous	Sum
1976: Carter				
all three debates	5	30	65	100
foreign policy debate	11	85	4	100
1976: Ford				
all three debates	12	26	62	100
foreign policy debate	35	63	2	100
1980: Carter	14	23	63	100
1980: Reagan	12	20	67	99

Table 7.5. Contents of speeches by the main candidates for president (percent)

Candidate	Year	USSR	Other foreign and defense matters	Domestic and miscellaneous	Sum
McGovern	1972	9	40	51	100
Carter	1976	9	35	56	100
Carter	1980	16	40	43	99
Nixon	1972	13	43	44	100
Ford	1976	7	28	65	100
Reagan	1980	10	20	71	101

Source: *New York Times.*

domestic issues between 1964 and 1976. When asked in 1976 about "the most important problems facing this nation," only 5 percent mentioned international problems and foreign policy, whereas 38 percent referred to the high cost of living and 24 percent to unemployment. However, other data show a heightened concern with several international issues between 1974 and 1976, including the "threat of communism" (Watts and Free 1978: 123–24).

The data, which obviously do not go very far, suggest on the whole that the Soviet Union remained a relatively but not overwhelmingly salient issue in the United States throughout the decade—much as in West Germany. There is some indication of an increase in salience toward the end of the 1970s—again, much as in West Germany.

7.1.3. The Soviet Union

Table 7.6 indicates the amount of attention devoted to the United States, West Germany, and the West in general in Leonid Brezhnev's major speeches to the CPSU congresses of 1971, 1976, and 1980. Table 7.7 provides similar data about all other statements by Brezhnev as well as by foreign minister Andrei Gromyko, and defense ministers Andrei Grechko and Dmitrii Ustinov made in these same years and reprinted in the *Current Digest of the Soviet Press* (*CDSP*).[3]

It goes without saying that there is a problem of validity with making inferences about salience from such data. First and foremost because of the nature of the Soviet political system, but also because Table 7.7 (but not Table 7.6) is based on a selection of texts made by the *CDSP*. In addition, it is difficult to determine the extent to which concern with the United States or with West Germany is implied in

Table 7.6. Contents of Brezhnev's reports to party congresses (percent of total text)

	1971	1976	1981
United States	3	4	3
West Germany	1	<1	1
Western Europe, including West Germany	2	3	2
The West, including the United States, West Germany and Western Europe but not imperialism in general	8	17	15
The West, including imperialism in general	17	24	19
Other foreign and defense matters	12	17	18

[3] This coding has also been done by Björsson; see note 1, above. The congress speeches have been coded as printed in *CDSP*. The number of categories is larger here than with regard to West Germany and the United States because in Soviet documents relations with single Western countries are implied to an unknown extent in general assessments about the West and imperialism.

Table 7.7. Contents of Soviet statements, excluding Brezhnev's reports to party congresses (percent of text about foreign and defense matters)

	1971	1976	1981
United States	9	13	29
West Germany	3	1	4
Western Europe, including West Germany	10	8	5
The West, including the United States, West Germany and Western Europe but not imperialism in general	37	59	68
The West, including imperialism in general	52	70	75

general statements about the West, imperialism, and so forth. The data are reported here in the hope that they are better than nothing at all as a basis for an assessment of the role of East-West relations as an issue in Soviet politics.

It can be seen in Table 7.6 that the allocation of attention to the various categories in the congress reports was rather stable over time. The proportion of the texts that dealt in general terms with imperialism decreased, however: in 1971 more than half of the text about the West was of this nature, but this dropped to about one-fifth in 1981. Moreover, somewhat more attention was devoted to the West in 1976 than in 1971 and 1981, which fits the common impression that controversy over policy toward the West was a particularly significant aspect of Kremlin politics in the mid-1970s (section 7.3.3). The table may suggest that relations with the West remained a relatively salient issue in Soviet domestic politics throughout the 1970s. It may possibly also suggest that the salience of relations with the United States and with Western Europe as separate issues in Soviet politics differed little.

In Table 7.7 two modifications are suggested. Note that the percentages are not based on the text as a whole, as in the other tables, but only on the text about foreign and defense policy. There were two trends, or two manifestations of a single trend. The proportion of the foreign and defense texts concerned with the West increased dramatically between 1971 and 1981; in 1981, two-thirds or three-fourths dealt with the West, whereas other foreign policy issues tended to disappear into the background. There was also—the other trend—a threefold increase in the attention devoted to the United States. In 1971 about the same amount of attention was devoted to the United States as to Western Europe, in 1981 about six times more.

The impression of a relatively high, and perhaps increasing, salience for East-West relations as an issue in Soviet politics fits with Bialer's suggestion that the role and weight of foreign policy in Soviet top-level policymaking increased: there was a visibly greater stress on foreign policy issues in the deliberations of top bodies, a greater interconnectedness of key domestic issues with foreign policy concerns, and an increasing recognition of this fact in the ideological and theoretical literature (1981: 414). It gains additional substantiation from Volten's study of Brezhnev's peace program, in which Brezhnev is quoted as saying in 1973 that "foreign policy is now the main problem of domestic policy" (1982: 109).

7.2. INSTITUTIONALIZATION

A policy may be institutionalized in three ways: by commitment in the form of declarations, by custom, and by investment (section 2.3). The following attempt to assess the extent to which détente became an institutionalized policy in West Germany, the United States, and the Soviet Union is limited to the study of commitment. The degree of commitment implied in policy declarations likely varies with the authority of the official making them, with their frequency, and with the context in which they are made (section 2.3). Here we shall limit ourselves to examining some top-level declarations made in 1972 (USSR: 1971), 1976, and 1980 (USSR: 1981); there is no attempt to go beyond highly authoritative statements made in quite commiting contexts, and frequency is taken into account only informally to suggest that which is particularly common in the documents.

This sort of primitive research design may suffice for the analyst who needs to acquire a reasonably systematic knowledge with a limited effort for a specific purpose. A more penetrating analysis, and one in which the uncertainty about the representativeness of the material were eliminated, would demand a research effort of different proportions. For such in-depth research the present effort may be useful as a pilot study, as pointed out previously.

The study of verbal commitment necessitates two distinctions. In the present context we are concerned with policy declarations because they represent commitments. They are not regarded as sources of information about other behavior: some argue that Soviet policy toward the West differed from the way in which it was described in

Soviet declarations, but that is irrelevant here. Nor are the declarations assumed to reflect the "real" calculations and plans of the three governments. We will take note of some differences between West German and U.S. statements on détente that represent a difference in commitment; these differences may or may not reflect differences in the thinking of the top leadership, but differences in thinking are not the object of study in this chapter.

The extent to which the West German and United States governments committed themselves to détente in the course of three election years will be examined. This, as pointed out previously, is an attempt to maximize the link between détente and domestic politics. However, in the case of the United States the approach raises a problem with the theoretical concept of institutionalization. All three incumbent presidents—Nixon, Ford, Carter—left office soon after the elections. Then, does a campaign statement by an incumbent president commit his successor, or should conclusions about institutionalization be based on the statements of successful challengers rather than on those of unsuccessful incumbents (and on those of vice presidents who become presidents rather than on those of presidents who leave office)?

It is at the core of the concept of institutionalization that commitment reduces the freedom of action of future governments whether their members have previously supported or opposed this policy. The assumption can be defended on two grounds. Commitment to a foreign policy creates expectations abroad and not just at home; inconsistency in foreign policy may incur foreign political costs; these may in turn incur domestic political costs. Moreover, the institutionalization of a policy may reduce the availability of planned alternatives. Policy proposals by the opposition carry neither of these effects. Rather, the former opposition, when coming into power, may be expected to strike a compromise between its own commitments in opposition and the "political reality" created by its predecessors in government. Of course, the less institutionalized a policy, the larger the freedom of action of the new government. A shift in government puts the stabilizers of foreign policies to the test, including the stabilizing effect of institutionalization.

It is important to note that I do not consider the Carter campaign of 1976 and the Reagan campaign of 1980 to be in any way irrelevant to the question of the stability of U.S. foreign policies. I have chosen to take the challengers into account within the concept of support, however, rather than institutionalization. As already pointed out (section 2.3), a policy can be both highly institutionalized and highly nonconsensual, an intriguing combination from the point of view of policy stability.

When setting out to explore the existence of commitments to détente, we have a choice between two approaches. One is to identify all policy commitments in the documents and then to decide a posteriori to what extent this amounts to a commitment to détente. The other is to start out with an a priori definition of détente and then to search for commitments to such a policy. In a small-scale study like the present one, only the latter approach is possible; what has been defined a priori as a policy of détente has been explained in chapter 4—basically restraint, arms control, and cooperation. The main limitation of this approach is that there is no systematic consideration of the extent to which the parties committed themselves also to contra-détente policies like rearmament and ideological combat.

Is this fatal? Recall that we are dealing with a relationship between adversaries; détente implies a way of managing such a relationship but not the disappearance of the adversity. It can be taken for granted that policies negative to the other party are highly institutionalized on both sides in such a relationship. The chief question is whether more positive policies are also institutionalized.

The documents used here to examine the institutionalization of détente—declarations by leaders like Willy Brandt, Richard Nixon, and Leonid Brezhnev—overlap those employed in the previous chapter to study cognitive stabilization. In principle, the documents are seen in different perspectives: the analysis in the previous chapter was based on the assumption that the declarations reflected widely shared ideas and could be given a psychological interpretation, whereas in the present chapter they are seen as political phenomena thought to be interesting because of their political effects. A contradiction indicates in the former case inconsistency and in the latter case a weakening of a commitment. In practice this distinction may become blurred. The problem of separating cognitive from political stabilization results from the difficulty of operationalizing the former without employing materials more suitable for the study of the latter.

7.2.1. West Germany

The following observations are based on four kinds of sources: (1) the election programs of the two government parties, the SPD and the FDP, (2) transcripts of the television debates held before the elections, (3) the 1972, 1976, and 1980 volumes of the *Bulletin*, a periodical issued by the government, and (4) the verbatim record of a key debate in the Bundestag held in February 1972 in connection with the first reading of the Eastern treaties. The three elections represent three phases in the history of the Ostpolitik: the struggle over its introduction, the confirmation of its continuation, and the renewed challenge to its future.

1972: The Struggle over the Ostpolitik   In 1972 the Bundestag ratified the Eastern treaties without the affirmative votes of the opposition, and the opposition failed in an attempt to oust the Brandt government. In the process of defending its Ostpolitik, the government could not but strengthen and sharpen its commitment to it.

The renunciation of force in the Eastern treaties was perhaps the element of détente most strongly emphasized in West German government statements at this time. The commitment to regard the current borders as inviolable (*unverletzlich*) was strongly reaffirmed. Détente was also said to be normalization, however. Normalization, foreign minister Walter Scheel said in the Bundestag debate, was the true political objective of the Eastern treaties. "Détente and normalization"—these were the pillars of the political process in Europe. The renunciation of force on the basis of the status quo created a basis for political dialogue and for mutually rewarding cooperation.[4] As Willy Brandt noted, once the treaties were ratified, the time had come to get rid of the artificial barriers in Europe, step by step.[5]

The treaties were ratified on May 17. In a typical statement, Brandt said that it was now a question of "filling the treaties with life" and continuing in this way "without over-reaching ourselves, to make peace in Europe securer."[6] In August the government published a favorable appraisal of the Soviet-German treaty, which was said to have introduced a period of understanding; a "visible sign of progressive normalization" was the "intensive exchange of opinions between the two states," as well as all the contacts in various fields (*Bulletin* [1972], 27: 205). The election program of the SPD presented an agenda for the following four years that included troop reductions and arms control, economic, technical, and cultural cooperation, and in general the application to Europe of the principles of peaceful coexistence "upon which president Nixon and secretary-general Brezhnev have come to an understanding" (SPD 1972: 12–13).

Thus the West German government committed itself quite clearly to

---

[4] *Verhandlungen des Deutschen Bundestages, 5. Wahlperiode, Stenographische Berichte, Band 79, 171–173. Sitzungen*, pp. 9742–52.

[5] *Verhandlungen*, p. 9740.

[6] *Bulletin* (1972), 20: 154. This and subsenquent quotations from German statements taken from the *Bulletin* reproduce the English of this publication. The remaining translations from the German have been made by the present author.

all three dimensions of détente. Let us now take note of three rhetorical devices that may have served to strengthen this commitment.

First, the new policy was described as a turning point in history. The Eastern treaties were of "historic importance" (*Bulletin* [1972], 7: 47). They marked the beginning of a "new epoch"; they were a "milestone" ([1972], 18: 136). It is politically difficult to depart from a policy declared to be a historic milestone.

Second, there was a strong dose of political realism. Brandt opened the Bundestag debate over the Eastern treaties by referring to the need for replacing confrontation with understandings about that which is "practically possible and necessary" without effacing the basic differences.[7] Scheel began his statement in the debate by referring to Nixon's visit to China. The Ostpolitik, he said, fitted a new pragmatic trend in international politics. The fact that the other system could not be changed in the short or even medium term was mutually recognized. Instead, a limited community of interest in communication and cooperation had emerged.[8]

Political realism of this kind places limited demands on the adversary. The Ostpolitik was not presented as a solution to the East-West differences. It was said to be possible in spite of, indeed, necessary because of, the enduring differences between the systems. Hence, the part to be played by the adversary was not dramatized. The Soviet Union was assumed to be a fair and reasonable partner in arms control and in cooperative undertakings; it takes two to tango. But the Ostpolitik was not made contingent on major change in Soviet foreign policy or in the Soviet political system.

The third rhetorical device simply was to use strong terms to describe the importance attached to the policy. According to the West German government, "the policy of pursuing closer understanding with the Soviet Union is close to the heart of the entire German people" (*Bulletin* [1972], 27: 205).

1976: Confirmation of the Ostpolitik   Angola cast its shadow over East-West relations in 1976. Helmut Schmidt, who had succeeded Willy Brandt as chancellor, admitted in an interview that Angola had led to a deterioration in the climate. However, "it would be a major error to deduce from this situation the shattering of détente" (*Bulletin* [1976], 9: 53). Foreign minister Hans-Dietrich Genscher reaffirmed his belief "in a relaxation of tensions, free of illusions" ([1976], 11: 70–

---

[7] *Verhandlungen*, p. 9740.
[8] *Verhandlungen*, pp. 9742–52.

71). The SPD's election program was categorical: "To the question of whether the global détente policy is finished we Social Democrats answer a clear 'no.' There are no alternatives to a policy of détente. Détente is not a matter of fashion but the expression of a vital interest" (SPD 1976: 45). The FDP's election program similarly stressed that the "realistic policy of détente" must continue. There was no alternative. "The Cold War must not return" (Verhengen 1980: 255). And in the television debate three days before the election, Schmidt maintained that détente demanded stubborn perseverance: "without the cultivation of the policy of détente and the permanent reproduction of its preconditions," the danger of a return to a situation similar to the early 1960s remained (transcript).

Thus, the basic commitment to détente was resoundingly reaffirmed. Note may be taken of three elements in the declarations that had not existed, or had not been as strong, in 1972.

The "political dialogue" that had developed since 1970 was said to be of "crucial importance." Consultations with the USSR were an established fact, and "there is no topic in our relations which we cannot discuss" (*Bulletin* [1976], 5: 27).

The Helsinki Final Act was said to outline "a future-oriented program that must be fully realized." The document did not "wipe away the fundamental differences" but did serve "to realize those possibilities of co-operation that exist despite those differences." Nobody had a greater interest in such developments than the Germans ([1976], 30: 217).

Finally, the emphasis on arms limitation was perhaps stronger than four years earlier. As a matter of fact, "military de-escalation" was said to be "the heart of détente" ([1976], 9: 53).

1980: The New Challenge   The Soviet invasion of Afghanistan was a turning point for Jimmy Carter (see next section), and this in turn put the Ostpolitik into question. Against this background it is interesting to read a major foreign policy speech given by Genscher in May 1980:

> If one realistically appraises the sense and the opportunities of détente policy, one cannot declare it to have failed even after Afghanistan, nor can one declare it to be superfluous for the future.
> It is important to see what détente policy can and cannot achieve. It does not promise to overcome the fundamental differences between East and West in their scale of values. Détente policy does not promise an innocuous world. It does not even promise steady progress free from any setbacks. It is not a substitute for the will to

defend oneself; in fact, it presupposes such a will. (*Bulletin*, [1980], 8: 4–7.)

Genscher went on to reaffirm all three dimensions of détente. Above all, he said, détente policy "must be marked by agreement to exclude the threat or use of force as means of resolving conflicts," to eliminate causes of tension by common effort or at least to defuse them so as to prevent escalation.

The international situation made détente more rather than less important—this was the basic theme of the SPD's election program. *Das wichtigste ist der Friede* (The main thing is peace) was the opening sentence of the program, which then went on to outline its "active peace policy" based on "détente and disarmament on the basis of a balance of power." The program made a very favorable evaluation of détente. This policy must continue, the program said; "especially in difficult times one must talk more to each other and not less." Confrontation must be avoided, cooperation must be increased, confidence building must go on in spite of foreign and domestic resistance and in spite of "irritation and reversals." The program also went into detail about arms limitation (SPD 1980: 1, 10–14).

The FDP's program was very similar: there was no working alternative to the détente policy; détente must go on "in spite of, or rather because of the threatening international situation" (Verhengen 1980: 601–2).

The commitment to détente may have become diluted in some respects under the impact of the international situation, pressure from Washington, and criticism by the CDU/CSU (section 7.3.1). Genscher, in the speech just quoted, emphasized both the necessity of participation by the superpowers in détente and the importance of preserving the balance between the two sides, thereby suggesting two conditions for West German pursuit of détente. Against this, however, could be set the resounding reaffirmation of détente as particularly justified "in difficult times." Afghanistan, even more than Angola, served to strengthen rather than weaken West Germany's commitment to détente.

Hence, a commitment, strong from the outset, had become even firmer by 1976 and had, by 1980, developed far in the direction of a well-established foreign policy institution. It was not peculiar that after the SPD had been ousted from power in 1982, the new chancellor Helmut Kohl went out of his way in his first news conference to emphasize the continuity in West German foreign policy (*New York Times*, October 5, 1982).

7.2.2. The United States

The following notes on détente in presidential declarations are based primarily on a perusal of the statements printed in the *New York Times* during 1972, 1976, and 1980 (January to election day). A major document from 1972 has been added: President Nixon's so-called State of the World Message to the Congress. Moreover, since the 1976 election is of particular interest for the comparison between the United States and West Germany—in 1972 both governments were prodétente, while in 1980 they differed strikingly; the intervening period may be crucial in accounting for the difference—a fuller coverage of what President Ford said about détente during his campaign has been sought. A few statements made by President Carter in 1980 and published in the *Department of State Bulletin* (*DSB*) have also been included. In an in-depth study of United States détente policy it would obviously be necessary to examine not just statements made by presidents in presidential election years but also statements by other spokespersons of the U.S. government and statements made in the intervening periods.

1972: Richard Nixon   This was *the* year of détente in U.S. politics. The State of the World Message, transmitted to the Congress on February 9, was intended to provide "an insight into our philosophy of foreign policy and our new approaches to peace." It stressed how strongly the administration had committed itself to "transform the U.S.-Soviet relationship so that a mutual search for a stable peace and security becomes its dominant feature and its driving force" (*DSB* 66, no. 1707 [1972]: 313, 320).

Then came Nixon's visit to Moscow in May and his triumphant return address to the Congress. Nixon surveyed the progress made in Moscow: the several agreements about concrete cooperation, which, he said, would create a growing vested interest on both sides in the maintenance of good relations; the expanded trade, which would increase the stakes both sides had in peace; the arms control agreements, particularly SALT; and the "landmark declaration" on basic principles, which committed both sides to avoid direct military confrontation and to exercise restraint. He used strong words to characterize the commitment to continue along this route: an "unparalleled opportunity" had been "placed in America's hands," and history laid on the United States "a special obligation to see it through," to seize the opportunity and "build a new structure of peace in the world" (*New York Times*, June 2, 1972). In his acceptance address at the

Republican convention, Nixon used a favorite phrase: the United States and the Soviet Union had "moved from confrontation to negotiation," and he needed a mandate to "continue these great initiatives" (*New York Times*, August 24, 1972).

Just as in contemporary West German declarations, the historic importance of the new policy was repeatedly emphasized. But there were also differences between American and West German détente rhetoric. None of them was pronounced, but some differences in nuance, if taken together, may have served to make Nixon's commitment to détente weaker than that of the West Germans.

First, Nixon's objectives were more ambitious. According to him it was not just a matter of "détente and normalization," which was a characteristic West German phrase. The State of the World Message referred to the "real and serious" issues dividing the United States and the Soviet Union. These were not "susceptible to solution by resort to mere atmospherics." There had to be "concrete agreements on the specific problems which cause the tension between our two countries." The "essence" of Nixon's approach was to "concentrate on the substance rather than the climate" and to "confront squarely the serious issues which divide us" (*DSB* 66, no. 1707 [1972]: 320–21). Precisely such a confrontation of the "real and serious" issues had begun during the Moscow summit, Nixon maintained. The foundation had been laid for "a new relationship between the two most powerful nations in the world." There had occurred a "solid record of progress on solving the difficult issues which for so long had divided our two nations and also have divided the world." The challenge was to go forward and "explore the sweeping possibilities for peace" that had opened up (*New York Times*, June 2, 1972).

Second, the necessity for Soviet responsiveness was emphasized. According to the State of the World Message, it was a basic principle of Nixon's foreign policy to judge the Soviet Union by its actions on the key issues. The Soviet Union had the choice "whether the current period of relaxation is to be merely another offensive tactic or truly an opportunity to develop an international system resting on the stability of relations between the superpowers" (*DSB* 66, no. 1707 [1972]: 322, 325). Similarly, according to a broadcast announcing the mining of North Vietnamese ports, the two countries were on the "threshold of a new relationship"; the United States was committed to "continue to build" this new relationship; the responsibility for failure would fall on the Soviet Union (*New York Times*, May 9, 1972). The West German declarations were less explicit about what was needed from the adversary.

Third, Nixon now and then pointed out that there were links between issues. "Accommodation is a process," he explained in the State of the World Message, and "the settlement of a major issue could not fail to improve the prospect for the settlement of others" (*DSB* 66, no. 1707 [1972]: 322). On his return from Moscow he recalled his objective of "creating a momentum of achievement in which progress in one area could contribute to progress in others" (*New York Times*, June 2, 1972).

Fourth, the importance of mutual self-restraint was emphasized in the State of the World Message. The United States did not expect the parties to give up the pursuit of their interests but did expect them to exercise self-restraint in pursuing them (*DSB* 66, no. 1707 [1972]: 322, 325).

A policy presented in this fashion is vulnerable to negative feedback. If your objectives are far-reaching, the likelihood of failure is great. If you stress that your policy—or its successful pursuit—is contingent on the adversary's showing restraint and being forthcoming on the key issues, it will likely be easy to justify a change in policy. If you add that issues are linked, you make the policy as a whole vulnerable to failure in its details. References to the adversary and to links are rhetorical devices likely to weaken commitments, especially if the declared objectives are ambitious.

It can be argued that Nixon was merely stating the obvious when he pointed out the necessity for Soviet responsiveness and restraint and the interrelations among issues. It must, therefore, be repeated that we are not comparing West German and American thinking about détente in the present context. The suggestion made here is that, regardless of the similarity or difference in thinking, the difference in presentation may have had an impact on the stability of the détente policy. With some exaggeration: the West Germans presented détente as unconditional normalization, whereas Nixon outlined fundamental but conditional change. Whether this reflected a difference in thinking is unclear but irrelevant at this point. It obviously takes two to tango, but when committing yourself to tango you may or may not emphasize this fact. Nixon did, and the West Germans did not. Moreover, the tango to which you commit yourself may be expert or average; Nixon's was the former, that of the West Germans the latter.

Henry Kissinger in his memoirs has rejected the charge of Nixon's "overselling" détente. Indeed, Kissinger has written, in all Nixon's speeches, statements, and interviews during this period there was a pattern of caution, "constantly pointing out the limits, the ambiguities, the competition inherent in the relationship, the requirement of vigilance, as well as the very real progress that had been made" (1979: 1255). Kissinger does take note of Nixon's escalating campaign oratory, however. Such oratory is apt to make a policy more vulnerable to the charge of failure (essentially this point is made by Hoffmann 1984).

1976: Gerald Ford   In interviews on December 31, 1975, and January 3, 1976, President Ford was asked about Angola and détente. He admitted that détente had not worked properly in Angola. However, it would be "very unwise for a president—me or anyone else—to abandon détente." Given the deep ideological differences and the military and industrial superpower of the Soviet Union, it was in the best interest of both countries "to work together to ease tensions, to avoid confrontation where possible, to improve relations on a worldwide basis." To "abandon this working relationship and go back to the cold war" would be very unwise. We "must continue rather than stop" (*DSB* 74, no. 1909 [1976]: 100–105).

Although he avoided using the word "détente," Ford made several similar statements during the campaign. "While I am president," he said in his acceptance speech, "we will not return to a collision course that could reduce civilization to ashes" (*New York Times*, August 20, 1976). "I don't believe we should move to a cold-war relationship," he said in the foreign affairs debate with Carter (*New York Times*, October 7, 1976). This is one of the formulations he used in 1976 to describe U.S. policy: "Through negotiations and constructive diplomacy, we are seeking to reduce the level of tensions with the Soviet Union. We share with them an interest in preventing a nuclear incineration, but we have no illusions that they have changed their political objectives or their essential world outlook" (*The Presidential Campaign 1976*, vol. 2: *President Gerald R. Ford* [1979], p. 622).

Nixon's commitment had been to historic change. Ford's was to avoid a return to the Cold War. The change in atmosphere is illustrated—but perhaps exaggerated—by the difference between the Republican platforms of 1972 and 1976. The 1972 platform affirmed that Nixon had begun "the difficult task of building a new relationship" with the Soviet Union and pledged to "build upon these promising beginnings . . . to establish a truly lasting peace" (Johnson and Potter 1973: 852). In 1976 the emphasis of the section on the Soviet Union was on the need for a "realistic assessment of the Communist challenge." A Republican administration would prevent a shift in the balance of power but would also "diligently explore with the Soviet Union new ways to reduce tensions and to arrive at mutually beneficial

and self-enforcing agreements in all fields of international activity."
The United States would "remain firm in the face of pressure, while at
the same time expressing our willingness to work on the basis of strict
reciprocity toward new agreements which will help achieve peace and
stability" (*Historic Documents of 1976*, pp. 659–61).

United States policy toward the Soviet Union, as presented by Ford,
remained one of détente. The ambition, however, was reduced from
creating a new epoch to avoiding confrontation and making agreements when possible. The Soviet Union had failed to satisfy Nixon's
conditions, and Ford's watered-down détente policy resulted.

1980: Jimmy Carter   On New Year's Eve, 1979, Jimmy Carter made
his famous statement that the Soviet invasion of Afghanistan had
changed his opinion of the Russians more drastically than anything
they had previously done during his presidency (*New York Times*, January 1, 1980). An "immediate and comprehensive evaluation of the
whole range of our relations with the Soviet Union" was announced
as early as January 4 (*New York Times*, January 5, 1980). In statement
after statement Carter laid down what was in effect a suspension of
détente; it was, in a common phrase, impossible to continue to do
"business as usual" with the invader of Afghanistan. "Neither we nor
our allies want to destroy the framework of East-West relations that
has yielded concrete benefits to so many people," Carter said. But the
United States must "impose the costs of aggression for as long as this
is necessary," even if this would mean "a protracted time of strain in
East-West relations" (*DSB* 80, no. 2038 [1980]: 5). "Détente with the
Soviets remains our goal," he explained, but it must be made clear that
America or Europe could not be "an island of détente while aggression
is carried out elsewhere" (no. 2041: 15).

Carter made one exception, however: nuclear arms control. "Especially now in a time of great tension" the effort to control nuclear
weapons must not be abandoned (*New York Times*, January 24,
1980). In the televised debate with Reagan, Carter made nuclear arms
control the most important issue in the election and the chief point of
difference between the candidates (*New York Times*, October 29,
1980).

THUS, while West Germany's Ostpolitik developed into a firm institution, the U.S. commitment to a policy of détente was scaled down.
Nuclear arms control was indeed an institutionalized part of U.S. foreign policy by 1980, but in other respects no particular policy toward
the Soviet Union appeared to be well established. Ronald Reagan's

freedom of movement in January 1981 was large in comparison with Helmut Kohl's in October 1982.

7.2.3. The Soviet Union

We will now examine how Brezhnev and his foreign and defense ministers presented Soviet policy toward the West in 1971, 1976, and 1981. The following observations are based on all such statements found in the *Current Digest of the Soviet Press* (*CDSP*). It bears repeating that it is unclear to what extent the process here called institutionalization exists in the Soviet Union.

1971: The Twenty-fourth Congress   Brezhnev, in his speech to the Twenty-fourth Congress of the CPSU, introduced what became known as his Peace Program. He pointed at a "substantial change for the better" in relations with West Germany and confirmed that the Soviet Union was prepared "to cover our part of the path toward . . . normalization and improvement." Generally, "cooperation on general questions of international policy" had increased with some capitalist countries. "Political consultations promoting better mutual understanding" had become "a regular practice," and economic, scientific, and technical "ties" had "acquired substantial scope." All of this accorded with the "principled line" of the Soviet Union with regard to capitalist countries: "consistently and fully to implement in practice the principles of peaceful coexistence, to develop mutually advantageous ties and—with those states that are ready to do so—to cooperate in the field of strengthening peace, making mutual relations with these states as stable as possible" (*CDSP* 23, no. 12 [1971]: 11–13).

The "principled line" was repeated in statement after statement (no. 21: 7; no. 24: 8; no. 44: 6–7). In addition to consultations and "ties," disarmament was a central feature of the documents. In terms of the sheer frequency of top-level declarations, the commitment to two dimensions of a policy of détente—arms control and cooperation—became substantial. With regard to the third dimension, restraint, the texts were less explicit.[9] A consideration of the Soviet détente rhetoric

[9] See Volten 1982 for a similar reading of the Peace Program. It may be objected that the conclusion is based on too literal an interpretation of the texts. Perhaps the Soviet leaders were committing themselves to restraint in a way that was clear to their Soviet audience, without this being obvious to a Western analyst insufficiently familiar with Soviet political language. It is nonetheless striking how difficult it is to find among all the references to arms control and cooperation anything reminiscent of Article 2 in the Nixon-Brezhnev Basic Principles Agreement, in which the parties commit themselves to "exercise restraint in their mutual relations." Of course, disagreement over the implica-

may suggest some additional strengths and weaknesses in the Soviet commitment to détente.[10]

On the one hand, détente with Western Europe was dramatized as a major change. Europe might be at "a turning point in history" (no. 44: 3); the "guaranteeing of a lasting peace in Europe" was becoming "a realistic prospect" (no. 39: 5); a start was being made on "the transition of Europe to a new historical phase" (no. 49: 12). Strong terms were used to demonstrate the importance attached to détente: the Soviet people were "vitally interested" in this matter (no. 44: 4).

On the other hand, just like Nixon but in contrast to the West Germans, Soviet declarations gave a decisive role to the adversary. The Soviet Union, Brezhnev said, was prepared to cover its part of "the path toward . . . normalization and improvement" of Soviet-West German relations, "provided, needless to say, that the other side acts in accordance with the letter and spirit" of the Soviet-German treaty (no. 12: 11–12). There were "great opportunities for active political cooperation"; "the more interest our partners show . . . the more extensive these opportunities will be and the easier it will be to realize them" (no. 24: 8). "The more realism there is in the Western countries' policies, the broader will be our common opportunities to continue improving the situation in Europe" (no. 49: 12).

The declarations about détente must also have been weakened by their containing at least as much about the continuing ideological struggle against imperialism as about détente. Soviet spokesmen insisted that the two were perfectly compatible, as shown in chapter 6. However, to deny the necessity for trade-offs between two lines of action is apt to dilute the commitment to both. A commitment to disarmament is weakened by arguing that rearmament is in fact compatible with, if not a means to, disarmament; this may be similar in the case of détente and ideological struggle.

Whereas statement after statement was made about the historical turning point in Europe, less was said about new relations with the United States (the war in Vietnam went on, and Nixon was not yet about to go to Moscow). According to Brezhnev, the principles of

---

tions of détente for superpower restraint in third areas became a chief cause of the détente crisis; see, e.g., George 1983: 107–16.

[10] I am aware of the risk of misunderstanding the political effect of rhetorical devices in a foreign political culture. The general need for more systematic research about verbal behavior in politics includes a need for crossnational study. The Soviet citizen or Western Sovietologist who may find my reading of Soviet texts to be erroneous is asked to contribute to the further development of systematic knowledge about verbal politics in the USSR.

peaceful coexistence were applicable also to the United States, but "we have to consider whether we are dealing with a real desire to settle questions at the negotiating table or with an attempt to pursue a 'positions of strength' policy" (no. 12: 13). According to Gromyko, the USSR favored "normal relations" with the United States, but Washington had to back up its statements in favor of talks by practical deeds (no. 17: 34).

1976: The Twenty-fifth Congress   In his report to the Twenty-fifth Congress of the CPSU, Brezhnev called attention to the Peace Program. Its purpose had been "to bring about a change of direction in the development of international relations. A change from the cold war to peaceful coexistence. . . . A change from tension, carrying the threat of explosion, to detente and normal, mutually advantageous cooperation." The accomplishments since 1971 had been "of truly permanent significance." The Soviet Union would "continue this policy with redoubled energy" (*CDSP* 28, no. 8 [1976]: 3–4).

When explaining what this meant in practice, Soviet declarations emphasized arms control and disarmament. The "materialization" of détente was also stressed, however: the "material fabric of peaceful cooperation" would "strengthen ties among European peoples and states and would give them an increasing stake in the preservation of peace for many years to come" (no. 26: 4).

Relations with West Germany were described in a rosy way. A "major shift" had occurred, Brezhnev told the congress. West Germany had become "one of our major partners" in business. Talks with West German leaders had "made it possible to improve mutual understanding and to advance cooperation." There were "complications": normalization was under attack from "rightist forces." Therefore, a stubborn struggle was still needed. The Soviet Union would wage this struggle. "We have a great goal before us, comrades: to make lasting peace the natural form of life for all European peoples" (no. 8: 9).

"We have," Brezhnev continued, "devoted a great deal of attention to the task of improving relations with the U.S." There had indeed been a "turn for the better." There was "an important fundamental mutual understanding . . . on the necessity of developing peaceful and equal relations." The treaties and agreements had laid a solid basis for cooperation and had lessened the danger of nuclear war "to a certain extent." However, the development had been "complicated by a number of rather important factors." Influential forces called for an intensified arms race, and attempts had been made to interfere in Soviet affairs by means of trade discrimination. "Needless to say, we could not tolerate this, and will not tolerate it." The Soviet Union nevertheless "firmly" intended to "pursue a course aimed at the further improvement of Soviet-American relations" (pp. 9–10).

On the issue of détente versus class struggle Brezhnev repeated that there was no contradiction. Détente meant "that disputes and conflicts between countries must not be settled by means of war or by means of the use of force or the threat of force. Detente does not in the slightest abolish, and it cannot abolish or alter, the laws of class struggle" (p. 14).

1981: The Twenty-sixth Congress   It has been "a stormy and complicated time," Brezhnev said at the beginning of his speech to the Twenty-sixth Congress of the CPSU. The "aggressiveness of imperialist policy" had "increased drastically" (*CDSP* 33, no. 8 [1981]: 3). How did this affect Soviet détente policy?

First, the basic commitment to détente was reaffirmed in several declarations of 1981. Détente was, in Brezhnev's words, "the most valuable achievement of the 1970s" (no. 19: 5–6). Even Defense Minister Ustinov maintained that "to preserve and deepen detente is a matter of honor and conscience" (no. 25: 6). Arms control and disarmament played at least as prominent a role in 1981 as in 1976; its urgency was stressed (no. 45: 3). The commitment to "ties," and particularly to trade, was also reaffirmed; "this, incidentally," Brezhnev said, "is a factor in the stabilization of international relations," and the only problem was the frequent use of economic ties for political purposes by the imperialists (no. 8: 6).

Soviet-West German relations were still described in positive terms. They had developed "favorably" (pp. 11–12). In fact, "what was accomplished in the 1970s is continuing to work for peace now too, in an aggravated international situation" (no. 31: 12). The Europeans were "making an invaluable contribution to the strengthening of peace by their day-to-day creative activity, by constantly expanding and strengthening fruitful peaceful ties"; "the material structure of peaceful cooperation in Europe is continuing to gain strength and to be enriched" (no. 44: 4).

Also in relation to the United States, the Soviet Union had pursued a "principled and constructive line." The Carter administration, however, "trying to put pressure on us," had undertaken to destroy "the positive elements that had been created." And the Reagan administration had continued to "poison the atmosphere." Brezhnev hoped, however, that American leaders would ultimately "see things more realistically." There was a "need for an active dialogue." The Soviet Union still wanted "normal relations" with the United States (no. 8: 11; see also no. 23: 8; no. 44: 4; no. 47: 10).

BY THE EARLY 1980s détente had been a declared object of Soviet foreign policy for many years. It appears, however, that Soviet commitment to détente was more selective than that of West Germany or the United States. It emphasized the dimensions referred to here as arms control and cooperation, but it said less about restraint. The commitment to détente may also have been weakened by its being explicitly conditional on the adversary and by the insistence that there was no contradiction between détente and class struggle.

A difference existed between détente with West Germany and détente with the United States, however. The commitment to détente was made in stronger terms, more unreservedly, and with less emphasis on the role of the adversary in the former case than in the latter. By 1981 détente with West Germany had developed far in the direction of a Soviet foreign policy institution, to the extent that such a thing is possible. In relation to the United States there was commitment merely to "normal conditions" and to the resolution of controversial issues, provided that there was sufficient "realism" on the part of the adversary.

7.3. SUPPORT

The following observations about support for and opposition to the policy of détente in West Germany and the United States are based on materials from the election campaigns of 1972, 1976, and 1980 in an attempt at getting at the fundamentals by a limited effort. As emphasized previously, this is scratching the surface, especially in the case of the United States (section 2.3). The campaign documents are supplemented by notes about interest organizations and public opinion. The observations about the extent of controversy over détente in the Soviet Union are based in their entirety on secondary sources.

7.3.1. West Germany

The sources for the view of the CDU/CSU about the Ostpolitik are the same as for government policy: the election programs, the television debates, and the Bundestag debate in February 1972.[11]

---

[11] Studies of the domestic politics of the Ostpolitik include Hacke 1975, Hanrieder 1970, and Niclauss 1977.

1972: Rainer Barzel   Rainer Barzel's main speech in the Bundestag debate about the Eastern treaties is a representative presentation of the CDU's reasons for failing to support ratification. Barzel said that he shared the vision of a Europe based on the unconditional prohibition of the use or threat of force, on mutual arms control and balanced disarmament, and on increased cooperation in all fields. A CDU-led government, however, would have demanded more from the Soviet Union in return for the treaties.

Thus, human rights was a major theme in Barzel's speech. Détente exists, he said, "only where the road to self-determination is eased and freedom of movement for persons, information, and ideas increasingly becomes a tangible reality." The CDU was in favor of making concessions to obtain a European charter that would make the frontiers more bearable and the systems more humane. It was opposed to measures cementing the status quo.

Self-determination in this context meant first of all German reunification, and the concern for individual freedoms was first a concern for the East Germans. The opposition maintained that the Eastern treaties established a definite solution rather than a modus vivendi, and they regarded freedom of movement for persons as the "proof" and the "criterion" of détente. "The real cause of tension," Barzel said, "is the denial of human rights in Germany and Europe, and nothing else."[12]

This was the heart of the matter. The chief disagreement between government and opposition concerned the causal relationship between détente and human rights. The government described détente as a means to promote human rights in East Europe. The opposition maintained that the realization of human rights was a precondition for détente. Hence their insistence that the government ought to have demanded more in return for the treaties.

The message of the election program was similar. The CDU/CSU wanted "good relations" with all states in Central and Eastern Europe and an increase in economic, cultural, and scientific exchanges. They favored mutual force reductions. They agreed that the unity of the German state could not be realized "for the time being"; they were prepared to negotiate step-by-step improvements in the freedom of movement within Germany, and the steps they proposed to take in this direction did not differ strikingly from government policy. However, the program also maintained that peace and cooperation were best served by realizing human rights: "We want détente in Germany through freedom of movement for persons, information, and ideas"

[12] *Verhandlungen*, pp. 9752–64.

(CDU 1972: 45–46). Human rights were hardly mentioned in the SPD's presentation of its Ostpolitik, and the CDU/CSU seemed intent on demonstrating that they were less willing than the government to pursue Realpolitik and to accept the status quo.

The Ostpolitik figured prominently in the campaign, but during the television debates at least the focus was on the DDR, and relations with the Soviet Union were mentioned only incidentally. In his first intervention in the debate on November 2, Barzel took the opportunity to repeat a key CDU/CSU position: "Our criterion of détente is, as you know, freedom of movement for persons, information, and ideas." In the debate on November 15, Franz Josef Strauss confirmed that a new government would respect the Eastern treaties—"there is no doubt about that"—but would strive for new and better agreements with more "sobriety," "matter-of-factness," and fewer illusions about the adversary (transcripts).

1976: Helmut Kohl   The CDU/CSU program of 1976 again proceeded from the thesis that "the freedom of all Europeans" was "an essential precondition for securing peace." The two parties favored an improved understanding with the Soviet Union, but there must be a reasonable relationship between what was conceded and what was given in return. The Ostpolitik must no longer be a "one way street." It must be based on a "sober assessment of the world political goals of Communist policy and the real intentions of the states of the Eastern bloc." And it must serve the interests of the people in these countries—people who remained deprived of their basic freedoms. An Ostpolitik that "conceals the lasting differences, denies one's own convictions, and strives for change by rapprochement (*Wandel durch Annäherung*) does not do service to peace" (CDU 1976: 7, 9–10).

This was similar to the message of 1972. A new theme, however, was skepticism as regards economic relations with the East: "We are opposed to a policy that supports the Communist plan economy with generous credits and quickens the rearmament of the Warsaw Pact states against free Europe" (p. 8).

In the final television debate, Helmut Kohl was asked about the Eastern policy of the CDU. His reply was that "we say a clear 'yes' . . . to a policy of détente, to a real policy of détente, to controlled disarmament, but a controlled, real détente." This meant that both sides must move; tit for tat (*Leistungen und Gegenleistungen*) must be the basic principle. Kohl added that he was in favor of trade with the East as long as it did not touch on the strategic field (transcript).

1980: Franz Josef Strauss   The CDU/CSU's election program of 1980 opened with a major attack on "Socialist détente policy." This must be replaced with a "realist peace policy," because "Soviet détente policy is the continuation of the Cold War by other means but with the same goals." In ten years of "Socialist détente policy" Soviet offensive capability had increased more than ever before. Since the beginning of "this wrongly conceived and deceptive policy of détente," the Soviet Union had been pursuing "worldwide power politics with increased vigor"— the opposite of a policy of security, cooperation, and détente. Because of "Socialist détente policy," peace had become more insecure than at any time since World War Two.

The CDU/CSU were ready to cooperate peacefully with Communist regimes, but as part of a Western foreign and defense policy characterized by "sobriety and vigilance." They favored mutual arms limitation and arms control but were aware that "for the Communist power-holders, détente and disarmament are parts of a power strategy."

Later in the program, the CDU/CSU reaffirmed that they favored a "real and lasting" détente. However, détente was no "one way street" and was "indivisible." Détente was possible only if the causes of tension were removed. They stressed that "without human rights and basic freedoms there is no security and also no peace worthy of the name." A CDU/CSU government would see to it that the West persisted on this issue (CDU 1980: 2–3, 8, 12–13).

Was this a break with the Ostpolitik? The final television debate failed to give an answer. On the one hand, Kohl reaffirmed that the CDU wanted "sensible and, if possible, good relations with the countries of Central and Eastern Europe." On the other hand, Strauss used most of his debating time for a major attack on West German foreign policy: coexistence, détente, and disarmament were "practical necessities" and not "semitheological dogmas"; the alternatives were not peace or war but peace in freedom or peace with absorption into the Soviet power system. Even though Helmut Schmidt persisted in pressing Kohl and Strauss about the substance of their alternative, they did not go into detail about the way in which their Eastern policy would differ from that of the SPD and the FDP (transcript).

No CONSENSUS over the Ostpolitik developed during the 1970s. On the contrary, both government and opposition told the 1980 electorate that they fundamentally disagreed over foreign policy and that this was the most important issue in the election. At the same time, the substantive distance between them was difficult to specify. This is not an uncommon situation in politics, and it may be more typical of foreign than of domestic policy. It is difficult for any opposition to develop a detailed foreign policy program that could be directly implemented. Their foreign policy alternative more likely consists in general principles about what to strive for in international interactions. It is impractical, precisely because foreign policy consists in interaction with other governments, to specify in advance what one will do.

The CDU/CSU kept demanding, throughout the decade, a balance between what was given to the East and what was conceded in return. Their Ostpolitik would be more active on human rights, they said, and they would prevent détente from becoming a cover for Soviet power politics. But they seem to have failed, understandably, to make clear what they thought should be done if the Soviet Union refused to concede anything. Would they bring the process of détente to a standstill? Would they even reverse it? Or would they rather do as the government had done: pay the price that had to be paid in order to obtain the advantages of détente? These were key questions for determining the substantive difference between government and opposition, and the material studied here provided no clear answers.

It has been argued that the CDU/CSU's original opposition to the Ostpolitik was based on a misreading of public opinion (Hacke 1975: 86). In fact, public opinion shifted in the direction of a new policy toward the East as early as the mid-1960s (Merkl 1981: 270–76). This shift was led not by the Social Democrats but by the churches (Griffith 1978: 126–27). Industry and business also helped to prepare the ground for the Ostpolitik, even though their associations and leaders were reserved about the Ostpolitik in their pronouncements (Burzig 1978; Krautheim 1974; Kreile 1974, 1980). The chief organized resistance came from the associations of the exiles, whose leadership proved unrepresentative of the members (Hacke 1975: 86).

Public opinion may have changed again in the 1970s, however. Garding, in a study of West German voters, distinguished between polarization, consensus, and dissension issues. He showed that the Ostpolitik was primarily a consensus issue in 1972 but had developed into a polarization issue by 1976 (Garding 1978). Baker et al. also reported increasing polarization as well as increasing support (1981: 135).

Thus, West Germany's policy of détente failed to acquire the protection of a broad national consensus during its first decade. The issue remained controversial in West German politics. The lack of clarity about the substantive difference between government and opposition may be important, however. Intense controversy that is substantively unclear—in such a situation sensitivity to the environment is presumably high, which is destabilizing, but no clear-cut policy alternative is put forward, which is stabilizing. The lack of consensus may have been less destabilizing than the election rhetoric suggested.

7.3.2. The United States

In 1972, West Germany's Ostpolitik had possessed a substance and had been a political issue for several years. The détente policy of the United States still consisted mostly of hopes and promises; it had no tradition as a major political issue; and it was launched in the midst of the Vietnam war. It is no wonder that détente encountered little opposition in the campaign of 1972. In fact, Nixon's use of détente had the appearance of a skillful exploitation of foreign policy for domestic purposes. In 1980, on the other hand, when the Ostpolitik had become firmly established in Bonn, most of détente had already been abandoned in Washington. The critical year, therefore, is 1976; the extent of controversy over détente in this presidential election is essential to the evaluation of the hypothesis that political consensus helps to stabilize a foreign policy.

What follows is based primarily on statements by the nonincumbent candidate in each election, as printed in the *New York Times*, and on their party platforms. Some material has been added from Jimmy Carter's campaign in 1976.

1972: George McGovern Most of what George McGovern said about the Soviet Union in the campaign of 1972 supported Nixon's "new departures." He and the Democrats may have been a shade more dovish than the president in stressing arms control and disarmament. They may have been a shade more hawkish in taking a more activistic stand with regard to "the oppressed peoples of Eastern Europe and the minorities of the Soviet Union" (Johnson and Potter 1973: 814); McGovern said in a speech that "we should press for justice for Soviet Jews rather than abandon them for a trade agreement" (*New York Times*, October 6, 1972). But there was no disagreement over fundamentals.

1976: Jimmy Carter As a candidate Jimmy Carter strongly supported the arms control dimension of the détente policy. His statements on détente were less favorable in other respects, as illustrated by several quotations. The first is from an interview in *U.S. News & World Report*:

> Q.: Do you feel that we should adopt a tougher approach in pursuing détente with the Soviet Union?

Carter: Yes, I think so. The Soviets would respect that approach. I would also make our commitments much more public. . . .

Q.: In what way would you be tougher toward the Soviet Union?

Carter: We should have been much more aggressive when we attended the Helsinki Conference—or should have been absent in the first place.

We now have in Eastern Europe at least a tentative endorsement by our country of the domination of that region by the Soviet Union. They didn't have that before the Helsinki accords. It was a very great diplomatic achievement for the Soviets to have our promise not to interfere in their control over Eastern Europe.

In response to our yielding on that point, there was an agreement on the Soviet Union's part that they would liberalize their policies toward human rights. They have not fulfilled those commitments.

As we sell the Russians things that they must have—food in their drought years, electronics equipment, heavy machinery—we ought to get a quid pro quo from the Soviets (*The Presidential Campaign 1976*, vol. 1: *Jimmy Carter* [1979], p. 742).

Next, from the television debate with Ford on foreign policy:

We've become fearful to compete with the Soviet Union on an equal basis. We talk about détente. The Soviet Union knows what they want in détente, and they've been getting it. We have not known what we wanted, and we've been outtraded in almost every instance. . . . [The] Helsinki agreement . . . may have been a good agreement at the beginning, but we have failed to enforce the so-called basket three part (*New York Times*, October 7, 1976).

Finally, an interview from *Playboy*:

Q.: In some respects, your foreign policy seems similar to that established by Kissinger, Nixon, and Ford. In fact, Kissinger stated that he didn't think your differences were substantial. How, precisely, does your view differ from theirs?

Carter: As I've said in my speeches, I feel the policy of détente has given up too much to the Russians and gotten too little in return. . . .

Q.: What do you mean when you say we've given up too much to the Russians?

Carter: One example I've mentioned often is the Helsinki agreement. I never saw any reason we should be involved in the Helsinki meetings at all. We added the stature of our presence and signature to an agreement that, in effect, ratified the take-over of eastern Europe by the Soviet Union. We got very little, if anything, in return. The Russians promised they would honor democratic principles and permit the free movement of their citizens, including those who wanted to emigrate. The Soviet Union has not lived up to those promises and Mr. Brezhnev was able to celebrate the major achievement of his diplomatic life (*The Presidential Campaign 1976*, vol. 1: *Jimmy Carter* [1979], p. 953).

It can be added that Carter signaled the use of American economic leverage in cases like Angola; he declined to single out grain as a bargaining weapon—"it would be a total withholding of trade" (*New York Times*, July 7, 1976).

The Democratic platform also reflected a relatively skeptical view of détente as this policy had been pursued in preceding years. A principal goal must be continued reduction of tension with the Soviet Union, it said. "This can, however, only be accomplished by fidelity to our principles and interests and through business-like negotiations about specific issues, not by the bad bargains, dramatic posturing, and the stress on general declarations that have characterized the Nixon-Ford administration's detente policy." The issue of oppression in Eastern Europe was emphasized. More extensive economic relations might be beneficial to both countries, but previous bargains had been overly favorable to the Soviet Union. "Our watch-word would be tough bargaining and concrete economic, political or other benefits for the United States" (*Historic Documents of 1976*, pp. 587–88).

Hence, the mood expressed in the Democratic campaign of 1976 was that the United States ought to have been tougher in the bargaining over détente and ought to have pressed more strongly for concessions on human rights. This was similar to the CDU/CSU's criticism of the Ostpolitik. Perhaps this is the natural position to take in opposition: tougher bargaining plus more idealism.

It is important to recall at this point that at least three presidential hopefuls had views on détente that were more skeptical than Carter's: Henry Jackson and George Wallace among the Democrats, and Ronald Reagan among the Republicans. Both of the former proved to have a significant following in the primaries (Moore and Fraser 1977: 170–80), and Reagan came close to capturing the Republican nomination (Witcover 1977: chap. 8). More radical criticism of détente than Carter's had a substantial political base in 1976.

1980: Ronald Reagan   The Republican platform of 1980 used strong words about foreign policy: "Never before in modern history has the

United States endured as many humiliations, insults, and defeats as it has during the past four years." The platform went on to argue that the "premier challenge . . . is to check the Soviet Union's global ambitions. This challenge must be met, for the present danger is greater than ever before in the 200–year history of the United States" (*Historic Documents of 1980*, pp. 571, 636).

Carter was attacked from all directions for having mismanaged foreign policy (Germond and Witcover 1981: 146–47). But Ronald Reagan criticized objectives as well as management. He advocated less restraint: "We've got to send some signals to the Soviet Union that there could be a confrontation down the road if they continue" (*New York Times*, February 21, 1980). He also wanted to go "all the way" with economic sanctions, if necessary (*New York Times*, October 2, 1980). The Republican platform pledged to "stop the flow of technology," to make emigration "a central issue in Soviet-American relations," to "insist on full Soviet compliance" with the Helsinki Final Act, and to "spare no efforts to publicize to the world the fundamental differences in the two systems" (*Historic Documents of 1980*, pp. 637–38).

The Republican position on arms control, the chief remnant of détente in Carter's policy, may be characterized as disarmament by rearmament. A precondition for arms limitation was to "reverse the trends now in favor of the Soviet Union," Reagan said (*New York Times*, August 21, 1980). "The one card that's been missing in these negotiations has been the possibility of an arms race"; the Soviets had been racing, "but with no competition" (*New York Times*, October 2, 1980).

Apart from arms policy, the massive Republican attack on détente did not seem to differ radically in substance from post-Afghanistan Carter policy. In the words of one observer, "both candidates sought to out-Cold War each other," and this "move Right" provided the basis for a "new Cold War consensus" (Cumings 1981: 213).

THE ORIGINAL near-consensus over détente, then, had dissolved already by 1976, when Ford's continuing commitment to a policy of the détente type proved controversial. The difference between him and Carter paralleled the one in Germany, but other critics of détente went further, and the policy advocated by Reagan even at this time seems to have more radically and specifically departed from détente than did the CDU/CSU's criticism of the Ostpolitik.

The concern here is not with the election campaigns per se. The assumption has been that the chief differences of opinion in American society are channeled through the elections to a sufficient extent for the differences and similarities between the main contenders to tell us the essentials about differences and similarities in the polity at large. This assumption is more audacious in the case of the United States than with regard to West Germany. Have we underestimated the support of détente by limiting ourselves to electoral politics?

It is clear, first of all, that the lack of a consensus over détente was reflected in Congress. Consistency and coherence in U.S. foreign policy, it has been argued, is most likely if there is centralization of congressional leadership, deference to the president on the big questions, and consensus over the Soviet threat. By the mid-1970s, however, congressional reform had decentralized power in both the Senate and the House; Congress had become a source of foreign policy initiative but had proved divided about key U.S.-Soviet issues. Congress had become "a volatile force on Soviet issues," even though "usually pressing presidents toward a tougher line" (Destler 1984: 55; see also Nye 1984: 334–36). The impact of congressional politics on détente, in other words, was destabilizing rather than stabilizing.

Hughes's study of the "domestic context" of American foreign policy includes a chapter about interest organizations. Hughes maintains, to begin with, that even though East-West trade is one of the issues dividing business, there is a basic business interest in expanding it. Labor, on the other hand, has tended to oppose détente. The agricultural organizations have differed among themselves on the crucial issues, including that of grain sales. The veterans' and military support organizations have been skeptical or opposed to détente, and the military-industrial complex has contributed to "the continuation of general public animosities and fears" related to the Cold War. The League of Women Voters has been active in supporting liberal foreign policies, but East-West relations are not among the several examples mentioned by Hughes. Nor does he report any organized support for détente among religious and ethnic groups (1978: 153–96). The impression is that the policy of détente was more weakly supported and more strongly opposed by interest organizations in the United States than in West Germany.[13]

---

[13] After having surveyed the opponents and the backers of détente, Cox came to the conclusion that they were about equal by the mid-1970s (1976: 171). His survey showed, however, that organized interests tended to be on the opposing rather than on the supporting side. According to Destler, the pressure for continuity in U.S. policy toward the USSR has been limited since the 1970s by the "relatively weak influence of interest groups with stakes in steady policies" (1984: 54). See also Hallenberg 1984: 197–206.

The absence of an elite consensus over foreign policy in the critical period—the mid-1970s—is confirmed in Holsti's and Rosenau's survey of about two thousand American leaders (1980: 296–98).

As regards public opinion, two types of polls are of particular interest here: those measuring the extent of "internationalism" and "isolationism" among the public (Watts and Free 1978; Free and Watts 1980), and those asking respondents whether they prefer defense increases or reductions (Watts and Free 1978; Kriesberg and Klein 1980; Richman 1981; Schneider 1983). The balance of opinion on the former issue can be computed by subtracting the isolationists from the internationalists, and on the latter issue by subtracting those who want to decrease spending from those who want to increase it. The way in which the two balances varied between 1964 and 1980 is shown in Figure 7.1.

This suggests that the U.S. pursuit of détente at first coincided with a period of relatively antimilitaristic internationalism. By the mid-1970s, however, a shift occurred in the direction of isolationism combined with a less skeptical view of defense spending. The change on the latter point, in the view of two researchers, was "little short of phenomenal" (Watts and Free 1978: 166). By 1980, public opinion had returned to the predétente state of a more militaristic internationalism.

Equally striking are the data on the item, "The U.S. should maintain its dominant position as the world's most powerful nation at all costs, even going to the brink of war if necessary." Fifty-six percent agreed with this statement in 1964, as against 39 percent in 1972 and 42 percent in 1974—but 52 percent in 1976 (p. 158). In 1980, moreover, a large majority supported a tough policy toward the Soviet Union (*Public Opinion*, 3, no. 1A [1980]: 22; see also Richman 1981: 44–46). These pieces of evidence suggest that détente had a broad support only for a brief period, that this period was about to end by the mid-1970s, and that there was relatively strong support for nondétente policies by the end of the decade.

Hence, there appears to have been less opposition to détente in the United States than in West Germany in 1972, but also less support. And when opposition developed, it became both more radical and more widespread in the United States.

7.3.3. The Soviet Union

Aspaturian (1971: 526–47), who proceeds from the assumption that different social and institutional groups have their own parochial interests in specific foreign policies, suggests a permanent polarization over détente: on the one hand, the party apparatus, the armed forces,

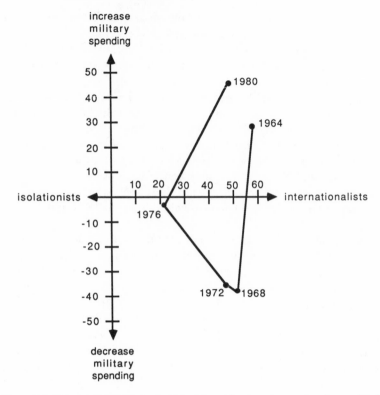

Figure 7.1. Balance of opinion in the United States between internationalists and isolationists and between supporters of increases and decreases in military spending (percentage differences). Source: Hallenberg 1984:193.

and heavy industry, who will likely benefit from tension; on the other hand, the state bureaucracy, light industry, agriculture, the cultural-professional-scientific groups, and the "consumers," who will likely benefit from détente.

Dallin, whose point of departure is the observation that cleavages over foreign policy have tended to be congruent with cleavages over other issues according to a left-right dimension, suggests that "the most important cleavage, in the present setting, of course deals with Soviet-American détente." He emphasizes that the division on détente has followed the traditional pattern (1981: 374).

In a study of Soviet writings in 1969, Jahn and Tiedke confirm the existence of different "tendencies" (*Strömungen*) on détente. They stress, however, that the détente policy did not seem to represent any particular social group or groups (pp. 76–77). Even though their classifications differ, several other authors similarly maintain that competing "tendencies" can be shown to exist in the Soviet Union with regard to policy toward the West, including Griffiths (1981) and Jönsson (1982).

Jackson (1981) has tried to map variations in the degree of controversy over policy toward the United States during the period with which the present study is concerned. He has examined Soviet images of the United States as a nuclear adversary, on the assumption that the way in which the adversary is described in a document is linked to the policy the author of the document wishes to promote. Hence, differences over policy are thought to be implied in differences with regard to the image of the adversary.

In Jackson's analysis, support for a policy of détente is associated with a "moderate" image of the United States. This image, in essence, is that powerful forces are at work in the United States for the revision of the Cold War policy, that the danger of war is decreasing, and that time is ripe for arms control. This is in contrast to a "conservative" image, according to which there is increasing militarism in the United States and a great danger of nuclear coercion and attack.

Jackson examines the image of the United States expressed in the writings and speeches of three groups: Arbatov and other Americanists, Grechko and other representatives of the military, and Brezhnev and other members of the Politburo. In the period 1970–72, Brezhnev and other political leaders avoided identifying themselves strongly with either the moderate line of the Americanists or the conservative line of the military; according to Jackson, this suggests that the issue was sensitive. In the period 1972–76, which is of particular interest here, Brezhnev came to endorse the moderate position, which was also supported by Gromyko and Aleksei Kosygin; the conservative position was upheld not just by Grechko but also by Aleksander Shelepin and Mikhail Suslov. After 1976 this polarization was replaced by an increasing consensus over what Jackson calls a "hardened moderate" image; by the end of the 1970s the substantive distance between the different groupings had decreased.

It is not possible, as Jackson points out, to infer the precise nature of differences over policy from differences over the image of the adversary. Jackson's analysis does suggest, however, that there was from the outset significant opposition to the policy of détente within the Kremlin. By the mid-1970s there seems to have developed a cleavage between supporters and opponents of détente reminiscent of those in Bonn and Washington. The consensus that apparently emerged toward the end of the 1970s was seemingly "bought" at the "price" of a hardening of the moderate position; important forces in the Soviet Union evidently remained skeptical about more far-reaching détente.

Volten, in his study of Brezhnev's Peace Program, argues that there was hesitation from the outset within the Soviet leadership (1982: 72–74). Support for the new policy increased at first as a result of its early successes, but in 1973 there were indications of a growing controversy within the polity. Of particular concern was Brezhnev's enthusiasm for a vast expansion of East-West economic cooperation, a line of action thought to have difficult institutional and ideological implications. By mid-1973 Brezhnev was on the defensive. The Politburo at first closed its ranks against the growing opposition, but in December 1974 the Central Committee decided to review the meaning and content of détente. The opponents succeeded in redirecting course along more conservative lines. A shift occurred from Brezhnev's personal conduct of foreign policy to collective rule, with defined limits to détente and interdependence (pp. 120–32). Brezhnev's policy package had been too complex and had antagonized too many elites. Unity was finally restored "at the expense of the active pursuit of normalization of East-West relations" (p. 233). Volten's analysis is similar to Jackson's: much opposition to radical détente from the outset and a compromise in the mid-1970s. Other analysts have confirmed that the utility of importing Western technology was one of the points at issue (Hardt and Tomlinson 1983: 170–71).

There is to my knowledge no study similar to Jackson's in which variations in the extent of controversy about West Germany are explored with regard to the entire period from the Eastern treaties to Afghanistan and Poland. It has been shown that there was disagreement over the new departure at the beginning of the 1970s (see the works cited in Jonson 1984: 12–13). Moreover, a study of the Soviet press in the period 1975–81 shows that even though the discussion took place within a narrow framework, some opposition to the policy of cooperation and contact with West Germany was voiced (pp. 144–46).

CHAPTER 8

The Administrative Stabilization of Détente

THE ADMINISTRATIVE STABILIZATION of East-West détente must have remained limited. Generally, the administrative stabilization of a foreign policy would seem apt to take a considerable time and to be contingent on previous international, political, and cognitive stabilization, as suggested previously (chapter 3). In the case of détente between Great Powers, moreover, there is special reason to expect administrative stabilization to occur at a late stage, if at all. Both parties to such a process have incentives to maintain their sensitivity to the environment as well as the availability of alternatives.

As explained previously (section 2.4), a distinction can be made between structural and substantive administrative stabilization. In the present theoretical sketch, the former is a matter of administrative fragmentation and decision structures, whereas the latter depends on the substance of the critical variables and of the response repertory. Everybody's interest in avoiding the administrative stabilization of a policy of détente has more obvious implications in the latter case than in the former.

Hence, a large number of variables are likely to remain critical, and the tolerable ranges are likely to remain small. Moreover, a stabilization bias against détente seems probable: the critical variables are more likely to include those that might indicate an increased threat than those that might indicate a reduced threat, and the tolerable ranges are likely to be smaller if it is a matter of an increase rather than a decrease in threat. Any relationship between two Great Powers seems unlikely to be stabilized by a mutual lack of attention—the Great Powers will always be each other's paramount consideration—but it will probably take even less to trigger a deterioration of the relationship than to bring about an improvement.

A superficial acquaintance with the intelligence community in Washington suffices to confirm that few variables are considered noncritical when the United States government sets out to analyze the Soviet Union. Soviet efforts to monitor the West can be assumed to be equally intense. Valenta, moreover, has provided several examples of small tolerable ranges in his study of the Soviet decision to invade Czechoslovakia (1979: 123–25). The West Germans, for their part, are situated right at the confrontation line, and "our antennas are big and are constantly operating," as a German observer has put it (author's interview).[1]

The existence of a stabilization bias to the detriment of détente is difficult to substantiate—a problem with the very concept of substantive administrative stabilization is that these matters are difficult to study empirically. However, U.S. intelligence has been officially reported to suffer from an overemphasis on "security defined narrowly in military terms" as against broader considerations (Commission on the Organization of the Government for the Conduct of Foreign Policy 1975: 4). Moreover, according to an experienced member of the intelligence community in Washington, analysts prefer to err on the conservative side with regard to the Soviet Union (author's interview); excessive optimism is apparently punished more severely than excessive pessimism. It is important to note, however, that a study of what the "Soviet estimate" has in fact been like over the years provides several examples not only of excessive pessimism but also of excessive optimism (Prados 1982); this indicates that the stabilization bias may be smaller than one is tempted to assume. It can be added that, according to Valenta's study, the decision to invade Czechoslovakia was influenced by an intelligence bias in favor of the interventionists (1979: 123–25).

Even more self-evident than large numbers of critical variables, small tolerable ranges, and a stabilization bias to the detriment of détente is the maintaining of the option of nondétente. By the early 1980s, to be sure, West German observers maintained that there was "no alternative" to the Ostpolitik. This assessment, however, may have reflected a political consensus rather than the emptiness of the response repertory.

So much for substantive stabilizers; these are virtually inaccessible to empirical observation but can be assumed to have been poorly developed in the case of East-West détente. The situation is different with regard to structural stabilizers. The need for a high sensitivity to the environment is an incentive for bureaucratic growth, and this in turn may lead to fragmentation. During a détente process, moreover, the relationship between the parties is likely to become increasingly multidimensional, and this is also apt to stimulate fragmentation.

---

[1] Interviews were made in Washington for this chapter in November 1982 and included talks with Raymond Garthoff, Leon Sloss, Helmut Sonnenfeldt, and Jim Timbie. Interviews were made in Bonn in September 1984; they included talks with Alexander Arnot, Egon Bahr, Karl Kaiser, Anton Rossbach, Eberhard Schulz, and Heinrich Vogel.

Now, even if it is in the interest of the parties to a process of détente to avoid stabilization by administrative fragmentation, the existence of what have here been called remedies—synthesizers, competition between synthesizers, and independent specialists—cannot be taken for granted. Similarly with regard to decision structures: even if it is essential for the parties to a détente process to maintain a capacity to respond to disturbances rationally and rapidly, and even if decision-making according to the leader-autonomous group model would be ideal, it cannot be assumed that this possibility will remain open.

In the present chapter, therefore, we are concerned with remedies against fragmentation and with decision structures in Washington, Bonn, and Moscow. It has been pointed out repeatedly that the empirical study of administrative stabilizers is difficult. These are suggestive theoretical concepts that do not lend themselves to easy operationalization. Serious empirical study, moreover, would presume a research effort beyond the scope of the present work, in which the administrative aspect is merely one of four. What can be reported here are the impressions gained from two kinds of sources: interviews with a number of well-informed and experienced people in Washington and Bonn,[2] and some of the literature about the making of foreign policy in the three countries. (Some of what follows is written in the present tense, since it has proven difficult to consistently separate the situation at the time of writing from the one obtaining during the 1970s.) Still, the following notes may suffice for the limited purpose of determining whether there is any indication at all of détente's being protected by "bureaucratic inertia."

8.1. THE UNITED STATES

Fragmentation   The U.S. intelligence community has been wrestling with the problem of fragmentation at least since the adoption of the National Security Act of 1947 (recent studies include Freedman 1977, Flanagan 1984, and Bowie 1984). A variety of agencies have been set up to serve the intelligence needs of separate government departments. This has created a need for a coordinating device. To find the optimum balance between fragmentation and coordination has been a continuing concern.

The complexity of the apparatus for monitoring the Soviet Union is impressive. Thousands of analysts comprise the Central Intelligence Agency (CIA), which is but one of several agencies. Foremost among

[2] See note 1, above.

the other intelligence organizations are the Defense Intelligence Agency (DIA) and the National Security Agency (NSA) in the area of the Department of Defense, and the Bureau of Intelligence and Research (INR) in the Department of State. However, the intelligence community also includes the Departments of Agriculture, Commerce, and Energy, the Treasury, the Bureau of the Census, the National Aeronautics and Space Administration (NASA), and others.

Fragmentation, moreover, need not be merely institutional. There is, I have been told, more crossagency contact between specialists on the Soviet navy than among them and specialists on other aspects of the Soviet Union. Such "functional" fragmentation, according to one participant in the process, became especially prevalent in the 1970s and made it increasingly difficult to form an overview of Soviet-U.S. relations.

It can be argued, however, that what are here called remedies against fragmentation have long been prominent features of United States foreign policymaking, particularly with regard to the Soviet Union.

There exists, to begin with, an institutionalized system for integrating the efforts of the intelligence community: a system for the production of so-called National Intelligence Estimates (NIES). The NIES are meant to provide the intelligence community's coordinated assessment of the situation in a particular country or with regard to a particular issue. Some NIES are issued annually, whereas others are updated as the need may arise. Differences of opinion among the participants in the NIE process are expressed in parallel texts or footnotes. There are two more forms for producing coordinated intelligence: the Special National Intelligence Estimates (SNIES) and the Interagency Intelligence Memoranda (IIMs), both of which apparently deal with more specific problems than the NIES (see Prados 1982 for a study of NIES).

The NIE process may be seen as bargaining between competing syntheses. A condition for this competition is the lack of a clear functional differentiation between what are known as the principal producers of finished intelligence: CIA, DIA, and INR. The three agencies are in large measure supposed to do the same thing, although from different perspectives. When considering U.S.-Soviet matters, they tend to analyze the same data but to arrive at different conclusions because of their different underlying views of the USSR: the INR is traditionally regarded as the least and the DIA as the most alarmist agency, with the CIA in the middle. This combination of similarity in mission and difference in inclination is a prototype of competitive synthesizing.

The NIE process is not the only arena where the chief agencies compete, however. There is a continuous flow of information from the various parts of the intelligence community ranging from news items to lengthy analyses of matters like the Soviet harvest or the Soviet leadership problem. The intelligence officer of a senior government official makes a selection from this variety of sources for his daily briefing; a senior official, I have been told, typically devotes fifteen minutes per day to routine briefing about the Soviet Union.

What needs to be emphasized is the combination of synthesis and competition. The production of intelligence in such a vast apparatus as the one in Washington is inevitably fragmented and hence apt to be cumbersome and standardized; this is likely to be true especially with regard to the Soviet Union, the dominating concern of the intelligence community. Because of the way in which the system is set up, however, there is a continuing competition between integrated views.

Outside experts, moreover, play an important role. The intelligence agencies have boards of external advisers, and the CIA has established several mechanisms for outside review of the NIEs and other products. Also important is the traffic back and forth between the agencies, the research institutes, and the universities.

The history of détente includes a famous example of the use of independent specialists to challenge established views: the B-Team episode. What became known as the B-Team was set up in 1976 by the president's Foreign Intelligence Advisory Board to compete with the regular NIE process. It was asked to write its own "estimate" on the basis of the information available to the regular intelligence community. The B-Team consisted of conservative critics of what they regarded as an arms control bias on the part of the CIA (Prados 1982: 250–57, Flanagan 1984). It is difficult to conceive of a more effective countermeasure to a threatening administrative stabilization of a policy of détente.

The sum of all this is an intelligence apparatus rather similar to the least stabilizing ideal type: competitive synthesizing plus the use of independent specialists. And yet concern has been repeatedly voiced over the risk of bureaucratization. A government study published in 1975 argued that "special efforts are constantly required to see to it that significant differences of views are spelled out rather than glossed over, and to make sure that unorthodox views and individual insights are encouraged rather than stifled by the system" (Commission on the Organization of the Government for the Conduct of Foreign Policy 1975: 29). The Carter administration actively strived to ensure that competing views would be available at the highest level (Hunter 1982). William Casey, director of central intelligence in the Reagan administration, reportedly felt that intelligence specialists tended to take a too narrow view of the world and to lose sight of the big picture. He initiated a procedure by which differences would be highlighted rather than papered over. He also wanted to improve the CIA's contacts with the academic community in order to "counter the bureaucratic tendency toward insularity and being satisfied with the conventional wisdom" (Taubman 1983).

That these worries were voiced may suggest that the policy of détente had in fact been protected to some extent by "bureaucratic inertia." However, the worries may also be taken to reflect a concern with this problem that contributed to preventing significant inertia from developing. The U.S. intelligence system seems in fact to be designed to prevent the United States from becoming tied to any particular policy toward the Soviet Union.

Decision Structure It would be useful to make a study of U.S. decisionmaking about détente-related matters, especially in the latter half of the 1970s, when the retreat from détente took place. The objective would be to examine whether the retreat was inhibited by the necessity of delegate decisionmaking or whether it was facilitated by the fact that decisions could be made according to the leader-autonomous group model.

In the absence of systematic study, we may first note that in the 1970s, the fragmenting potential of the U.S. system of government was given full sway in the foreign policy area with the demise of the "imperial presidency" and the general "democratization" of political institutions. The tradition of "deference to the president on the big things" no longer held (Destler 1984; Nye 1984: 334–40). This caused policymaking on détente-related matters to be more complex than previously. At least the decision structure associated with arms and arms control policy may have tended toward the delegate model. That decisionmaking about East-West matters was becoming increasingly complex is also suggested by one of Jimmy Carter's first actions as president: to set up a special coordination committee headed by his national security adviser (Hunter 1982: 17–24, 106–7). One reason apparently was a feeling that détente risked getting out of the president's control.

However, presidential control proved to be substantial when put to the test in 1980. The Soviet invasion of Afghanistan made it impossible to continue to do "business as usual," in Carter's words. This is precisely the kind of change that the stabilization of détente would be expected to render difficult: vested interests would offer resistance, bargaining would be required, and the result would take time and would be a compromise. In fact, ending business as usual was easy. It appears that Carter ordered a list of all ongoing activities from the

Department of State and then simply decided on cutbacks (cf. Roney 1982: 128).

There is in general little indication that the complexity of the decision structure inhibited the retreat from détente. The effect was rather to make it difficult for the United States to pursue a coherent foreign policy of any kind (Nye 1984). Moreover, the stabilizing effect, if any, may have been limited to noncrisis situations. The complexity of the decision structure possibly helped to protect the détente policy against disturbances in the form of gradual changes in conditions or incremental negative feedback—disturbances such as Soviet rearmament and activities in Africa. However, if a stabilizer is effective only in noncrisis conditions, its ability to protect a policy of détente is limited.

FURTHER RESEARCH, however useful, seems unlikely seriously to challenge the conclusion that the U.S. policy of détente was undermined rather than stabilized by administrative features. It is important to question whether these features are rooted in the U.S. political system and hence form a built-in impediment to stable détente between East and West. A tentative answer is suggested in chapter 9.

8.2. WEST GERMANY

Our object in this section is to compare the administration of West Germany's Ostpolitik with that of U.S. détente policy. Was there a difference that may help explain why the former fared better than the latter?

Fragmentation   One difference between West Germany and the United States lies in the sheer size of their respective foreign policy bureaucracies. The potential for fragmentation is smaller in Bonn than in Washington.

The West German foreign policy apparatus is also complex, however. By the mid-1970s, the growing complexity of security policy had led to an increase in specialization within the two traditional agencies—the Auswärtiges Amt and the Ministry of Defense—and had at the same time increased the security policy relevance of other agencies (Haftendorn 1977: 339). The institutional structure of security policy also included the Bundeskanzlersamt as well as the Bundestag with its several committees and parties (p. 343, diagram 1). What is more, the making of West German security policy was in large measure internationalized and took place multilaterally in NATO and the European

Community as well as bilaterally with each of the main allies (pp. 347–50).

According to Haftendorn, there was reason to question the ability of this system to produce a synthesis. No agency existed to pull the strings together. Neither the Bundessicherheitsrat nor the Bundeskanzleramt was concerned with integrated planning. There was a tendency for decisions on security policy to be made at lower levels and for options not to be forwarded to the top (pp. 339, 342).

One dimension of the Ostpolitik seems to be kept apart from the rest, moreover: East-West trade. This aspect of West Germany's relations with the East is managed by the Ministry of Economics rather than by the Auswärtiges Amt—a reflection of a deliberate, consensual policy to the effect that even in East-West relations, business is business and not politics.

Competition in intelligence seems to be less intense in Bonn than in Washington. The position of the Auswärtiges Amt is unrivaled. The Ministry of Defense has tried to attain a position similar to the Pentagon's, but the effort has failed (p. 342). The Bundeskanzlersamt, moreover, is staffed mainly by people from the ministries and not by political appointees; therefore, its foreign policy sections do not tend to represent a way of thinking basically different from the one that prevails in the Auswärtiges Amt.

As regards the use of independent specialists, several government-funded institutes specialize in Soviet and Eastern European research. An organization has been set up to "ensure the relevance of the research" at these institutes and to keep the ministries up to date with findings and projects. About eighty scholars were active in 1982 at these institutes or at specialist departments of general academic institutes (Buchholz 1982: 80–81). Several seminars, moreover, are organized every year at which scholars meet high-level bureaucrats and politicians. The foreign minister may himself devote a whole day to such an event.

It nevertheless appears to be a common view in Bonn that the impact of the academics is small.[3] According to Haftendorn, well-informed journalists are more important (1977: 346–47). In the early days of the Ostpolitik, one of its veterans has told me, the politicians found the best academic experts to be less knowledgeable than the Soviet specialists of the Auswärtiges Amt; he felt that the impact of the academics had decreased even further since then.

Furthermore, whereas American academics tend to disagree about

[3] This was explained to me at length during several of the interviews.

the Soviet Union and to form opposing schools of thought (Hallenberg 1983), this may be less true with regard to their West German counterparts. There is among the latter a consensus over a complex view of the USSR, I have been told, rather than a "confrontation between simplistic views," as in the United States.

This does not mean that contending views are never heard. The internationalized character of West German policymaking appears to be important from this point of view; West German academics, as one of them put it in a conversation, form a national monopoly that is, however, exposed to international competition. Nevertheless, whereas the pluralism obtaining in Washington would seem to undermine any policy toward the Soviet Union, it cannot be excluded that the less competitive situation in Bonn has contributed somewhat to stabilize the Ostpolitik.

Decision Structure If, by the mid-1980s, knowledgeable people in Bonn were asked how a decision about a modification of the Ostpolitik might be made, their first response was to point out that the question was irrelevant, since nobody wanted a change and since "there is no alternative." If the questioner insisted, they were prone to argue that the process of decisionmaking could not be predicted. No particular decision structure, in other words, was thought to be associated with the Ostpolitik; everything would depend on the political situation obtaining at the time. The decision might, for example, be made by the Bundeskanzler in a way similar to Carter's after the Soviet invasion of Afghanistan.

Still, two factors might complicate West German decisionmaking in such a situation.

First, there is West Germany's greater stake in East-West economic relations. A decision to shift foreign policy away from détente might be difficult to make without the support of banks, business, labor, and perhaps other organized interests. It seems a reasonable presumption that if Helmut Schmidt had followed Jimmy Carter's example and ordered the Bundeskanzlersamt or the Auswärtiges Amt to produce a list of on-going East-West acitivities from which countermeasures against the invasion of Afghanistan might be chosen, his freedom of action would have been more circumscribed than Carter's with regard to at least some of the items.

The other complication is that decisions might have to be made multilaterally or in consultation with the main allies. West Germany's freedom to act alone is smaller than that of the United States. The internationalized character of its foreign and security policy may provide the Ostpolitik with some protection in the form of an elaborate decision structure.

TO SUMMARIZE, there are hints of a difference between the United States and West Germany with regard to the administrative stabilization of détente. In Bonn the remedies against the stabilizing effects of fragmentation may have been somewhat less far-reaching; the likely decision structure may have been somewhat closer to the stabilizing type; and there may in addition be reason to suspect that the monitoring of the Soviet Union has been somewhat less biased against détente (namely, the leading role of the Auswärtiges Amt).

8.3. THE SOVIET UNION

The Soviet Union has been described as a "bureaucracy writ large" (Meyer, quoted from Hough 1980b: 7). Western scholars have drawn varying conclusions from this observation. On the one hand, "a bureaucratized society is particularly susceptible to being directed, organized or mobilized." From this point of view, bureaucratization has provided the Soviet leaders with an instrument that can be used to implement whatever they decide to do. On the other hand, "if we are going to try to understand the Soviet Union in terms of a bureaucratic model, we need to move well beyond any conception that depicts bureaucracy solely as a passive instrument." This is so because there is a conflict in bureaucratic responsibilities between "acceptance of superior orders and adherence to professional standards or long-standing rules" (Hough 1977: 56–58). The latter is necessary in order for the bureaucracy to be an effective instrument of the rulers but may at the same time pave the way for a bureaucratic influence on their decisions.

Bureaucracy-as-instrument would seem to imply less "bureaucratic inertia" than bureaucracy-as-policymaker. The following notes about remedies against fragmentation and about decision structures in Soviet policy toward the West may be seen against the background of the larger issue of the implications of the bureaucratization of Soviet society.

Fragmentation The Soviet intelligence community appears to be about as fragmented as the one in Washington. In addition to the Ministry for Foreign Affairs with its various sections there are in particular the foreign section of the Committee of State Security (KGB) the Chief Intelligence Directorate of the General Staff, and several Central Committee departments (Valenta 1979: 123–24, Cutler 1984, Brown

1985, Mackintosh 1985). The academic institutes may also be regarded as part of the intelligence community, as well as the media (Cutler 1984).

It does not seem fruitful to speculate about the extent of synthesizing in this system. Western scholars have been more concerned with its degree of pluralism. As pointed out previously (sections 2.3 and 7.3.3) it is common to suggest that there are competing schools of thought, or "opinion groups," or "tendencies" with regard to the West. It is controversial, however, whether the differences in views coincide with institutional differences or cut across them. In Sovietologist discourse, the issue is whether governmental agencies act as "interest groups," or whether the only "interest groups" in the USSR are those that can be identified on the basis of common attitudes (Skilling 1983).

This is related to the question paramount in the present context— namely, whether competition between synthesizers exists. Presumably, such competition is more likely, or more likely to be intense, if con- tending views are represented by contending agencies. The interest group controversy suggests that it may be precipitate to presume dif- ferences in outlook between, say, the Soviet Ministry for Foreign Affairs, the KGB, and the general staff running parallel to those between the INR, the CIA, and the DIA in Washington. There is at any rate reason to suspect that their competition takes place within a narrow framework. To quote a classic text on the Soviet Union, the "tendency to embrace data that confirm established predilections while rejecting the unpalatable facts that offend one's preconceptions is a weakness . . . [to] which . . . totalitarian societies appear to be par- ticularly susceptible. . . . Every dictatorship has a tendency to breed sycophancy and discourage independence in its bureaucratic hier- archy" (Fainsod, quoted in Aspaturian 1971: 609). According to a more recent study, "at all levels, within the institutions of the Soviet state, cautious conformity is likely to produce moderate reward with minimal risk, while dissent will sharply increase the risk, with little likelihood of compensating reward"; the institutions are concerned "either with the implementation of centrally determined policy, or, in the case of those that are responsible for policy formation, with the pursuit of Soviet interests by the application of doctrinal precedent and accepted practice." Hence the rigidity of Soviet policy (Keeble 1985: 230–31).

Much attention has been devoted in Western literature to the role of the Soviet academic institutes (see, for example, Hough and Fainsod 1979: 396–99). This is the Soviet version of what are called inde- pendent specialists in the theoretical sketch. However, several of the institutes are subordinated to their ministries and state committees, and they are meant to provide in-house research. Even some of the scientific academies are closely associated with specific ministries. The institutes of the USSR Academy of Science have a more independent position, and their role in foreign policy seemed to increase in the 1970s; they include the Institute of World Economy and International Relations (IMEMO) as well as the Institute of the U.S.A. and Canada. Disagreements are aired in journals and at roundtables held at the institutes in which Foreign Ministry officials, Central Committee cadres, and leading journalists may participate, and the scientific councils of the institutes also include such people (Cutler 1984).

To specify the independence of these independent specialists is difficult. Needless to say, there is less academic freedom in the Soviet Union than in the West; "the operational conception of Soviet foreign policy research . . . will remain, for a long time to come, very different from the Western conception of academic endeavor" (Eran 1979: 276). In fact, the heads of the foreign policy institutes have usually been recruited from the Central Committee apparatus or the Ministry of Foreign Trade (Hough and Fainsod 1979: 399). Their staffs do operate outside the party and government bureaucracies, however, and it may be simplistic to regard them as mere appendixes of the latter.

Western scholars sometimes ascribe the role of interest groups to the Soviet institutes. IMEMO, for example, is reported to have supported trade with the West in opposition to other institutes (p. 399), and the Institute of the U.S.A. is suggested to have been a virtual lobby for détente in the 1970s (Schwartz 1978): 162. The examples suggest a difference in the role of U.S. and Soviet academics with regard to détente. In the United States, independent specialists helped to undermine détente, just as their participation in policymaking tends to undermine any policy. In the Soviet Union, their role, if any, was rather to increase the stability of the détente policy.

Decision Structure   A variety of "models" of Soviet policymaking have been put forward in the Western literature (Meyer 1984). It has been suggested that the validity of each "model" has varied over time. The latter half of the Brezhnev period, of particular interest here, was "cartelistic," to use Roeder's term. Decisionmaking in the Politburo had the appearance of consensus-seeking within an oligarchy, but there was at the same time a tendency for individual members to keep control of their own policy area and to defer to their colleagues in other matters (Roeder 1984: 177–78). Hough similarly argues that the Brezhnev era was marked by an increase in the deference to the views of specialized elites and hence by the playing of a more decisive role by individual members of the Politburo in their own areas of special responsibility (Hough and Fainsod 1979: 477).

This decision structure is different from the leader-autonomous group type, which is here assumed to be the least stabilizing one. It was not a matter of Brezhnev's deciding after having heard the views of independent advisers. Whether the Politburo functioned in a way reminiscent of the stabilizing delegate group type is less clear.

In his study of the Soviet decision to invade Czechoslovakia in 1968, Valenta argues that the invasion was preceded by a long process of coalition building. He maintains that the building of a majority in the Soviet political system requires not just compromise but "engagements in various kinds of maneuvers: trading, internal bargaining, and persuading wavering or uncommitted leaders. It also calls for appealing to various pressure groups . . . and to a broader forum of supporters" (1979: 17). This suggests that policymaking about fundamental East-West matters may approach the type here called delegate decision-making. Two comments are due, however, in addition to the obvious one that one should not generalize from a single case. First, in the early Brezhnev period, decisionmaking was "oligarchic" rather than "cartelistic" (Roeder 1984: 176–77); the Czechoslovak decision was made in a period when consensus building was generally more complex than it became during the chief years of détente. Second, it may not be clear to what extent the central decisionmakers functioned as delegates of external groups. Perhaps the Czechoslovak case demonstrated the difficulty of reaching a decision on an important and ambiguous issue rather than the necessity to make policy by means of bargaining among interests.[4]

THE "BUREAUCRATIC INERTIA" in Soviet defense policy has been emphasized by Alexander (1984), among others; it would not be easy, he argues, to bring about "major change in the political-military sphere." It cannot be determined to what extent this was true with regard to the policy of détente. The Soviet system of government may be more susceptible to "bureaucratic inertia" in foreign policy than those of the United States and West Germany. However, it may be precipitate to exclude the possibility that there is a degree of competitive synthesizing, although presumably within a narrow framework; the persistent finding of Sovietologists that there are contending opin-

[4] See Mackintosh 1985 for a discussion of the role of the military and of the KGB in Soviet decisionmaking.

ions points in this direction. There is also some use of what may be regarded as independent specialists, even though their independence is more limited than in the West. Similarly, even though the striving for consensus during the Brezhnev period might have rendered decisions difficult to make, signs of a less cumbersome decision structure emerged by the 1970s, and it is not clear that decisionmaking was ever close to the most stabilizing delegate type. This amounts to no more than a couple of questionmarks to the view that when the bureaucratic Soviet society has begun to pursue a particular foreign policy, such as détente, this line of action is not easily changed.

THIS IS THE END of the experiment with applying the theoretical sketch to empirical data. It has been shown, I believe, that international, political, and cognitive stabilizers can in fact be examined empirically in meaningful ways. The distance between theoretical concept and operationalization seems mostly to be manageable. Improvements can be made, but the chief limitation of the study remains its small scope. It would have been desirable to be able to examine a larger material in a more systematic fashion. Still, even a limited empirical study seems capable of providing meaningful results.

However, this is less true with regard to the administrative stabilizers. The present chapter has been more impressionistic and journalistic than the preceding three. The experiment on this point suggests that it may not be possible to draw meaningful conclusions about the extent of administrative stabilization on the basis of a relatively small research effort. Moreover, it is not entirely clear what a large effort would be like. This part of the theoretical sketch needs to be reconsidered in a more fundamental manner than the rest.

CHAPTER 9

Evaluation of the Détente Experiment

9.1. How Stabilized Did Détente Become?

AN EVALUATION of the experiment with détente of the kind called skeptical in chapter 4 assumes, among other things, that the détente construction put to the test in the 1970s was maximally advanced. On this assumption, the 1970s proved that the best that can be obtained is not good enough and that stable détente is impossible.

We set out in previous chapters to examine what the détente construction was like. The theoretical sketch of foreign policy stability introduced in Part One was used as a guide. The results are summarized in Table 9.1.

In the table, it is first suggested what a highly stabilized process of détente would be like:

- There would be binding treaties prescribing détente in a precise and noncontradictory fashion.

- Both parties would have become highly dependent on continued détente.

- Détente among them would be supported by strong common enmities and friendships.

- Détente would be based on consistent ideas on both sides.

- Détente would occupy a central position in the belief systems of the parties.

- Détente-related beliefs would be of the inherent good faith type or otherwise untestable.

- The détente policy would be highly institutionalized on both sides.

- There would be strong support for détente, and no opposition against it.

- The issue of détente would be highly salient in domestic politics on both sides.

- The administration of détente would be fragmented without remedies.

Table 9.1. The stabilization of détente in the 1970s: summary of findings

Stabilizer	Highly stabilized détente policy	United States détente policy	West German détente policy	Soviet détente policy
Normative regulation	Noncontradictory, unambiguous, binding treaty.	Extensive regulation by the mid-1970s, but mainly in legally nonbinding forms and with internal contradictions and problems of application.		
Dependence	Strong dependence on continued détente.	Very limited.	Some by the mid-1970s.	Very limited in relation to the U.S., some in relation to West Germany by the mid-1970s.
Third parties	Strong common enmities and friendships.	Western European-Soviet détente.	U.S.-Soviet détente, until the mid-1970s.	Possibly China in the early 1970s but decreasingly a common enemy and decreasingly important militarily.
Consistency	Perfect consistency.	"Dual track" problem, ideological problem after the mid-1970s.	Mild "dual track" problem, no serious ideological problem.	Neither a "dual track" nor an ideological problem in the official doctrine.
Centrality	Highly central.	Not central.	Quite central.	Quite central.
Testability	Untestable.	Partly testable.	Partly testable.	Partly testable.

Institutionalization	Highly institutionalized.	Relatively weak and decreasing commitment.	Relatively strong and increasing commitment.	Relatively weak and selective commitment but stronger toward West Germany than toward the U.S.
Support	Consensus.	Considerable opposition after the mid-1970s.	Considerable opposition throughout the 1970s, but substantive differences unclear.	Considerable controversy in the early 1970s, consensus over a compromise by the mid-1970s, at least with regard to the U.S.
Salience	High.	Relatively high.	Relatively high.	Relatively high.
Fragmentation	High, no remedies.	High, strong remedies.	Moderately high, moderate remedies.	High, remedies cannot be assessed.
Critical variables	Few and with large tolerable ranges.	Have not been studied but may be assumed to be several with small tolerable ranges, and with a bias to the detriment of détente (except perhaps in West Germany).		
Response repertory	No alternatives.	Have not been studied but may be assumed to have included alternatives to détente (perhaps decreasingly in West Germany).		
Decision structure	Delegate decisionmaking.	Leader-autonomous group decisionmaking in crisis, delegate decisionmaking in non-crisis on some matters.	Leader-autonomous group decisionmaking perhaps less likely than in the U.S., and decreasingly likely.	Difficult to assess. Both leader-autonomous group and delegate decisionmaking appear unlikely.

- The critical variables would be few, and the tolerable ranges would be large.

- There would be no alternative in the response repertory of either party.

- On both sides, decisions about whether and how to modify the détente policy would have to be made by a decisionmaking process of the delegate type.

What needs to be considered, first of all, is whether Soviet-West German relations approached this ideal type more closely than did Soviet-U.S. relations. If they did not, the utility of the theoretical sketch is put in doubt. If they did, the specific differences between the two relationships may suggest the critical variables for stabilizing a process of détente.

Three observations can be made:

1. The stabilizers of U.S. détente policy were on the whole less well developed than those of West Germany's Ostpolitik.

We have shown, first of all, to what a limited extent U.S. détente policy became stabilized in the 1970s (see Table 9.1). This was essentially a nonstabilized policy—cognitively, politically, administratively. The "dual track" problem in the American view of the Soviet Union, the cognitively noncentral position of the policy of détente, the testability of détente-related beliefs, the weak points in the Nixon administration's commitment to détente, the rapid growth of domestic opposition, and the destabilizing features of the administrative apparatus— all contributed to rendering détente vulnerable. Moreover, the United States did not become significantly dependent on pursuing this policy; the only indication to the contrary was the difficulty of stopping the grain sales. Only two stabilizers on the checklist appeared to be well developed: the rather considerable normative regulation, and the fact that the allies in Europe continued to pursue détente.[1] This did not suffice when the strains and stresses multiplied.

It was different with the Ostpolitik. The "dual track" problem was less marked; the centrality of the Ostpolitik in West German thinking was obvious; its institutionalization was less qualified and continued to increase throughout the 1970s; even though polemics went on

---

[1] Salience was also relatively high but is here thought to have a stabilizing impact only indirectly—by reinforcing the effect of the other political stabilizers, both of which were rather poorly developed with regard to U.S. détente policy (see section 2.3 about the role of salience as a foreign policy stabilizer).

throughout the decade, the substantive differences between government and opposition were unclear; the administration of the Ostpolitik may have been somewhat stabilizing; and economic dependence on the Ostpolitik seemed to have become large enough by the mid-1970s to have an impact. American détente policy had more protection than the Ostpolitik only in one respect, and that was in terms of third parties: from Bonn's point of view, the retreat from détente on the part of the United States substituted a disturbance for the stabilizing impact of a détente-minded ally.

To this can be added that the Westpolitik of the Soviet Union seemed more stabilized vis-à-vis West Germany than toward the United States. Such a difference was obvious with regard to economic dependence. The commitment to détente, moreover, seemed to be less qualified in the former case than in the latter.

The parallel between the existence of stabilizers and what happened to détente suggests that the theoretical sketch does help to explain why détente failed in the U.S.-Soviet case but partly succeeded in the West German-Soviet case.

2. Except with regard to dependence and centrality, the differences in détente stabilization between the United States and West Germany were small, subtle, or ambiguous.

Few of the differences in stabilization between U.S. and West German détente policy were large, obvious, and well confirmed. As regards cognitive consistency, there was American reasoning about the necessity to combine détente with deterrence and with resistance against aggression vis-à-vis West German phraseology about the need for equilibrium; this is a subtle distinction. The suggestion that there was a difference in stabilization by domestic politics rests mainly on some peculiarities of Nixon's way of selling détente to the American people and possibly on some differences between the way in which the Ronald Reagans and the Franz Josef Strausses campaigned against détente; it remains a mere hypothesis that rhetoric à la Nixon is rather strongly destabilizing, whereas opposition à la CDU/CSU is only mildly destabilizing. The suggestions about administrative differences, moreover, are speculative. The only unquestionable differences in stabilization were those with regard to economic dependence and cognitive centrality. In the latter half of the 1970s, moreover, the difference in political stabilization became increasingly evident, but then the retreat from U.S.-Soviet détente had begun.

Hence, even though most of the indications were in the right direction, only a few were strong and clear. This may suggest that dependence and centrality were more important than other factors in bringing about the difference in outcome between the Soviet-West German and the Soviet-U.S. cases. Whether this is true of foreign policy stabilization in general cannot be determined on the basis of this instance.

3. The degree of stabilization was low even with regard to Soviet-West German détente.

A comparison between the ideal type of highly stabilized détente and the reality of Soviet-West German relations suggests that even this dyad had a relatively weak détente construction. Even though extensive, the normative regulation of détente had weaknesses. Even though important, Soviet-West German economic relations did not become vital for either party. There was little third party stabilization. The underlying beliefs were not protected by untestability. The institutionalization of the policy of détente in Moscow was selective, and the very mechanism of domestic institutionalization may be insignificant in a nondemocratic society. There were polemics over détente in Bonn and opposition to far-reaching détente in Moscow. The degree of "bureaucratic inertia" may be presumed to have been modest. It is perhaps remarkable that a measure of détente survived the disturbances to which it was exposed.

This third observation supports the view of the détente optimist. That which is significant appears to be within reach. The Soviet-West German experience suggests stable détente to be practicable and not utopian. This, however, raises two questions. First, how far can a process of détente stabilization go? Is it possible for a détente construction to become significantly stronger than the one between the Soviet Union and West Germany? Second, how far can the Soviet-West German experience be generalized? Can a similar development occur between the Soviet Union and the United States, or is there a structural difference between the superpower relationship and other international relations?

The optimist's argument goes like this. In the Soviet-West German relationship there was more economic interdependence, and détente was cognitively more central and became more firmly embedded in domestic politics. This suggests the outline of a general strategy for détente: economic transactions will render the policy of détente increasingly central on both sides and will at the same time strengthen the prodétente forces in the domestic politics of both, which will pave the way for a further intensification of economic relations, and so on.

The thought can be elaborated in the following way. An interde-

pendence-beliefs-politics feedback circle is contingent on tangible benefits. This idea is commonplace; it was, for example, at the core of
Henry Kissinger's détente philosophy (Gaddis 1982: 291–94). Tangible benefits change political beliefs and increase political support. If
you want your adversary to continue to pursue a given policy even in
the face of disturbances, it is in your own interest to pursue a policy of
giving tangible benefits to him. One reason for the failure of Soviet-
U.S. détente—this is the optimist's interpretation—was that the parties
failed to see to it that important interests gained sufficiently from, or
did not lose too much from, détente—and not just important interests
at home. The Soviet-West German experience, in the optimist's view,
demonstrates the feasibility of the strategy of stabilizing the foreign
policies of others by influencing their thinking and intervening in their
domestic politics with tangible benefits.

There are two principal ways in which the skeptic might challenge
this analysis.

First, the nature of the rivalry between the United States and the
Soviet Union—the two superpowers of a bipolar international system
and the main representatives of two competing ideologies—is qualita-
tively different from other international relations. The American and
Soviet empires, moreover, are less dependent on their environment
than other nations; they are inevitably tied together by their nuclear
rivalry, but otherwise the potential for their becoming significantly
dependent on one another is comparatively small.

Second, some features of the Soviet and U.S. political systems make
stable détente especially unlikely between the two. As argued previously, the absence of democratic control is likely to render institutionalization ineffective: commitments are inexpensive to violate in a political system like that of the USSR. Therefore, it likely takes more to
institutionalize a policy in the USSR than in the West. If given sufficient
time, a foreign policy may become an institution even in Moscow, but
a Soviet foreign policy is apt to be more vulnerable to early disturbances and, therefore, less likely ever to be stabilized than a Western
foreign policy.

A feature of politics in the United States, on the other hand, is
chronic instability. Not only have radical shifts in government been
common in Washington at least since 1961—there were four presidents in the decade after SALT I—but even within single administrations coalitions have tended to be unstable and the turnover among
top people to be considerable. In the turbulence of Washington in the
1970s, conditions did not favor détente's—or any foreign policy's—

acquiring a firm political basis. There was remarkable governmental stability in both Bonn and Moscow during this period.

The difference was not accidental; it was not a matter merely of Watergate. Openness, complexity, and lack of a firm structure combine to render governmental stability less likely in the United States than in other major countries. In U.S. politics the processes of institutionalization and consensus building keep being disturbed to an uncommon extent, it appears.

The stabilization of Soviet-American détente, therefore, may be inhibited by the fact that a foreign policy is difficult to stabilize in a society as pluralistic as the United States and is time-consuming to stabilize in an authoritarian society like the Sovet Union. It may be easier for foreign policies to become protected by their embedment in domestic politics when it is a matter of a parliamentary system of the Western European type, and this may in turn increase the time available for the stabilization of the policy pursued by an authoritarian adversary. The skeptic may argue that this obstacle to Soviet-American détente was demonstrated in the 1970s.

Our examination of the East-West détente construction cannot decide between the two interpretations of the 1970s, but it may have clarified the issue. A key question is whether special impediments exist to the operation of an interdependence-beliefs-politics feedback circle in the relationship between the superpowers. Even if there are no special impediments, however, the general question remains of how far a process of détente stabilization can go between any two adversaries in an international system like the present. This is further considered in Part Three, in which détente is seen as a critical problem of anarchic systems and not merely of current East-West relations.

9.2. Implications for the Theoretical Sketch

So far the theoretical sketch introduced in chapter 2 has been used as a tool for studying détente. There is reason now to turn the tables around and consider what the empirical results imply for the theoretical sketch.

The basic finding remains that almost all differences in stabilization between the Soviet-U.S. and Soviet-West German relationships were found to run parallel to the difference in the survivability of détente. The confirmation offered by this single test is not strong (see Appendix), but the result does support the hypothesis that the variety of phenomena included in the sketch help to stabilize foreign policies.

This overall conclusion needs to be qualified in three respects, however.

First, the overall fit between theory and data has two clear exceptions. The normative regulation of U.S.-Soviet détente was found to be about as extensive as in the West German-Soviet case. Third party stabilization, moreover, was found to obtain in the U.S. case but not in the West German case. In a way, neither the most "idealist" nor the most "realist" part of the theoretical sketch was compatible with the evidence.

It obviously cannot be concluded on this basis that norms and third parties are unimportant for foreign policy stabilization. It does seem, however, that neither phenomenon is treated satisfactorily in the theoretical sketch as it now stands. The analysis of international norms as foreign policy stabilizers needs to be made more subtle. Similarly, it needs to be reconsidered whether the stabilizing impact of third parties can be accounted for in terms of structural balance theory, which is the device used here (section 2.1). Other reasons for a reconsideration of the concept of third party stabilization have also been discovered (section 5.3).

Second, the notion of administrative stabilization, which also has a basis in what must be considered established theory, has proven difficult to apply empirically. The difficulties suggest a need for a rather fundamental reconsideration of this aspect of the theoretical sketch.

Third, when applying the theoretical sketch to United States, West German, and Soviet foreign policy, frequent references have been made to features of their respective political systems as conditioning the political and administrative stabilization of their foreign policies. This appears to be such an important background variable that it should be systematically incorporated in the theoretical sketch rather than treated ad hoc, as in the present study.

Hence, the empirical application has confirmed the basic soundness of the theoretical sketch but has also suggested a relatively demanding agenda for its improvement. Further empirical study is probably the best method for coming to grips with these theoretical demands.

PART THREE

The Stabilization of Détente: A Scenario

Détente in Anarchy

ANARCHY is a basic feature of the international system, according to traditional international politics theory. This system lacks a central authority with a monopoly on the use of force, and therefore, in this common view, international politics is characterized by war and conflict rather than by peaceful cooperation. The lack of a machinery for enforcing collective decisions renders conflict resolution difficult, especially since conflicts are apt to touch on the power of the parties and ultimately on their supremely important interest in security and survival. Moreover, since anarchy necessitates military preparedness, it is difficult for states to avoid threatening one another even if they want to, and war remains an ever-present possibility. This is why the problem of how to bring about peaceful coexistence without conflict resolution—amity between enemies, "détente"—is acute in anarchy. At the same time, the very anarchy that creates the need for détente renders this condition difficult to achieve.

The so-called Anarchy Model of international politics is here accepted as a plausible account of a lasting, even though not necessarily eternal, condition for international politics. A policy of détente can be seen as an attempt to cope with this condition—an attempt with a significant probability of failure.

To decrease tensions is not the only difficulty. There is the additional problem of keeping them at low levels—of preventing processes of détente from being reversed. Anarchy inhibits the stabilization of processes of détente, and not just their onset. Because of anarchy, moreover, processes of détente are exposed to frequent disturbances. Hence, there may be insufficient time for détente relations to become stable enough to survive.

In this chapter I propose to consider in more detail the conditions for stable détente. Such coexistence may, in the very long run and under uncommonly favorable circumstances, develop into a security community—a relationship, that is, in which war is unthinkable (Deutsch et al. 1957: 5–6). A consideration of the factors rendering this outcome implausible may improve our understanding of how international anarchy works. It may also to some small extent improve our ability to cope with anarchy.

This must not be taken to imply an assumption to the effect that stable détente should be sought under all circumstances. First, many parties to many conflicts consider it more important to stand up against the enemy than to reduce the probability of war, and it is not for me or anybody else to say that this is always the wrong priority. Moreover, even if a *condition* of stable détente is thought to be desirable it does not follow that a *policy* of détente ought to be pursued. What could be gained from such a policy if it were successful must be weighted against what might be lost if it were tried without success; the credibility of a policy of deterrence may be undermined by the pursuit of a policy of détente, and in some circumstances stable deterrence cannot be dispensed with. What is assumed here is merely that it may be desirable in some circumstances to achieve a stable détente and that it is therefore useful to examine the feasibility of a policy designed to bring it about.

The problem of the feasibility of stable détente in anarchy is similar to the one considered by Robert Axelrod in his path-breaking work, *The Evolution of Cooperation* (1984). Axelrod begins with the question: "Under what conditions will cooperation emerge in a world of egoists without central authority?" He then presents a theory of cooperation in Prisoners' Dilemma situations. The evolution of cooperation, according to this theory, benefits from the adoption of strategies that are "nice" (that is, cooperate on the first move, and defect only if the other party has defected), "provocable" (that is, defect if the other party defects), and "forgiving" (that is, reciprocate renewed cooperation).

What renders this theory insufficient as an analysis of détente in anarchy is, among other things, its assumption that the parties can remain sufficiently perceptive and flexible to be provocable and yet nice and forgiving—and capable of being credibly provocable and credibly nice and forgiving at the same time. The present study is concerned with a number of factors—"stabilizers"—reducing the ability of a party to switch from cooperation to defection and back as the need arises. I hope to show what insights can be gained from taking these factors into account.

10.1. Four Assumptions

The following consideration of the problem of détente in anarchy departs from four assumptions which have been made throughout the book but need to be spelled out here:

1. The analysis is concerned with the conditions for stable non-tense relations between states that remain adversaries, as pointed out previously. It is not concerned with conflict resolution but with conflict management. Continued adversity is taken for granted.

The terms *tension* and *détente* are used in the way explained in chapter 4. The degree of tension, roughly, is a function of the extent of mutual threat perceptions. A policy of détente, roughly, is one calculated to reduce the threat perceptions of the adversary. Détente in East-West relations had three main dimensions, which have here been called restraint, arms control, and cooperation; in what follows it is assumed that they are the main dimensions of international détente generally.

2. A government begins to pursue a policy of détente under the impact of the distribution of power between their own country and the adversary. Other considerations may be involved, and other factors may be triggers, but a policy of détente is always an intendedly rational response to the balance of power. Expressed in terms of the present conceptual framework, a particular state of the balance of power is always the condition, or one of the conditions, for a policy of détente.

As should be obvious, "balance" of power here denotes merely the power of one party compared with the power of the other. This comparison is all that is implied in the term balance. There is no assumption to the effect that détente presumes the distribution of power to be even. Power refers to power bases in the broadest sense (see Goldmann 1979b), but it is assumed that the power balance to which a policy of détente is a response is mainly a matter of military capabilities. The term balance of power is sometimes used below as a synonym to the military situation.

3. When a government sets out to pursue of policy of détente, reciprocity from the adversary is a condition for its continuation. Unilateral détente is incompatible with the demands of anarchic politics—all governments are here assumed to share this view.

4. A policy of détente is likely to be exposed to stress from several sources: shifts in the balance of power, disappointment in the adversary, crises, and shifts in government. It is, first of all, difficult to freeze the original power situation. Even if the parties manage to stop their arms race, technology will continue to develop, economic conditions will continue to change, and alliances will change in both composition and cohesion. Second, it is almost inconceivable that a lack of sufficient reciprocity would not be perceived by at least one party to an adversary relationship in a condition of anarchy, where mutual confidence is low. Third, crises will inevitably occur, and they are likely to be considered by one party or the other to offer opportunities too

tempting not to be taken or risks too great not to be averted. Fourth, a policy of détente can hardly avoid becoming exposed to at least some stress as a result of the demise of those who launched it.

On these assumptions, what will happen to a relationship of détente depends on whether stabilizers develop in time to protect it against disturbances that are inevitable or highly probable. Our object in this chapter is to consider what a process of détente stabilization may be like and whether it is likely or unlikely to succeed.

10.2. A Détente Scenario

Suppose that a process of détente has begun between two long-standing enemies. Something has occurred to destabilize their mutual policies of enmity—a shift in the balance of power, perhaps, as when the Soviet Union joined the United States in possessing an unquestionable second strike capability; or rethinking by one of the parties, as when Anwar Sadat went to Jerusalem; or a crisis dramatizing the dangers of the confrontation, such as the Cuban Missile Crisis; or a shift in government within one of the parties from hawks to doves, or from ideologues to pragmatists. Much may be needed to trigger an improvement in the relations between long-standing enemies under conditions of anarchy; more about this below. Suppose, however, that this has occurred.

I propose to outline a scenario for a maximally successful continuation of this process and then to consider the extent to which such a scenario is realistic. The scenario about to be suggested—this must be repeated—is not meant to describe how a process of détente might come about. It assumes that such a process has started and is concerned with its stabilization. The stabilization of détente is assumed to consist in the gradual strengthening of the various phenomena included in the inventory of foreign policy stabilizers introduced in chapter 2. As suggested previously, these phenomena are unlikely to be independent of one another. Moreover, whereas some may develop easily, the emergence of others may take a considerable time. The basic pattern, as hypothesized, is from international, to cognitive and political, to administrative stabilizers. A model of the process of foreign policy stabilization was outlined in chapter 3.

This model forms the point of departure for the détente scenario. A process of détente stabilization will be assumed to have four main phases representing the likely sequence in which the stabilizers will become significant. The division into phases is not meant to suggest that there are distinct borderlines between one phase and the next. The phases are assumed to overlap and are kept apart only for analytical purposes.

In the presentation of each phase of the scenario, its basic features are first summarized. Then its plausibility is discussed—that is, the likelihood that the various stabilizers would in fact emerge as assumed. Finally, the stabilizing impact of such a development is considered— that is, the extent to which a policy of détente would be protected by the stabilizers if they emerged as assumed.

Phase One: Traditional International Politics

Basic Features   Once the parties have begun to pursue a policy of détente toward each other, they begin—in this scenario—to conclude explicit agreements to this effect. They do it in order to constrain the adversary and to ensure reciprocity. Informal rules of the game, more-over, begin to develop. This is an inevitable consequence of the mutual pursuit of a policy of détente; all foreign policies are self-stabilizing to some extent.

At the same time a growing third party stabilization occurs. Common enmities are strengthened, and the allies are drawn into the détente process. This is so because of a propensity of all international relations to adapt to the new situation. The process of détente, then, is increasingly protected by structures of the my-enemy's-enemy-is-my-friend type as well as the my-friend's-friend-is-my-friend type.

Plausibility   The formalization of parallel decisions to pursue détente seems to be likely, and the emergence of customary rules of the game is automatic. Whether third party stabilization will also take place is more uncertain. Traditional international politics reasoning would seem to assume or imply that the my-enemy's-enemy and my-friend's-friend mechanisms operate. However, the dynamics of Great Power relations in recent decades have in large measure failed to operate according to these rules of triangular politics (see section 5.3). The main case in point is the U.S. effort to pursue détente toward the Soviet Union and the People's Republic of China at the same time. An excep-tion from the my-friend's-friend rule, moreover, is the difference between the United States and its European allies about how to respond to the détente crisis of the late 1970s. Third party stabilization cannot be taken for granted, it appears.

Stabilizing Impact   The Anarchy Model, with its emphasis on the lack of a central government in the international system and on the conse-quent importance of power politics, would seem to imply that the impact of normative regulation is small, whereas that of third parties is substantial.

Apart from the general question of the impact of international norms, which was touched on in section 2.1, there are particular problems with outlawing the offense while permitting or prescribing the defense. This familiar dilemma in international law is directly connected with the anarchy of the international system and with the premise that national independence is a supreme value. The dilemma was illustrated in the 1970s, as shown in section 5.1. The Helsinki Final Act and other documents of this period indicated the limits of what can be obtained. They even showed that the normative regulation of a détente process may be counterproductive. The act created expectations all over Europe of a new type of politics. When the expectations proved premature, governments were put under a pressure to protest, and the protests put détente under stress. In effect a mechanism was created in Helsinki for institutionalized increases in East-West tension.

Hence, there is reason to expect the stabilizing impact of the normative regulation of détente to be small. As regards third party stabilization, even though traditional theory suggests this to be important, the 1970s told a different story. This experience showed that third party stabilization is neither necessary nor sufficient to protect a policy of détente (see section 5.3).

In summary: what has here been journalistically called traditional international politics is unlikely to provide much protection to an emerging relationship of détente. Norms are easily created, but their effectiveness as détente stabilizers is in doubt. The plausibility as well as the effectiveness of third party stabilization of détente is uncertain; an equally likely possibility may be the emergence of a flexible game of multipolar politics, as in the U.S.-Soviet-China triangle.

Phase Two: Interdependence and Institutionalization

Basic Features   During Phase Two, two more factors are becoming significant: interdependence and institutionalization. On both sides, breaking off the relationship would necessitate increasingly complex readjustment. On both sides, moreover, a considerable commitment to the policy of détente is accumulating; by now, both governments would have to pay a high political price for deviating from détente. Institutionalization, moreover, is helped along by dependence; the substantive and the political costs of deviation tend to increase together.

Plausibility   The Anarchy Model may be taken to imply that international interdependence has a limit. It assumes national independence to be a prime concern of all governments. There should in particular be a limit to the extent to which a nation can accept dependence on its adversaries. Interdependence, moreover, implies that both parties are making gains, and there is presumably a limit to the gains you are willing to let your adversary make from cooperating with you. Since all governments argue in this way, mutual dependence is unlikely to be a significant factor in adversary relationships, it may be argued.

The argument can be turned around, however. Even if you are growing dependent on your adversary, your adversary is also growing dependent on you. Even if your adversary is gaining from cooperating with you, you are also gaining from cooperating with him. Your interest is to avoid becoming dependent on your adversary while making the adversary dependent on you, and to yourself obtain the gains of cooperation while denying them to him. It is a matter of having your cake and eating it. There is no a priori reason why governments, faced with the necessity for choice, would prefer denying gains to the adversary to obtaining gains for themselves, the détente optimist may argue.

The counterargument of the skeptic is that the optimist's reasoning can be expected to hold only in the case of perfect symmetry. One party will in most cases risk more than the other and will therefore be concerned to prevent the process of cooperation from going too far. The counter to this is in turn that it cannot be taken for granted that governments will be governed by considerations of symmetry.

Soviet-West German relations in the 1970s suggest that the built-in limit to economic interdependence among adversaries need not be very low. The limit, if there is one, is perhaps to be found where interdependence shades over into integration rather than during the early stages of a détente process. Of course, the development of economic cooperation between adversaries also depends on their economic compatibility, trends in their domestic economies, and other factors; the point here is that the fact of adversity does not necessarily set a low limit to interdependence and that therefore the détente scenario need not be unrealistic on this point.

Is it an equally plausible suggestion that détente will be strongly institutionalized on both sides?

A degree of institutionalization, as pointed out previously, is inherent in the very concept of policy. There is reason to expect more than this minimum, however. Commitment by policy declaration is likely to have become considerable by Phase Two, especially if there has been a need to reassure not only the adversary but also the allies, if the domestic opposition has been attacking the policy, and if the issue has been salient in domestic politics—a plausible combination of circumstances, exemplified by West Germany's Ostpolitik in the 1970s.

A commitment may be more apparent than real, however. Policy declarations play different roles in different countries, and in different circumstances. Moreover, the very rhetoric of a commitment may weaken as well as strengthen it (both American and Soviet declarations about détente provide examples). The extent to which a policy of détente is likely to be institutionalized would seem to vary with such background factors as political systems and cultures as well as with personalities and situations. This problem is in need of further study.

Stabilizing Impact: The Problem of Interconnected Stabilization   Every foreign policy is stabilized to some extent by dependence and institutionalization. In the case of a policy of détente there is a complication, however. It may be called the problem of interconnected stabilization.

Suppose that we are concerned with two nations, A and B, who are pursuing policies of enmity toward each other. Suppose, moreover, that both A and B would prefer the adversary to be amicable rather then enimical. Then A's propensity for behaving amicably toward B is affected by whether A expects B to reciprocate amicable behavior. The more stabilized B's policy of enmity, the less reason for A to expect B to reciprocate amicable behavior. Hence, the more stabilized B's policy of enmity toward A, the more stabilized A's policy of enmity toward B, and vice versa. The stabilizers of their mutual policies may be said to be positively interconnected: the stabilizers of A's policy are indirect stabilizers of B's policy, and vice versa. It follows that the more stabilized their respective policies of enmity, the more stable their relationship of enmity.

Suppose instead that A and B, even though adversaries, pursue amicable policies toward each other, and that—as in the previous case—both prefer the other to continue in this fashion. Then the consequences for A of the stabilization of B's policy are more complex. On the one hand, it may provide reassurance: uncertainty about B's amity may compel A to consider preemption, and the more stabilized B's policy of amity, the less A's uncertainty. On the other hand, the stabilization of B's policy of amity may weaken deterrence: the possibility that B may reply in kind helps to deter A from deviating from his policy of amity toward B, and the more stabilized B's policy of amity, the less credible the threat of retaliation. From the point of view of deterrence, then, the more stabilized B's policy of amity toward A, the less rather than more stabilized A's policy of amity toward B, and vice versa. The stabilizers of their mutual policies of amity are negatively rather than positively interconnected to some extent. The effects of the stabilization of their respective policies of amity on the stability of the amicability of their relationship are intriguing. The stabilization of policies of amity does not necessarily serve to stabilize relationships of amity.

There is a contradiction between inter-state action-reaction and foreign policy stabilization: the latter hinders the former. The implication for an enimical relationship is straightforward: foreign policy stabilization increases the difficulty of breaking out of such a relationship. The mechanism of interconnected stabilization adds to the difficulty of getting a process of détente underway. A cold war has built-in stability, so to speak. The implication for an amicable relationship between adversaries is less obvious, since the stabilization of the policy of one party may undermine the stability of the policy of the other. It is less evident how to strengthen amities than enmities. A détente process is self-destabilizing to some extent.

Normative regulation of détente—and of international violence in general—circumvents the paradox of destabilizing stabilization by prohibiting the offense but permitting or prescribing the defense. The norms prohibit deviations from a policy of détente except in response to a deviation by the adversary; they are designed, as it were, to provide reassurance without weakening deterrence. Matters are different with interdependence. This stabilizer affects deterrence as well as reassurance. The more interdependence, the higher the cost of deviating from détente but the smaller the probability that the cost will actually be incurred—since the other party, the one who would have to break off the relationship, has more to lose from breaking it off the more dependent he is on its continuation. It is impossible to strengthen a relationship of détente by means of mutual dependence without also weakening it to some extent.

This is reminiscent of nuclear deterrence. If both parties have a credible second strike capability, nuclear retaliation may appear so incredible that moves at lower levels are not deterred; the risk of mutual annihilation may invite blackmail and brinkmanship just as well as caution, according to the logic of the situation. The well-known paradox of nuclear deterrence—not only the offense but also the defense may be deterred, and because the defense may be deterred, deterrence of the offense may fail—is applicable also to the question of interdependence as a stabilizer of détente. Interdependence provides both parties with a weapon that may lack credibility because it is too costly to use.

The argument rests on the assumption of a particular kind of rationality. If both parties are assumed to be rational in this particular sense, it is indeed impossible to determine if deterrence will work at lower levels, whether it is a matter of a nuclear or an economic balance of terror. On this assumption, the effect of interdependence on détente is indeterminate.

A way out of the impasse has been proposed by Morgan (1983). After having argued that rational models cannot fully account for the fact that deterrence works, he suggests that we assume decisionmaking to be "sensible" rather than rational. Risk is the key element in sensible decisionmaking. Nuclear confrontation implies the possibility of enormous, indeed "unacceptable," costs to both parties, and the sensible decisionmaker is anxious to avoid taking this risk. Analogously, interdependence carries advantages to both sides, and the larger they are, the less willing the sensible decisionmaker presumably is to take the risk that the adversary will forego them. Hence, deterrence may work at lower levels, even if the cost of retaliation is disproportionately high.

On the assumption of sensible rather than rational decisionmaking, interdependence does help to protect a détente relationship. Its stabilizing impact cannot be specified, since the concept of sensibility is vague. What can be said with some confidence, however, is that the impact is reduced by virtue of the mechanism of negative interconnections between stabilizers.

The question of the relationship between economic ties and détente is an aspect of the larger question—one of the chief issues in international politics theory—of the relationship beween "high politics" and "low politics." This is an absolutely central research area for the further study of the conditions for stable détente.

Interdependence, like normative regulation, is a bilateral stabilizer in the sense that it can come about only by joint action between the parties. Institutionalization, on the other hand, is unilateral. Such a stabilizer may obtain on one side without obtaining on the other. It is in principle possible for détente to be a highly institutionalized policy within nation A but a minimally institutionalized policy within A's adversary B. Such radical asymmetry may even be difficult to avoid because of differences between political systems. Whereas West Germany's Ostpolitik could not avoid becoming an institutionalized part of West German politics, similar institutionalization of the USSR's Westpolitik could hardly have taken place because of the nature of the Soviet political system, however much the Soviet leadership may have wanted to reassure the West.

It may be taken for granted that symmetrical institutionalization has a stabilizing impact on a relationship of détente, even though the impact is reduced by the mechanism of negative interconnections (this presumes that the gain in stability from the institutionalization of nation A's policy of détente exceeds the loss in stability from the decrease in the credibility of retaliation resulting from the institutionalization of the détente policy of nation B). Suppose, however, that the situation is asymmetrical and that a policy of détente is highly institutionalized only in B and not in A. Then the institutionalization of B's policy of détente cannot but render A's détente policy even more unstable. The final result, other things being equal, is to increase the likelihood that B's policy of détente will become subject to stress from A's behavior. Hence, the less symmetrical institutionalization is, the smaller its efficiency as a stabilizer of a détente relationship is likely to be.[1]

ANARCHY necessitates deterrence. Therefore, a problem with the stabilization of détente is that it may weaken the credibility of retaliation. The mechanism of negative interconnections presumably operates with regard to all stabilizers except normative regulation, but the problem may be particularly significant in Phase Two, and that is why it has been considered here. As long as the relationship remains in Phase One, the problem has limited relevance, since normative regulation is one feature of this phase and the other feature, third party stabilization, seems unlikely to have a large impact anyway. In Phases Three and Four, on the other hand, deterrence may have begun to play a less vital role, since the détente relationship is then fairly well established. Phase Two is special in that deterrence remains paramount but is becoming undermined. This may be one of the chief problems with the stabilization of détente in anarchy.

This, it may be added, is also the point where the notion of foreign policy stabilization suggests a modification of Axelrod's theory of cooperation. The détente scenario, which is in the process of being presented, is for the most part a detailed exploration of what a process of evolving cooperation à la Axelrod might be like in practice—a consideration of the likelihood that this process might be sustained by a number of international, cognitive, political, and administrative factors. The possibility of negative interconnections between stabilizers points in a new direction, however. The stabilization of policies of cooperation may undermine what Axelrod calls the provocability of

[1] In the case of asymmetrical stabilization much may depend on who A and B are. See Goldmann 1983b for a comment on this point.

the parties, and provocability is essential for the evolution of cooperation in his theory. The possibility that the evolution of cooperation
may be self-defeating in this fashion is not considered by Axelrod. This
would seem to be a problem primarily during the early or middle part
of the process, since at a later stage the inclination to defect may have
been reduced to such an extent that provocability is less essential.

Phase Three: Cognitions, Consensus, and Bureaucratization

Basic Features   The continued pursuit of détente is having a growing
impact on underlying beliefs. Détente is increasingly assumed to be
linked to other policies and therefore occupies an increasingly central
position in the political thinking of the parties. At the same time, the
inconsistency in their détente-related beliefs is progressively reduced—
there is a decreasing inclination to take disadvantages and uncertainties into consideration. Moreover, their détente-related beliefs are getting less and less testable as specific expectations are replaced by a view
of the adversary approaching the "inherent good faith" model.

Moreover, this increasingly central and consistent, and decreasingly
testable, belief in détente is becoming the one held by all important
actors in domestic politics. Active opposition to détente is disappearing; there is growing active support by both the political opposition and the interest organizations; and public opinion is becoming
overwhelmingly favorable. It is now becoming unthinkable for a
leading politician to come out against détente.

Finally, the growing network of relations with the adversary has
given rise to administrative growth. There now exists a vast bureaucracy to manage this policy area. Hence, there is a decreasing sensitivity to the environment because of fragmentation, and decisionmaking on matters related to the policy is getting increasingly
complex.

Plausibility   The plausibility of these developments can be questioned
on several grounds.

It is not self-evident, first of all, that a policy of détente will gain in
cognitive centrality over time. To be sure, some links to other policies
are likely to become stronger; the more cooperation, the more likely
the perception that this cooperation is useful from more than one point
of view. However, it is also possible that the policy of détente has originally been intended to serve objectives that have then lost their significance. The Ostpolitik was at the outset linked to the goal of improving
West Gemany's international standing (section 6.2); by the early

1980s, this had become a less urgent concern of West German foreign policy. Generally, whereas it seems plausible that links to economic policy will become stronger over time, it is difficult to justify a similar assumption about the centrality of détente in other respects.

Is the assumption of increasing consistency equally questionable? It can be argued that cognitive inconsistency is inherent in the very notion of peaceful coexistence between adversaries. One cognitive difficulty is the "dual track" problem: the need to combine détente with deterrence (section 6.1). If the other party is not merely an ordinary adversary but an ideological or religious anathema, there is the additional cognitive problem of dealing with the devil. Détente, in a way, may be cognitively problematical from the point of view of both the pragmatist and the ideologue.

The essence of the pragmatist's problem is that in order for détente to be rational, an image of the adversary is assumed according to which deterrence inhibits détente; in order for deterrence to be rational, on the other hand, an image of the adversary is assumed according to which détente is dangerous (see section 6.1). This, it may be argued, is a concomitant of anarchy.

The essence of the ideologue's problem is that détente is beneficial to the adversary as well as to yourself. If you engage in cooperation with him, his repugnant system is likely to be strengthened, as well as his ability to pursue successfully his unacceptable policies. A trade-off must be made between your own gains and those of the adversary, and this is particularly unpleasant if the conflict is ideological or religious.

The East-West experience suggests, however, that these inhibitions to the cognitive stabilization of a policy of détente are not inevitable. The dual track problem was rather evident in American texts, but in West German pronouncements détente tended to go together with the maintenance of a systemic equilibrium rather than with deterrence of the adversary, and in Soviet statements deterrence was assumed to help rather than to hinder détente by making the adversary more rather than less cooperative. Moreover, the problem of dealing with the devil was absent or uncommon in both American and West German statements about détente, and it was ameliorated in Soviet statements by an assumption to the effect that détente would weaken rather than strengthen the adversary; détente, in other words, was pictured either as ideologically irrelevant or as a subversive tactic. Hence, even though a degree of cognitive inconsistency may be inherent in the notion of peaceful coexistence between adversaries, ways of ameliorating the problem exist.

The fact of anarchy seems to render the scenario quite unrealistic in another respect, however, and that is the suggestion of an increasing inclination to apply an "inherent good faith" model to the adversary. Single politicians in single countries may perhaps be shown to have had such a tendency, but a more reasonable expectation is that international suspicion will remain considerable.

The comments that can be made to the scenario's assumption of an increasing political support run parallel to those with regard to its presumption of an increasing cognitive stabilization. The two phenomena can be assumed to be interconnected. The factors tending to increase the cognitive centrality of a policy are also likely to increase the amount of political support. By the same token, to the extent that cognitive inconsistency is a concomitant of détente in anarchy, this is true also about political opposition to such a policy. Now, can it be maintained that since it appears possible to avoid strong cognitive inconsistency, a relative political consensus is also within reach?

The evidence from the 1970s suggests that the answer is "no": a relatively high degree of consistency in the ideas on which governments base a policy of détente seeems easier to attain than a political consensus over such a policy. There was considerable opposition to détente throughout the decade in the United States and West Germany as well as in the Soviet Union. The case of the United States is particularly illuminating. The ideological aspect, as we have noted, was conspicuously absent in Richard Nixon's and Henry Kissinger's declarations about détente. However, it did not take long for an ideological opposition to détente to gain ground—partly in the form of a rightwing ascendancy, partly in the shape of Jimmy Carter's emphasis on human rights. Moreover, in both the United States and West Germany the dual track problem and the ideological problem took the political form of the accusation that détente had been a "one way street." The opposition to détente eventually began to fade away in West Germany but became government policy in the United States.

It is easy to explain why international anarchy should be expected to inhibit the stabilization of détente by political consensus. At a minimum, anarchy would seem to render military establishments or "military-industrial complexes" unavoidable, and this means that there will always be important domestic actors interested in avoiding far-reaching détente. These actors will get political support because of the threat posed by the adversary; the existence of such threats, of course, is the essence of the Anarchy Model. The support will be especially large if the adversary is also an ideological opponent. There appears to be no similarly built-in support of détente. National unity in support of non-détente is easier to imagine than an overwhelming national consensus over détente.

The continuation of political opposition to a policy of détente may in turn check its cognitive stabilization to some extent. The existence of an opposition that keeps emphasizing the disadvantages and uncertainties may have an impact on the thinking of those in power. This is perhaps the chief way in which international anarchy renders cognitive consistency difficult—but apparently not impossible—to achieve.

It also seems implausible that the increasing administrative fragmentation assumed to take place during Phase Three would lead to an increase in "bureaucratic inertia." Governments have strong incentives to prevent the analysis of their main adversaries from degenerating into a mass of disorganized detail and to prevent decisionmaking about such matters from being bogged down in complex structures. There is reason to expect that countermeasures to bureaucratic inertia will be taken (see section 2.4). They may be more effective in some political systems (such as that of the United States) than in others (such as that of the Soviet Union), and it cannot be taken for granted that bureaucratic inertia will be averted (see chapter 8). Still, this is one more aspect of the third phase of the scenario that seems difficult to reconcile with international anarchy.

Stabilizing Impact: Crises as Disturbances   Suppose now that in spite of the obstacles a policy of détente has gained the protection of cognitive consistency and centrality as well as of political consensus and bureaucratic inertia. How effective is this protection? The answer may vary with the situation. The difference between crisis and noncrisis is likely to be crucial. Cognitive, political, and administrative stabilizers of a policy of détente may have a considerable impact in noncrisis situations and may yet be unimportant in crises.

A crisis, according to a common definition, is a situation in which there is a threat to important values, restricted decision time, and surprise.[2] This usage will be adopted here, with one addition. Policy stability is affected not only by risks but also by opportunities. Not only

[2] Hermann 1969, Hermann 1972, Holsti 1972. For a survey of definitions, see Robinson 1972. Brecher (1980: 1–8) has proposed a definition that differs in part from Hermann's and Holsti's. The chief difference is that Brecher adds perceived high probability of involvement in military hostilities as a necessary condition for crisis. If we were to make this addition, we would in effect define away our research problem, which concerns the effects of crisis on tension. Brecher also omits surprise as a necessary condition, but for the purposes of the present study it has appeared more useful to limit the analysis to situations in which some such element is present.

an unanticipated risk of suffering a large loss but also an unanticipated chance of making a large gain may put a policy under stress, especially if decision time is restricted. A crisis may be positive as well as negative, so to speak.

All kinds of disturbances may take the form of a crisis: changes in conditions and feedback as well as residual events. However, a particularly interesting situation from the point of view of the stabilization of détente is one in which a residual crisis and a feedback crisis combine. Especially in this kind of situation the stabilizers assumed to have gained prominence in Phase Three may prove insufficient to protect a relationship of détente.

The situation I have in mind has three features: an event occurs that (1) is unexpected by both parties, (2) implies a large opportunity or risk for at least one party, an opportunity or a risk that can be averted only by deviating from détente, and (3) provides restricted decision time.

Suppose that the event implies an opportunity or a risk for A rather than B. Then A's détente policy rather than B's is directly affected by the event. If A does deviate from détente, this deviation in turn serves to put B's policy of détente under stress. We may say that B's policy of détente risks coming under indirect stress from the original crisis. Developments in Poland in 1980 and 1981 put the Westpolitik of the Soviet Union under direct stress and the Ostpolitik of West Germany under indirect stress (Goldmann 1983b).

The question now is: How is the impact of the stabilizers of a détente relationship affected by the fact that the respective policies of détente are put under stress from a crisis?

Constraints on the actor's sensitivity to the environment, to begin with, are likely to be less important in crisis situations than otherwise. Cognitive, political, and administrative factors contributing to a reduction of the sensitivity to the environment may indeed help to protect policies against gradual and ambiguous disturbances, such as a shift in the balance of power or incremental change in the behavior of the adversary. A crisis, on the other hand, is highly visible; this is true almost by definition. It can be assumed to be taken note of.

The unavailability of alternatives may also be a less important factor in crises than otherwise. It is commonly hypothesized that whereas moderate stress helps to increase creativity and improve performance, severe stress tends to reduce the consideration of alternatives (Brecher 1980: 377; Holsti 1972: 14–15, 17, 22–23). If this were true, the lack of doubts inherent in cognitive consistency, the lack of debate following from a political consensus, and the impediments to innovation resulting from administrative growth would be apt to be particularly stabilizing in crisis situations. However, both simulation and interview studies have failed to support the hypothesis (Hermann 1972: 198–99; Lentner 1972: 128). A feature of decisionmaking in crisis, rather, is the substitution of small ad hoc units at the top for normal routines, and a search for alternatives typically constitutes a substantial portion of decisionmaking time (Lentner 1972: 120; Paige 1972: 45, 51; Robinson 1972: 26, 34). Crisis appears to encourage rather than to restrain creativity and innovation. The suggestion is not that brilliant ideas are more likely to obtain in a crisis but that new ideas, whether brilliant or foolish, are more likely to be put forward and to be accepted in a crisis than if it is a matter of responding to a more gradual or ambiguous disturbance.

To this must be added the fundamental fact that the cost of adhering to previous policy by definition is higher in a crisis than otherwise. Therefore, the cost of deviating from it must also be unusually high in order for stabilization to be effective. Even very considerable cognitive and political costs may be insufficient to prevent a deviation from détente if the pressure for change comes from a crisis situation. As already noted, moreover, decision structures tend to be of the least stabilizing type in such situations.

All policies are likely to be more vulnerable to crises than to other disturbances. This does not mean that they cannot endure. It remains relevant whether they are protected by a consistent body of ideas linking them to other policies in combination with a strong political commitment, a national consensus, and a complex administrative apparatus. Still, even as late in the process of détente stabilization as during Phase Three, the occurrence of a crisis may render the combined impact of these factors insufficient to prevent a change in policy.

Phase Four: The Disappearing of the Alternatives

Basic Features   During the final stage of the process of détente stabilization there develops not just structural but substantive "bureaucratic inertia" (this distinction was first made in section 2.4). Structural inertia refers to the factors here called fragmentation and decision structure. Such factors are assumed to have already become important during Phase Three. By substantive administrative stabilizers are meant, on the one hand, critical variables and their tolerable ranges, and, on the other hand, response repertories.

During Phase Four, intelligence and planning are increasingly carried out as if policy change were unthinkable. Few variables are considered critical, and the tolerable ranges on these variables are very large. The response repertory is becoming poor on both sides. We are now approaching the point where the process of détente is completed. A security community is about to be substituted for the adversary relationship.

Plausibility   Examples can in fact be found of foreign policies protected by the kind of factors assumed to become significant only in Phase Four. United States policy toward the People's Republic of China in the 1950s and most of the 1960s may be one; the Swedish policy of neutrality is another. As regards a policy of détente, however, Phase Four seems quite unlikely to be attained. The fact of international anarchy would appear to be not just a constraint but a powerful inhibition against the advanced administrative stabilization of détente. The possibility should not be entirely discounted: security communities have been formed. Still, it seems unlikely that both parties to an adversary relationship would stop being concerned with the possibility that their coexistence might cease to be peaceful. They are more likely to continue to consider several variables to be critical, to keep the tolerable ranges relatively narrow, and to remain prepared for the eventuality of nondétente.

Stabilizing Impact   If Phase Four were nevertheless attained, huge disturbances would be needed to bring about a change in policy. Not even a maximally stabilized foreign policy is unchangeable, however. When it is a matter of a policy of détente, it is particularly important to note that the stabilizers attaining prominence in Phase Four belong to those rendered ineffective in crises. As already suggested, there is likely to be less dependence on preexisting intelligence routines and on a preexisting response repertory when pressure for change comes from a crisis than in other situations.

A fifth phase during which the adversaries cease to be adversaries can be imagined. If a process of détente were to end with a security community, anarchy-related constraints would lose most of their relevance, and the door would be open for further integration, which could continue until the infringement on national autonomy would threaten to become unacceptable in the view of one party or both.

10.3. The Uses of the Scenario

The above scenario is hypothetical—a mere thought-experiment made with the help of a sketchy theory and inspired by some observations about East-West relations. It is meant to have three uses: as an aid in diagnosing international relations, as a clarificaton of some points in the Anarchy Model, and as a basis for considering whether and how to pursue a policy of détente.

The diagnostic use is straightforward. There is sometimes reason to be concerned with the likelihood of violent conflict between adversaries who coexist for the moment—between Bonn and Moscow, Cairo and Jerusalem, Moscow and Beijing. There are several ways of measuring how the degree of tension in an inter-state relation has developed in the past,[3] but this is not always the information we seek. If the question is what would likely happen to the relationship if it were put under stress, the degree of détente stabilization rather than the past or even the current level of tension is our chief concern.

The scenario may serve as a standard with which the actual state of affairs can be compared. Since it is hypothetical, it is not fully reliable as a yardstick. Because it is based on relatively detailed and explicit considerations, however, it should represent an improvement over more intuitive notions of what constitutes stable détente. The scenario suggests, for example, that even relatively extensive institutionalization and interdependence may be insufficient to protect the relation against plausible disturbances—but that, on the other hand, a relationship of détente that has acquired a firm basis in beliefs and domestic politics on both sides may be seriously vulnerable only to a major crisis. It is my impression that by the mid-1980s Jerusalem-Cairo remained in Phase One although their détente process began several years ago. This remained true also with regard to the process of détente stabilization between Moscow and Beijing. The stabilization of détente between Moscow and Bonn, on the other hand, seemed to be as far advanced as Phase Three. The scenario suggests what this may imply for the future.

The scenario clarifies the Anarchy Model by examining its explanatory power. The Anarchy Model would seem to assume highly stabilized détente to be unlikely, and the scenario elaborates on this assumption by specifying a number of anarchy-related constraints. They include (1) the problem of proscribing the offense while permitting or prescribing the defense, (2) the mechanism of negative interconnections between stabilizers, and (3) the implausibility of cognitive consistency with regard to détente, of political consensus over détente, and of a high degree of administrative stabilization of détente. It is,

[3] See Goldmann 1974 for a relatively early attempt that was continued in Goldmann and Lagerkranz 1977 and in Goldmann 1979a, and see Frei and Ruloff 1983 for a more sophisticated effort.

however, less obvious that there are significant anarchy-related limitations to the degree of international interdependence, political institutionalization, and cognitive centrality. Hence, the scenario does not only serve to specify some constraints on détente that may be inherent in anarchy but also points at some of the possibilities that may nevertheless exist.

This brings us to the third way in which the scenario may be useful: as a "handbook" for détente stabilization. Your first problem, if you want to improve relations between yourself and your adversary—or between two adversaries, if you yourself are a third party—is whether his policy of enmity can be destabilized. Discussions about the feasibility of détente are often concerned with the question of whether such destabilization will occur or can be made to occur. The issue is commonly assumed to be whether and how to change conditions, and whether and how to persuade the adversary—or both contenders, if you are a third party—that the feedback of current policies is negative.

This is not the issue with which the above scenario is concerned. The position taken here is that it is impossible to generalize about the process of policy destabilization (see section 3.2) and, therefore, that a standard scenario for the destabilization of policies of enmity cannot be constructed. The best way to destabilize a relationship of enmity depends on the specifics of the situation, according to this assumption.

Suppose, however, that the relationship between yourself and your enemy has improved, that you want this improvement to continue, and that you are therefore eager to do what can be done to stabilize your adversary's recent, more amicable policy. How can this be achieved?

According to the model of the process of policy stabilization with which we are experimenting here (see chapter 3), the stabilization of a relationship of amity among enemies is a race between the incidence of disturbances and the progressive growth of stabilizers. The trick is to reduce the amount of stress in the short run so as to gain time for stabilization that can protect détente later on—and, at the same time, to help the process of stabilization along in order for détente to become as invulnerable as possible as soon as possible. This is a difficult task under conditions of anarchy, but the process of détente stabilization may be aided by a careful pursuit of restraint, arms control, and cooperation.

What happened in U.S.-Soviet relations in the decade following the agreement on "basic principles" in 1972 suggests a number of steps that might have reduced the stress on their emerging détente but were not taken. The USSR carried out a rearmament program that altered the military balance. The two parties failed to go much beyond SALT I in limiting their arms race. They could have shown more restraint in a series of crises. There was a reluctance to satisfy the adversary's expectations of the benefits of cooperation.

International anarchy inhibits restraint, arms control, and cooperation. Everyday international politics—the 1970s were not exceptional—cannot but expose attempts at détente to a variety of stresses and strains. Still, the Anarchy Model should not be considered deterministic. Anarchy renders enduring détente implausible but does not make it impossible. Governments can do more to avoid disturbing a fragile, newly begun détente process than the United States and the Soviet Union did in the 1970s.

If avoiding premature stress is one pillar of a policy of détente, policy stabilization is the other. The purpose of pursuing a policy of restraint, arms control, and cooperation is not only the short-term avoidance of stress but also the long-term stabilization of the détente policy of your adversary.

Apart from taking the obvious measure of normative regulation, your chance lies in influencing the adversary's dependence on détente, his beliefs about détente, and his domestic politics. These variables may be tied together in a positive feedback circle (this was suggested at the end of chapter 9), and you may be able to reinforce it. If you want détente stabilization, you have an interest in giving your adversary reason to believe that long-term détente is vital to him and to give détente as powerful a constituency as possible within his society. This link between international and domestic politics—the deliberate manipulation of somebody else's domestic politics by means of cooperation rather than intervention—may have been insufficiently studied.

The argument adds up to three rules for the pursuit of a policy of détente.

First, *do not change the balance of power.* As has been pointed out repeatedly, a policy of détente may be seen as an intendedly rational response to a particular power situation between you and your adversary. A change in your favor cannot but be a source of stress on your adversary's policy of détente. If your objective is to stabilize your adversary's policy of détente, it is in your own interest to avoid improving your power position on his account.

Second, *be restrained in crisis.* Crises will inevitably put your policy of détente under stress by offering opportunities or creating risks. These are likely to be the most important sources of stress on an emerging détente relationship. The greater your restraint and caution in such situations, the less the stress on your adversary's détente policy.

Joint crisis prevention and crisis management is very much in the interest of those who want to pursue a policy of détente.

Third, *reward your adversary*. It is important to devise your policy of détente so as to maximize your adversary's gains and minimize his costs. There are several reasons for this. First, a lack of reward may be perceived as a disappointment and hence may be a source of stress. Furthermore, cooperation may lead to interdependence, and this is likely to help to stabilize the détente policy of your adversary. Above all, it is in your own interest to embed détente in your adversary's beliefs and domestic politics and, therefore, to demonstrate the several ways in which détente can help him attain his various objectives.

There are, as pointed out previously, two arguments against following these rules.

First, the probability of success may be considered too small. Reciprocity cannot be assumed, disturbances cannot be avoided, and the fact of anarchy sets limits to both the plausibility and the impact of détente stabilization. There is also the dilemma due to the mechanism of negative interconnections. A condition for the stabilization of a policy of détente on the part of your adversary is presumably the progressive stabilization of your own; you can hardly hope for the stabilization of your adversary's policy while preserving maximum flexibility for yourself. This, however, may undermine deterrence, which is also a sort of a stabilizer of a nonenimical policy on the part of your adversary. The dilemma is rooted in the anarchic structure of the international system.

Second, détente in relation to a particular adversary may simply be found to be undesirable. Can we really be expected to do business with, and in effect help to maintain, a regime that is violating or threatening our most cherished values? The problem of détente is ultimately one of desirability and not merely one of feasibility.

IT IS PERHAPS POSSIBLE to discern three standard views about détente toward an adversary. The advocates of détente often base themselves on what may be called an optimistic realism. They assume that even though the conflict may continue to exist and deterrence may remain necessary, the risk of war can be reduced by restraint, arms control, and cooperation. Since they give a high priority to peace and security in relation to other objectives, they are ready to deal with the devil and to offer him benefits.

The opponents of détente appear to consist of two different groups: the zealots and the skeptical realists. The former hesitate to deal with the devil, to coexist with the imperialists, to do business with the

Soviets. The latter argue that détente, even though desirable, will not work and that straightforward deterrence is the only possibility.

This study has no relevance for the arguments of the zealots. Nor does it come out clearly in favor of either the optimistic or the skeptical realists. What has been presented here is both a program for détente stabilization and an explanation of why this may be a Sisyphean task in many cases. For reasons that can be traced back to the structure of the international system, relatively primitive détente stabilization is unlikely to suffice and relatively advanced détente stabilization is unlikely to occur. This is the skeptic's case. Still, a détente relationship can be sufficiently stabilized in time for it to survive the unavoidable disturbances, and our adversary's policy of détente can become sufficiently stabilized to more than compensate for the loss in the credibility of our own deterrence. That is the optimist's view. This study can contribute by specifying some of the trade-offs and uncertainties.

A Note on the Utility of
Weak Theory and Weak Tests

THE THEORY presented in this book is sketchy and is essentially a mere checklist of factors assumed to be important in accounting for change and stability in foreign policy. It is not tested in a strict sense but is merely applied to historical developments studied for their intrinsic interest rather than for their ability to test the theory; détente is examined with the help of the theoretical sketch rather than for the purpose of testing it, and thus Part Two of the book is of the type Eckstein calls "disciplined-configurative study" in his seminal essay on "Case Study and Theory in Political Science."[1] Both theory and empirical design, in other words, are weak in comparison with the canons of empirical science.

This raises the question whether a weak theory can be useful for other purposes than as a stepping-stone on the road to strong theory—whether it can be useful, for example, in wrestling with a specific problem like détente in spite of its weakness. It also raises the question of the extent to which weak theory can be strengthened by such a primitive empirical design as the present.

These questions are commented on in this note. My object is to specify what the imperfections imply and hence what a study such as this can achieve in spite of its imperfections. Since both weak theory and weak tests are common in international relations research, the note may have some relevance beyond the present study.

THE UTILITY OF WEAK THEORY

A theory is here taken to consist of assertions about relations between concepts. The strength of a theory is taken to be a function of three features:

1. Its precision—that is, the degree to which the relationships are specified. At one extreme the theory consists in a mere enumeration of

[1] Eckstein 1975: 99–104. This is similar to what Lijphart calls "interpretative case studies" (1971: 692).

concepts assumed to be relevant. At the other extreme the relationships are given a precise mathematical formulation.

2. Its explanatory power—that is, the amount of variance the theory can explain within its area of applicability, or its ability to anticipate unknowns (Eckstein 1975: 88–89).

3. Its degree of empirical confirmation.

Strong theory is obviously useful. Scholars who are motivated by concern with international problems sometimes assume, even though for the most part implicitly, that they can achieve by their research a theory strong enough to provide precise and valid policy-oriented conclusions. Decisionmakers and bureaucrats, moreover, sometimes seem to expect this kind of advice from scholars. Economics appears to be the model: it is assumed that the analysis of international relations should strive to approach the standards of the discipline of economics, where precise conclusions about policy can be deduced, or are thought to be deducible, from a theory that is strong or is thought to be strong.

Strong international relations theory is presently uncommon, however. For this reason the utility of weak theory is an important question.

Hoffmann's (1960) distinction between theory as answers and theory as questions may be introduced at this point. Strong theory can provide precise, comprehensive, and well-founded answers to important questions. The answers provided by weak theory, in contrast, are by definition imprecise, incomplete, and tentative. Whereas a biologist's view of the impact of fertilizers on wildlife may be termed scientific, a political scientist's position on nuclear strategy is more properly termed an educated guess.

The utility of weak theory lies in its ability to pose questions rather than to provide answers. To ask the right—the "fruitful"—questions is essential for developing strong theory, and weak theory can help theory-oriented research along by conceptualizing an area of investigation and providing a framework into which new results may be integrated. What is perhaps less self-evident is that the ability of weak theory to ask questions renders it useful for nontheoretical purposes even though it cannot provide good answers to the questions.

Explanation, prediction, and even mere description presume by logical necessity decisions about what to include and what to leave out and about how to structure what is included. Weak theory—and of course strong theory—can improve both the selection and the structuring of data by providing explicit criteria. There are three reasons for being guided by weak theory rather than by no theory at all.

1. It is not necessary to begin from scratch with each problem of selection and structuring.
2. There is a reduced risk of the inadvertent omission of relevant dimensions.
3. The criteria for selection and structuring are accessible to a critical examination and hence to improvement.

In other words, even though it cannot provide good answers, weak theory can render the asking of questions less time-consuming, less arbitrary, and more amenable to control.

Weak theory can perform these functions better the stronger it is, of course. The mere enumeration of concepts assumed to be relevant is less useful than if there are reasonably precise assertions about the relations between them. The larger the explanatory power, the better. Moreover, the utility of weak theory depends on whether its concepts are sufficiently operational to permit empirical application. To "test" a weak theory largely means to improve it in these respects by applying it to empirical data—to make it more precise, comprehensive, and operational.

Some weak theories are more amenable to improvement than others. A weak theory containing falsifiable propositions about the way in which changes in some variables will affect other variables may be described as underdeveloped rather than inherently weak. On the other hand, if a theoretical construct merely provides a "framework" or "perspective" and essentially consists in definitions—if, in other words, the construct is causally more or less empty—its weakness is inherent. A term like *theoretical sketch* may be used to denote the former and a term like *analytical framework* to denote the latter.

Part One of this book opens with a mere framework of analysis intended to specify the problem with which the study is concerned, and particularly its core concept of foreign policy "stabilizer." The subsequent reasoning about what phenomena function as foreign policy stabilizers has causal content and forms a theoretical sketch. It remains weak theory, however, and its utility therefore lies in its ability to ask questions rather than to provide answers. I hope, of course, that the sketch can be improved, which is one reason for publishing an effort of this kind. I also hope, however, that even in its present shape, the sketch may be useful as a tool for the analysis of specific problems. The construction of such tools seems to be one of the neglected tasks of international relations research; the emphasis has been on the development of strong theory on the one hand and on nontheoretical analysis on the other.

THE UTILITY OF WEAK EMPIRICAL TESTS

Soviet-U.S. and Soviet-West German relations in the 1970s were selected for study because this promised to provide insights into the problem of détente. The argument was not that this was the best way of testing the general theory of foreign policy stability that had been sketched. If that had been a chief consideration, the empirical design would probably have been different. The study that was carried out nontheless permitted a sort of test of the theoretical sketch. The object of this section is to consider what such weak tests can and cannot do for weak theory.

The most basic distinction between research designs is the one between case study, where N = 1, and comparative study, where N > 1 (Eckstein 1975: 81–86). A further distinction can be made between two types of comparative study: what may be called comparative case study, where N exceeds 1 but remains too small for statistical purposes, and statistical study, where N is sufficiently large for statistical analysis. A statistical study is based on what are presumed to be all instances of a phenomenon or a sample that is in some sense representative. Single and comparative case studies may also shed light on the validity of a general theory, but their ability to do this depends on the theory as well as on the selection of cases; the weaker the theory, the weaker the criteria for selection.

It can be discussed whether the present study is single case or comparative case. It does compare two or three instances: U.S.-Soviet and West German-Soviet relations, or U. S., West German, and Soviet foreign policy. From the point of view of the problem of détente stabilization, the method followed in this study is similar to "focused comparison" as outlined by George (see George and Smoke 1974: 94–97, app.; George 1979). From the point of view of developing a general theory of foreign policy change and stability, détente in the 1970s is rather a single case. At any rate, this is not a statistical study; it has not been designed to identify the statistical correlates of foreign policy change and stability. Eckstein (1975: 129–31) claims that a properly designed single case study may be equivalent or even superior for testing theory. However, case study, whether single or comparative, is logically insufficient for a strict test of probabilistic or weakly specified multivariate theory. Since the present theoretical sketch is both, the failure to use a statistical design is indeed a limitation.

It is worth pointing out, however, that a statistical design does not always provide a decisive advantage over case study research in the field of international relations, even when it is a matter of testing probabilistic or multivariate theory. My own previous research about Great Power relations (Goldmann 1974; Goldmann and Lagerkranz 1977; Goldmann 1979a), which was the point of departure for the present study, gave an insight into the limitations of statistical designs. The research was based on year-by-year data about the level of tension and some other variables. It proved to be common for the variables to remain essentially constant for long periods and then to jump to a new level, where they then remained essentially constant for a considerable time. What the correlations between such data series measure largely is whether a small number of important events tended to occur together or at different times. Such research is statistical in form more than in content. Or, better, the statistical design improved the descriptive quality of the research, which was important enough, but the improvement in our ability to test theory was modest.

It may be noted that the far more ambitious and successful Correlates of War project has a similar problem insofar as warfare since 1815 has to a large extent been concentrated to a small number of major events like World War I and World War II (Small and Singer 1982: 146, 150). It has been pointed out that in Michael Wallace's much-discussed research on the relationship between arms races and war, which is based on data from the Correlates of War project, the two world wars account for over 80 percent of the explanatory capability (Diehl 1983).

What is reflected here is less the poverty of the statistical method than the poverty of history—the lack of a sufficient variety of historical instances of that which needs to be studied in order to evaluate probabilistic or multivariate theory (cf. Eckstein 1975: 121). And if history is poor, the difference between a statistical and a nonstatistical design is reduced.

What can be positively achieved by applying a weak theory to one or a few historical cases?

First, the mere application of a set of concepts to empirical data is a means to conceptual refinement. In a sense, a concept is "tested" by being applied. The "test" may lead to an improved understanding of the problems and possibilities of operationalization. Operationalization, of course, is a prerequisite for a theory's being useful even for asking questions. Therefore, the application of weak theory to empirical data is ipso facto a way of improving its utility. This is reminiscent of, or a weak form of, Eckstein's suggestion that the minimum objective of a case study intended as a "plausibility probe" is to "establish that a theoretical construct is worth considering at all, i.e., that an apparent empirical instance of it can be found" (p. 109).

Second, as is often pointed out, case studies may be useful for generating new theoretical ideas (this usage of the case study method is emphasized by Lijphart 1971: 692). To carry out "exploratory" or "heuristic" research is in large measure to improve a theoretical sketch by adding new variables and new hypotheses about the relations between variables.

Third, it may perhaps be argued that even other propositions than those about necessities and sufficiencies can be empirically assessed on the basis of case studies. If X is hypothesized to be "essential" for Y— this kind of proposition is typical of weak theory—and if we find a case in which Y occurs but not X, or that there is no difference with regard to Y between one case with X and another case without X, we may be justified in concluding that the credibility of the proposition has been reduced, especially if there has been a proper selection of a case or cases.[2] This would seem to be a stronger form of what Eckstein calls a "plausibility probe."

Even though they were selected on nontheoretical grounds, the comparison between the Soviet-U.S. and Soviet-West German cases reported in Part Two may be taken to give a rough indication of the general validity of the theoretical sketch. It also helps us to some small extent to distinguish between "essential" and "non-essential" stabilizers of foreign policy—a "test," if you wish, of the hypothesis that the phenomena included in the theoretical sketch are "essential." The study also serves an "exploratory" or "heuristic" function by suggesting ideas about background variables (this can be seen in chapters 9 and 10). Mainly, however, Part Two is simply a practical experiment with applying the theoretical concepts to an empirical problem. That is perhaps the chief way in which the empirical research reported in this book is theoretically useful.

[2] George's argument about the utility of plausibility testing would seem to go along with the point made here (George and Smoke 1974: 639).

Adomeit, Hannes. 1981. "Consensus versus Conflict: The Dimensions of Foreign Policy." In Seweryn Bialer, ed., *The Domestic Context of Soviet Foreign Policy.* Boulder, Colo.: Westview.

Agnelli, Giovanni. 1980. "East-West Trade: A European View." *Foreign Affairs* 58, no. 5: 1016–33.

Albright, David E. 1977. "The Sino-Soviet Conflict and the Balance of Power in Asia." *Pacific Community* 8, no. 2: 204–34.

Alexander, Arthur J. 1984. "Modeling Soviet Defense Decisionmaking." In Jiri Valenta and William Potter, eds., *Soviet Decisionmaking for National Security.* London: George Allen & Unwin.

Allison, Graham T. 1971. *Essence of Decision: Explaining the Cuban Missile Crisis.* Boston: Little, Brown.

Almond, Gabriel A. 1950. *The American People and Foreign Policy.* New York: Harcourt, Brace.

Anckar, Dag. 1978. "Politikprocesser och politikinnehåll: till frågan om politik som orsak och policy som verkan." *Politiika* 20, no. 2: 99–128.

Antal, Endre. 1980. "Der Ost-West-Handel am Scheidenweg." *Osteuropa* 30, no. 3: 221–38.

Armstrong, John A. 1980. "The Domestic Roots of Soviet Foreign Policy." In Eric P. Hoffmann and Frederic J. Fleron, eds., *The Conduct of Soviet Foreign Policy.* New York: Aldine.

Aspaturian, Vernon V. 1971. *Process and Power in Soviet Foreign Policy.* Boston: Little, Brown.

Axelrod, Robert, ed. 1976. *Structure of Decision: The Cognitive Maps of Political Elites.* Princeton: Princeton University Press.

Axelrod, Robert. 1984. *The Evolution of Cooperation.* New York: Basic Books.

Baker, Kendall L., Russel J. Dalton, and Kai Hildebrandt. 1981. *Germany Transformed: Political Culture and the New Politics.* Cambridge, Mass: Harvard University Press.

Bergson, Abram. 1980. "Comment." In Egon Neuberger and Laura D'Andrea Tyson, eds., *The Impact of International Economic Disturbances on the Soviet Union and Eastern Europe: Transmission and Response.* New York: Pergamon.

Bethkenhagen, Jochen, and Heinrich Machowski. 1982. *Entwicklung und Struktur des deutsch-sowjetischen Handels: Seine Bedeutung für die Volkswirtschaften der Bundesrepublik Deutschland und der Sowjetunion.* Deutsches Institut für Wirtschaftsforschung, Sonderheft 136. Berlin: Duncker & Humblot.

Bialer, Seweryn, ed. 1981. *The Domestic Context of Soviet Foreign Policy.* Boulder, Colo.: Westview.

Bianco, Lucien. 1979. "Rappel historique et perspectives d'évolution du conflit sino-soviétique." *Défense nationale* 35 (November): 7–16.

Birnbaum, Karl E. 1973. *East and West Germany: A Modus Vivendi.* Farnborough, Hants.: D. C. Heath.

Blacker, Coit D. 1983. "The Kremlin and Détente: Soviet Conceptions, Hopes, and Expectations." In Alexander L. George, ed., *Managing U.S.-Soviet Rivalry: Problems of Crisis Prevention.* Boulder, Colo.: Westview.

Blainey, Geoffrey. 1973. *The Causes of War.* New York: Free Press.

Bornstein, Morris. 1979. "East-West Economic Relations and Soviet-East European Relations." In U.S. Congress, Joint Economic Committee, *Soviet Economy in a Time of Change,* vol. 1. Washington, D.C.: U.S. Government Printing Office.

Bowie, Robert R. 1984. "The President and the Executive Branch." In Joseph S. Nye, Jr., ed., *The Making of America's Soviet Policy.* New Haven and London: Yale University Press.

Brandt, Willy. 1972. *Der Wille zum Frieden: Perspektiven der Politik.* Hamburg: Hoffmann und Campe.

Brecher, Michael. 1980. *Decisions in Crisis: Israel, 1967 and 1973.* Berkeley and Los Angeles: University of California Press.

Brown, Archie. 1985. "The Foreign Policy-Making Process." In Curtis Keeble, ed., *The Soviet State: The Domestic Roots of Soviet Foreign Policy.* Aldershot, Hants.: Gower.

Buchholz, Arnold. 1982. *Soviet and East European Studies in the International Framework: Organization, Financing and Political Relevance.* Berlin: Berlin Verlag.

Burzig, Arno. 1978. "Ostpolitik und Osthandel: Das Zusammenwirken von Regierung und Wirtschaftsverbänden in der Ost-West-Wirtschaftspolitik." In Helga Haftendorn, et al., eds., *Verwaltete Aussenpolitik: Sicherheits- und entspannungspolitische Entscheidigungsprozesse in Bonn.* Cologne: Verlag Wissenschaft und Politik.

Buzan, Barry, and R. J. Barry Jones, eds. 1981. *Change and the Study of International Relations: The Evaded Dimension.* London: Frances Pinter.

Byrne, Angel O., et al. 1982. "U.S.-U.S.S.R. Grain Trade." In U.S. Congress, Joint Economic Committee, *Soviet Economy in the 1980's: Problems and Prospects, Part 2.* Washington, D.C.: U.S. Government Printing Office.

Caldwell, Lawrence T., and William Diebold, Jr. 1981. *Soviet-American Relations in the 1980s: Superpower Politics and East-West Trade.* New York: McGraw-Hill.

Carlsnaes, Walter. 1985. Review of Jan Hallenberg, *Foreign Policy Change: United States Foreign Policy toward the Soviet Union and the People's Republic of China, 1961–1980.* In *Cooperation and Conflict* 20, no. 3: 211–27.

Carrère d'Encausse, Hélène. 1979. "Visées et possibilités de Moscou en Asie." *Défense nationale* 35 (November): 17–28.

CDU (Christlich-Demokratische Union). 1972. *Wir bauen der Fortschritt auf Stabilität*. Bonn.

———. 1976. *Aus Liebe zu Deutschland*. Bonn.

———. 1980. *Für Frieden und Freiheit in der Bundesrepublik Deutschland und in der Welt*. Bonn.

———. 1983. *Arbeit, Frieden, Zukunft: Miteinander schaffen wir's*. Bonn.

China's Army—Ready for Modernization. 1985. Beijing: Beijing Review.

Cohen, Bernard C. 1969. "National-International Linkages: Superpolities." In James N. Rosenau, ed., *Linkage Politics*. New York: Free Press.

———. 1973. *The Public's Impact on Foreign Policy*. Boston: Little, Brown.

Cohen, Bernard C., and Scott A. Harris. 1975. "Foreign Policy." In Fred I. Greenstein and Nelson Polsby, eds., *Handbook of Political Science*, vol. 6: *Policies and Policy-Making*. Reading, Mass.: Addison-Wesley.

Cohen, Raymond. 1981. *International Politics: The Rules of the Game*. London: Longman.

Commission on the Organization of the Government for the Conduct of Foreign Policy. 1975. *Appendices*, vol. 7. Washington, D.C.: U.S. Government Printing Office.

Cooper, William H. 1982. "Soviet-Western Trade." In U.S. Congress, Joint Economic Committee, *Soviet Economy in the 1980's: Problems and Prospects, Part 2*. Washington, D.C.: U.S. Government Printing Office.

Cox, Arthur Macy. 1976. *The Dynamics of Détente: How to End the Arms Race*. New York: W. W. Norton.

Cumings, Bruce. 1981. "Chinatown: Foreign Policy and Elite Realignment." In Thomas Ferguson and Joel Rogers, eds., *The Hidden Election: Politics and Economics in the 1980 Presidential Campaign*. New York: Pantheon.

Cutler, Robert M. 1981. "The Cybernetic Theory Reconsidered." *Michigan Journal of Political Science* 1, no. 2: 57–63.

———. 1984. "Organizational Process in Soviet Foreign Policy-Making." Paper presented at the annual convention of the International Studies Association, Atlanta, Ga., March 28–31.

Dallin, Alexander. 1980. "Soviet Foreign Policy and Domestic Politics: A Framework for Analysis." In Eric P. Hoffmann and Frederic J. Fleron, eds., *The Conduct of Soviet Foreign Policy*. New York: Aldine.

———. 1981. "The Domestic Sources of Soviet Foreign Policy." In Seweryn Bialer, ed., *The Domestic Context of Soviet Foreign Policy*. Boulder, Colo.: Westview.

Destler, I. M. 1984. "Congress." In Joseph S. Nye, Jr., ed., *The Making of America's Soviet Policy*. New Haven and London: Yale University Press.

Deutsch, Karl W., et al. 1957. *Political Community and the North Atlantic Area*. Princeton: Princeton University Press.

Deutsch, Karl W., and Lewis J. Edinger. 1959. *Germany Rejoins the Powers*. Stanford: Stanford University Press.

Diehl, Paul F. 1983. "Arms Races and Escalation: A Closer Look." *Journal of Peace Research* 20, no. 3: 205–12.

Dittmer, Lowell. 1981. "The Strategic Triangle: An Elementary Game-Theoretical Analysis." *World Politics* 33, no. 4: 485–515.

Dohan, Michael R. 1979. "Export Specialization and Import Dependence in the Soviet Economy, 1970–77." In U.S. Congress, Joint Economic Committee, *Soviet Economy in a Time of Change*, vol. 2. Washington, D.C.: U.S. Government Printing Office.

Dunér, Bertil. 1977. *Autonomi: Skiss till teoretisk referensram och illustration av dess tillämpning*. Stockholm: Swedish Institute of International Affairs.

East, Maurice A., Stephen S. Salmore, and Charles F. Hermann, eds. 1978. *Why Nations Act*. Beverly Hills, Calif.: Sage.

Eckstein, Harry. 1975. "Case Study and Theory in Political Science." In Fred I. Greenstein and Nelson W. Polsby, eds., *Handbook of Political Science*, vol. 7: *Strategies of Inquiry*. Reading, Mass: Addison-Wesley.

Eran, Oded. 1979. *Mezhdunarodniki: An Assessment of Professional Expertise in the Making of Soviet Foreign Policy*. Ramat Gan, Israel: Turtledove.

Farrell, R. Barry, ed. 1964. *Approaches to Comparative and International Politics*. Evanston, Ill.: Northwestern University Press.

Faurby, Ib. 1976. "Premises, Promises, and Problems of Comparative Foreign Policy." *Cooperation and Conflict* 11, no. 3: 139–62.

Festinger, Leon. 1957. *A Theory of Cognitive Dissonance*. Stanford: Stanford University Press.

Fisher, Roger. 1961. "Bringing Law to Bear on Governments." *Harvard Law Review* 74, no. 6: 1130–40.

———. 1969. *International Conflict for Beginners*. New York: Harper & Row.

Flanagan, Stephen J. 1984. "The Coordination of National Intelligence." Paper presented at the annual convention of the International Studies Association, Atlanta, Ga., March 28–31. Forthcoming in Duncan L. Clarke, ed., *Public Policy and Political Institutions: United States Defense and Foreign Policy, Coordination and Integration*. Greenwich, Conn.: JAI Press.

Fraser, Angus M. 1979. "Military Modernization in China." *Problems of Communism* 28, no. 5–6: 34–49.

Free, Lloyd, and William Watts. 1980. "Internationalism Comes of Age . . . Again." *Public Opinion* 3, no. 2: 46–50.

Freedman, Lawrence. 1977. *U.S. Intelligence and the Soviet Strategic Threat*. London: Macmillan.

Frei, Daniel, and Dieter Ruloff. 1983. *East-West Relations*. Cambridge, Mass.: Oelgeschlager, Gunn & Hein.

Fritsch-Bournazel, Renata. 1980. "Gefahren für die Entspannung in Europa." In Josef Füllenbach and Eberhard Schulz, eds., *Entspannung am Ende?*

Chancen und Risiken einer Politik des Modus vivendi. Munich: Oldenburg.

Gaddis, John Lewis. 1982. *Strategies of Containment: A Critical Appraisal of Postwar American National Security Policy.* Oxford: Oxford University Press.

Garding, Hartmut. 1978. "Ostpolitik und Arbeitsplätze: Issues 1972 und 1976." In Dieter Oberndörfer, ed., *Wählerverhalten in der Bundesrepublik Deutschland.* Berlin: Duncker & Humblot.

Garver, John. 1980. "Chinese Foreign Policy in 1980: The Tilt towards the Soviet Union." *China Quarterly* 82: 214–49.

GATT (General Agreement on Tariffs and Trade). 1979. *International Trade 1978/79.* Geneva.

Gelman, Harry. 1979. "Outlook for Sino-Soviet Relations." *Problems of Communism* 38, no. 5–6: 50–66.

George, Alexander L. 1979. "Case Studies and Theory Development: The Method of Structured, Focused Comparison." In Paul Gordon Lauren, ed., *Diplomacy: New Approaches in History, Theory, and Policy.* New York: Free Press.

———. 1980a. *Presidential Decisionmaking in Foregn Policy: The Effective Use of Information and Advice.* Boulder, Colo.: Westview.

———. 1980b. "Domestic Constraints on Regime Change in U.S. Foreign Policy: The Need for Policy Legitimacy." In Ole R. Holsti, Randolph M. Siverson, and Alexander L. George, eds., *Change in the International System.* Boulder, Colo.: Westview.

———. ed. 1983. *Managing U.S.-Soviet Rivalry: Problems of Crisis Prevention.* Boulder, Colo.: Westview.

George, Alexander L., and Richard Smoke. 1974. *Deterrence in American Foreign Policy: Theory and Practice.* New York: Columbia University Press.

Germond, Jack W., and Jules Witcover. 1981. *Blue Smoke and Mirrors: How Reagan Won and Why Carter Lost the Election of 1980.* New York: Viking Press.

Gilpin, Robert. 1981. *War and Change in World Politics.* Cambridge: Cambridge University Press.

Goldman, Marshall I. 1976. "Autarchy or Integration—The U.S.S.R. and the World Economy." In U.S. Congress, Joint Economic Committee, *Soviet Economy in a New Perspective.* Washington, D.C.: U.S. Government Printing Office.

———. 1982. "Interaction of Politics and Trade: Soviet-Western Interaction." In U.S. Congress, Joint Economic Committee, *Soviet Economy in the 1980's: Problems and Prospects, Part 1.* Washington, D.C.: U.S. Government Printing Office.

Goldmann, Kjell. 1971. *International Norms and War between States: Three Studies in International Politics.* Stockholm: Läromedelsförlagen.

———. 1974. *Tension and Détente in Bipolar Europe.* Stockholm: Esselte Studium.

Goldmann, Kjell. 1979a. *Is My Enemy's Enemy My Friend's Friend? From Bipolarity to Ambiguity in Great Power Relations.* Lund: Studentlitteratur.

————. 1979b. "The International Power Structure: Traditional Theory and New Reality." In Kjell Goldmann and Gunnar Sjöstedt, eds., *Power, Capabilities, Interdependence: Problems in the Study of International Influence.* London: Sage.

————. 1981. *Stormaktspolitik och kulturklimat.* Lund: Studentlitteratur.

————. 1982. "Change and Stability in Foreign Policy: Détente as a Problem of Stabilization." *World Politics* 34, no. 2: 230–66.

————. 1983a. "Avspänningen: utvärdering av en försöksverksamhet." In Bo Huldt and Erik Holm, eds., *Fred och säkerhet: Debatt och analys, 1982–83.* Stockholm: Akademilitteratur.

————. 1983b. "Détente and Crisis." *Cooperation and Conflict* 18, no. 4: 215–32.

Goldmann, Kjell, and Johan Lagerkranz. 1977. "Neither Tension nor Détente: East-West Relations in Europe, 1971–1975." *Cooperation and Conflict* 12, no. 4: 251–64.

Graber, Doris A. 1976. *Verbal Behavior in Politics.* Urbana, Ill.: University of Illinois Press.

Griffith, William E. 1978. *The Ostpolitik of the Federal Republic of Germany.* Cambridge, Mass.: MIT Press.

Griffiths, Franklyn. 1981. "Ideological Development and Foreign Policy." In Seweryn Bialer, ed., *The Domestic Context of Soviet Foreign Policy.* Boulder, Colo.: Westview.

Guillermaz, Jacques. 1980. "La politique chinoise de défense après Mao Zedong." *Politique internationale* 8: 135–46.

Hacke, Christian. 1975. *Die Ost- und Deutschlandpolitik der CDU/CSU.* Cologne: Verlag Wissenschaft und Politik.

Haftendorn, Helga. 1977. "Management der Sicherheitspolitik: Ein Beitrag zum Entscheidigungsprozess der Bundesrepublik Deutschland." In Klaus-Dieter Schwarz, ed., *Sicherheitspolitik: Analysen zur politischen und militärischen Sicherheit.* Bad Honnef: Osang Verlag.

————. 1983. *Sicherheit und Entspannung: Zur Aussenpolitik der Bundesrepublik Deutschland, 1955–1982.* Baden-Baden: Nomos.

Hallenberg, Jan. 1983. "Sovjetbilden i amerikansk debatt och politik." In Bo Huldt and Erik Holm, eds., *Fred och säkerhet: Debatt och analys, 1982–83.* Stockholm: Akademilitteratur.

————. 1984. *Foreign Policy Change: United States Foreign Policy toward the Soviet Union and the People's Republic of China, 1961–1980.* Stockholm: Department of Political Science, University of Stockholm.

————. 1986. *The Domestic Political Context of the Making of America's Soviet Policy: A Review of the Literature.* Stockholm: Department of Political Science, University of Stockholm.

Hanrieder, Wolfram F. 1967. *West German Foreign Policy, 1949–1963: International Pressure and Domestic Response*. Stanford: Stanford University Press.

———. 1970. *The Stable Crisis: Two Decades of German Foreign Policy*. New York: Harper & Row.

Harary, Frank. 1961. "A Structural Analysis of the Situation in the Middle East." *Journal of Conflict Resolution* 5, no. 2: 167–78.

———. 1977. "Graphing Conflict in International Relations." *Peace Science Society (International)*, Papers 27: 1–9.

Harary, Frank, Robert Z. Norman, and Dorwin Cartwright. 1965. *Structural Models: An Introduction to the Theory of Directed Graphs*. New York: John Wiley.

Hardt, John P., and Kate S. Tomlinson. 1983. "Soviet Economic Policies in Western Europe." In Herbert J. Ellison, ed., *Soviet Policy toward Western Europe: Implications for the Atlantic Alliance*. Seattle: University of Washington Press.

Hart, Thomas G. 1983. "Sino-Soviet State Relations, 1969–1982: An Attempt at Clarification." *Cooperation and Conflict* 18, no. 2: 79–100.

Healey, B., and A. Stein. 1973. "The Balance of Power in International History: Theory and Reality." *Journal of Conflict Resolution* 17, no. 1: 33–62.

Heiskanen, Ilkka, and Tuomo Martikainen. 1974. "On Comparative Policy Analysis: Methodological Problems, Theoretical Considerations, and Empirical Applications." In Stein Rokkan and Helen V. Aareskjold, eds., *Scandinavian Political Studies*, vol. 9. Oslo: Universitetsforlaget, and Beverly Hills, Calif.: Sage.

Heiss, Hertha W., Allen J. Lenz, and Jack Brougher. 1979. "United States-Soviet Commercial Relations since 1972." In U.S. Congress, Joint Economic Committee, *Soviet Economy in A Time of Change*, vol. 2. Washington, D.C.: U.S. Government Printing Office.

Hermann, Charles F. 1969. "International Crisis as a Situational Variable." In James N. Rosenau, ed., *International Politics and Foreign Policy*. 2d ed. New York: Free Press.

———. 1972. "Threat, Time, and Surprise: A Simulation of International Crisis." In Charles F. Hermann, ed., *International Crisis: Insights from Behavioral Research*. New York: Free Press.

———. 1978. "Foreign Policy Behavior: That Which Is To Be Explained." In Maurice A. East, Stephen S. Salmore, and Charles F. Hermann, eds., *Why Nations Act*. Beverly Hills, Calif.: Sage.

Hewett, Ed A. 1983. "Foreign Economic Relations." In Abram Bergson and Herbert S. Levine, eds., *The Soviet Economy: Toward the Year 2000*. London: George Allen & Unwin.

Historic Documents of 1976. 1977. Washington, D.C.: Congressional Quarterly.

Historic Documents of 1980. 1981. Washington, D.C.: Congressional Quarterly.

Hoffmann, Eric P., and Frederic J. Fleron, eds. 1980. *The Conduct of Soviet Foreign Policy.* New York: Aldine.

Hoffmann, Stanley. 1960. *Contemporary Theory in International Relations.* Englewood Cliffs, N.J.: Prentice-Hall.

———. 1984. "Détente." In Joseph S. Nye, Jr., ed., *The Making of America's Soviet Policy.* New Haven and London: Yale University Press.

Holsti, Kalevi J., ed. 1982. *Why Nations Realign: Foreign Policy Restructuring in the Postwar World.* London: George Allen & Unwin.

Holsti, Ole R. 1976. "Foreign Policy Formation Viewed Cognitively." In Robert Axelrod, ed., *Structure of Decision: The Cognitive Maps of Political Elites.* Princeton: Princeton University Press.

———. 1972. *Crisis, Escalation, War.* Montreal: McGill-Queens University Press.

Holsti, Ole R., and James N. Rosenau. 1980. "Cold War Axioms in the Post-Vietnam Era." In Ole R. Holsti, Randolph M. Siverson, and Alexander L. George, eds., *Change in the International System.* Boulder, Colo.: Westview.

Holsti, Ole R., Randolph M. Siverson, and Alexander L. George, eds. 1980. *Change in the International System.* Boulder, Colo.: Westview.

Hopmann, P. Terrence. 1981."Détente and the European Force Reduction Negotiations." Paper presented at the 22d annual convention of the International Studies Association, Philadelphia, March 18–21.

Hough, Jerry F. 1977. *The Soviet Union and Social Science Theory.* Cambridge, Mass: Harvard University Press.

———. 1980a. "The Evolution in the Soviet World View." *World Politics* 32, no. 4: 509–30.

———. 1980b. *Soviet Leadership in Transition.* Washington, D.C.: Brookings Institution.

Hough, Jerry F., and Merle Fainsod. 1979. *How the Soviet Union Is Governed.* Cambridge, Mass: Harvard University Press.

Hughes, Barry B. 1978. *The Domestic Context of American Foreign Policy.* San Francisco: W. H. Freeman.

Hunter, Robert E. 1982. *Presidential Control of Foreign Policy: Management or Mishap?* New York: Praeger.

Iger, Svante. 1974. *Ekonomiskt beroende i ett maktperspektiv: En teoretisk diskussion och en operationalisering.* Stockholm: Swedish Institute of International Affairs.

Jackson, William D. 1981. "Soviet Images of the U.S. as Nuclear Adversary, 1969–1979." *World Politics* 33, no. 4: 614–38.

Jacobsen, Carl G. 1981. *Sino-Soviet Relations since Mao: The Chairman's Legacy.* New York: Praeger.

Jahn, Egbert, and Jutta Tiedke. 1979. "Politische Strömungen in der sowjetischen Entspannungspolitik." In *Friedensanalyse für Theorie und Praxis* 9. Frankfurt am Mein: Suhrkamp.

Jervis, Robert. 1976. *Perception and Misperception in International Politics.* Princeton: Princeton University Press.

Joffe, Ellis. 1979. "The Army after Mao." *International Journal* 34, no. 4: 568–84.

———. 1981. "Defense Modernization and Civil-Military Relations in China." *International Political Science Review* 2, no. 3: 317–25.

Johnson, Donald Bruce, and Kirk H. Potter, eds. 1973. *National Party Platforms, 1840–1972.* Urbana, Ill.: University of Illinois Press.

Jones, R. J. Barry. 1981. "Concepts and Models of Change in International Relations." In Barry Buzan and R. J. Barry Jones, eds., *Change and the Study of International Relations: The Evaded Dimension.* London: Frances Pinter.

Jones, R. J. Barry, and Peter Willets, eds. 1984. *Interdependence on Trial: Studies in the Theory and Reality of Contemporary Interdependence.* London: Frances Pinter.

Jonson, Lena. 1984. *Sovjetisk utrikesdebatt: Politiken mot Västtyskland— grupperingar i sovjetisk press, 1975–1981.* Lund: Dialogos.

Jönsson, Christer. 1982. "Foreign Policy Ideas and Groupings in the Soviet Union." In Roger Kanet, ed., *Soviet Foreign Policy and East-West Relations.* New York: Pergamon.

Keeble, Curtis, ed. 1985. *The Soviet State: The Domestic Roots of Soviet Foreign Policy.* Aldershot, Hants.: Gower.

Keohane, Robert O., and Joseph S. Nye, Jr. 1977. *Power and Interdependence: World Politics in Transition.* Boston: Little, Brown.

Kerr, Donna H. 1976. "The Logic of 'Policy' and Successful Policies." *Policy Sciences* 7, no. 3: 351–63.

Kissinger, Henry. 1979. *White House Years.* Boston: Little, Brown.

Klingemann, Hans D., and Charles Lewis Taylor. 1978. "Partisanship, Candidates, and Issues." In Max Kaase and Klaus von Beyme, eds., *Elections and Parties.* Beverly Hills, Calif.: Sage.

Krause, Joachim, and Lothar Wilker. 1980. "Bureaucracy and Foreign Policy in the Federal Republic of Germany." In Ekkehard Krippendorff and Volker Rittberger, eds., *The Foreign Policy of West Germany: Formation and Contents.* Beverly Hills, Calif.: Sage.

Krautheim, Hans-Jobst. 1974. "Ostpolitik und Osthandel: Das Problem von auswärtiger Politik und Aussenhandel in den Publikationen der Wirtschaftspresse und des BDI (1963–72)." In Egbert Jahn and Volker Rittberger, eds., *Die Ostpolitik der Bundesrepublik: Triebkräfte, Wiederstände, Konsequenzen.* Opladen: Westdeutscher Verlag.

Kreile, Michael. 1974. "Ostpolitik und ökonomische Interessen." In Egbert Jahn and Volker Rittberger, eds., *Die Ostpolitik der Bundesrepublik: Triebkräfte, Wiederstände, Konsequenzen.* Opladen: Westdeutscher Verlag.

Kreile, Michael. 1980. "Ostpolitik Reconsidered." In Ekkehart Krippendorff and Volker Rittberger, eds., *The Foreign Policy of West Germany: Formation and Contents.* Beverly Hills, Calif.: Sage.

Kriesberg, Louis, and Ross Klein. 1980. "Changes in Public Support for U.S. Military Spending." *Journal of Conflict Resolution* 24, no. 1: 79–110.

Kühne, Winrich. 1977. "Die Schlussakte der KSZE: Zur Bedeutung, Auslegung und Anwendung von Verhaltensregeln in den Ost-West-Beziehungen." In Jost Delbrück, Norbert Ropers, and Gerda Zellentin, eds., *Grünbuch zu den Folgewirkungen der KSZE.* Cologne: Verlag Wissenschaft und Politik.

Kuper, Ernst. 1978. "Der Wandel der westdeutschen Entspannungskonzeption wärend der sozialliberalen Koalition." In Helga Haftendorn, et al., eds., *Verwaltete Aussenpolitik: Sicherheits- und entspannungspolitische Entscheidigungsprozesse in Bonn.* Cologne: Verlag Wissenschaft und Politik.

Lange, Christian L. 1919. *Histoire de l'internationalisme.* Part One. Christiania, Norway: H. Aschehoug.

Lentner, Howard H. 1972. "The Concept of Crisis as Viewed by the United States Department of State." In Charles F. Hermann, ed., *International Crisis: Insights from Behavioral Research.* New York: Free Press.

Levine, Steven I. 1979. "Some Thoughts on Sino-Soviet Relations in the 1980s." *International Journal* 34, no. 4: 649–67.

Lijphart, Arend. 1971. "Comparative Politics and the Comparative Method." *American Political Science Review* 55, no. 3: 682–93.

Mackintosh, Malcolm. 1985. "The Military Role in Soviet Decision-Making." In Curtis Keeble, ed., *The Soviet State: The Domestic Roots of Soviet Foreign Policy.* Aldershot, Hants.: Gower.

McGowan, Patrick J. 1974. "Problems in the Construction of Positive Foreign Policy Theory." In James N. Rosenau, ed., *Comparing Foreign Policies: Theories, Findings, and Methods.* New York: Sage.

McWhinney, Edward. 1978. *The International Law of Détente: Arms Control, European Security, and East-West Cooperation.* Aalphen aan den Rijn: Sijthoff and Noordhoff.

Merkl, Peter H. 1981. "Die Rolle der öffentlichen Meinung in der westdeutschen Aussenpolitik." In Wolfram F. Hanrieder and Hans Rühle, eds., *Im Spannungsfeld der Weltpolitik: 30 Jahre deutsche Aussenpolitik, 1949–1979.* Stuttgart: Bonn-Aktuell.

Meyer, Stephen M. 1984. "Soviet National Decisionmaking: What Do We Know and What Do We Understand?" In Jiri Valenta and William Potter, eds., *Soviet Decisionmaking for National Security.* London: George Allen & Unwin.

Moore, Jonathan, and Janet Fraser, eds. 1977. *Campaign for President: The Managers Look at '76.* Cambridge, Mass.: Ballinger.

Morgan, Patrick M. 1983. *Deterrence: A Conceptual Analysis.* 2d ed. Beverly Hills, Calif.: Sage.

Müller, Friedemann. 1977. "Sicherheitspolitische Aspekte der Ost-West-Wirtschaftsbeziehungen." In Jost Delbrück, Norbert Ropers, and Gerda Zellentin, eds., *Grünbuch zu der Folgewirkungen der KSZE*. Cologne: Verlag Wissenschaft und Politik.

Municio, Ingegerd. 1982. "Implementationsforskning." *Statsvetenskaplig tidskrift* 85, no. 3: 183–90.

Niclauss, Karlheinz. 1977. *Kontroverse Deutschlandpolitik*. Frankfurt am Main: Alfred Metzner.

Nogee, Joseph L., and Robert H. Donaldson. 1981. *Soviet Foreign Policy Since World War II*. New York: Pergamon.

Nye, Joseph S., Jr. 1984. *The Making of America's Soviet Policy*. New Haven and London: Yale University Press.

Nygren, Bertil. 1984. *Fredlig samexistens: Klasskamp, fred och samarbete. Sovjetunionens detente-doktrin*. Stockholm: Department of Political Science, University of Stockholm.

———. 1986. *Approaches to Soviet Foreign Policy in Sovietology*. Stockholm: Department of Political Science, University of Stockholm.

Nygren, Bertil, with Donald Lavery. 1981. *Cooperation between the Soviet Union and Three Western Great Powers, 1950–1975*. Stockholm: Swedish Institute of International Affairs.

OECD (Organization for Economic Cooperation and Development). 1984. *East-West Technology Transfer*. Paris.

Paige, Glenn D. 1972. "Comparative Case Analysis of Crisis Decisions: Korea and Cuba." In Charles F. Hermann, ed., *International Crises: Insights from Behavioral Research*. New York: Free Press.

Politics. 1985. China Handbook Series. Beijing: Foreign Languages Press.

Prados, John. 1982. *The Soviet Estimate: U.S. Intelligence Analysis and Russian Military Strength*. New York: Dial Press.

Problèmes politiques et sociaux. 1978. *La documentation française, no. 337*.

Reynolds, Philip A., and Robert D. McKinlay. 1979. "The Concept of Interdependence: Its Uses and Misuses." In Kjell Goldmann and Gunnar Sjöstedt, eds., *Power, Capabilities, Interdependence: Problems in the Study of International Influence*. Beverly Hills, Calif.: Sage.

Richman, Alvin. 1981. "Public Attitudes on Military Power." *Public Opinion* 4, no. 6: 44–46.

Riker, William H. 1962. *The Theory of Political Coalitions*. New Haven and London: Yale University Press.

Robinson, James A. 1972. "Crisis: An Appraisal of Concepts and Theories." In Charles F. Hermann, ed., *International Crisis: Insights from Behavioral Research*. New York: Free Press.

Robinson, Thomas W. 1979. "Chinese-Soviet Relations in the Context of Asian and International Politics." *International Journal* 34, no. 4: 624–48.

Roeder, Philip G. 1984. "Soviet Policies and Kremlin Politics." *International Studies Quarterly* 28, no. 2: 171–94.

Rokeach, Milton. 1968. *Beliefs, Attitudes, and Values: A Theory of Organization and Change.* San Francisco: Jossey Bass.

Roney, John C. 1982. "Grain Embargo as Diplomatic Lever: A Case Study of the U.S.-Soviet Embargo of 1980–81." In U.S. Congress, Joint Economic Committee, *Soviet Economy in the 1980's: Problems and Prospects, Part 2.* Washington, D.C.: U.S. Government Printing Office.

Rose, Richard. 1973. "Comparing Public Policy." *European Journal of Political Research* 1, no. 1: 67–93.

———, ed. 1976. *The Dynamics of Public Policy: A Comparative Analysis.* Beverly Hills, Calif.: Sage.

Rosefielde, Steven. 1980. "Was the Soviet Union Affected by the International Economic Disturbances of the 1970s?" In Egon Neuberger and Laura D'Andrea Tyson, eds., *The Impact of International Economic Disturbances on the Soviet Union and Eastern Europe: Transmission and Response.* New York: Pergamon.

Rosenau, James N. 1961. *Public Opinion and Foreign Policy.* New York: Random House.

———. 1963. *National Leadership and Foreign Policy.* Princeton: Princeton University Press.

———, ed. 1967. *Domestic Sources of Foreign Policy.* New York: Free Press.

———, ed. 1969. *Linkage Politics.* New York: Free Press.

———. 1980. *The Scientific Study of Foreign Policy.* London: Frances Pinter, and New York: Nichols Publishing Company.

———. 1981. *The Study of Political Adaptation.* London: Frances Pinter, and New York: Nichols Publishing Company.

Sagan, Scott D. 1985. "Nuclear Alerts and Crisis Management." *International Security* 9, no. 4: 99–139.

Saint-Vincent, René. 1977. "La défense chinoise après Mao." *Défense nationale* 33 (July): 89–102.

Schelling, Thomas C. 1960. *The Strategy of Conflict.* Cambridge, Mass.: Harvard University Press.

Schneider, William. 1983. "Conservatism, Not Interventionism: Trends in Foreign Policy Opinion, 1974–1982." In Kenneth Oye, Robert Lieber, and Donald Rothchild, eds., *Eagle Defiant: United States Foreign Policy in the 1980s.* Boston: Little, Brown.

Schütz, Hans-Joachim. 1977. "Probleme der Anwendung der KSZE-Schlussakte aus Völkerrechtlicher Sicht." In Jost Delbrück, Norbert Ropers, and Gerda Zellentin, eds., *Grünbuch zu den Folgewirkungen der KSZE.* Cologne: Verlag Wissenschaft und Politik.

Schwartz, Morton. 1978. *Soviet Perception of the United States.* Berkeley and Los Angeles: University of California Press.

Segal, Gerald. 1981. "China's Nuclear Posture for the 1980s." *Survival* 23, no. 1: 11–18.

Skilling, Gordon. 1983. "Interest Groups and Communist Politics Revisited." *World Politics* 34, no. 1: 1–27.

Small, Melvin, and J. David Singer. 1982. *Resort to Arms: International and Civil Wars, 1816–1980*. Beverly Hills, Calif.: Sage.

SPD (Sozialdemokratische Partei Deutschlands). 1972. *Mit Willy Brandt für Frieden, Sicherheit und eine bessere Qualität des Lebens*. Bonn.

———. 1976. *Weiter arbeiten am Modell Deutschland*. Bonn.

———. 1980. *Sicherheit für Deutschland*. Bonn.

Stankovsky, Jan. 1981. *Ost-West-Handel 1980 und Aussichten 1981*. Vienna: Wiener Institut für Internationale Wirtschaftsvergleiche, Forschungsberichte no. 68.

Starr, Harvey. 1984. *Henry Kissinger: Perceptions of International Politics*. Lexington, Ky.: University of Kentucky Press.

Steinbruner, John D. 1974. *The Cybernetic Theory of Decision: New Dimensions of Political Analysis*. Princeton: Princeton University Press.

Stent, Angela. 1981. *From Embargo to Ostpolitik: The Political Economy of West German-Soviet Relations, 1955–1980*. Cambridge: Cambridge University Press.

Stubbe Østergaard, Clemens. 1983. "Multipolarity and Modernization: Sources of China's Foreign Policy in the 1980s." *Cooperation and Conflict* 18, no. 4: 245–67.

Tan Eng Bok, Georges. 1978. "La modernisation de la défense chinoise et ses limites." *Défense nationale* 34 (May): 69–84.

Taubman, Philip. 1983. "Casey and his C.I.A. on the Rebound." *New York Times Magazine*, January 16.

The Presidential Campaign 1976. Vol. 1: *Jimmy Carter*. 1979. Washington, D.C.: U.S. Government Printing Office.

The Presidential Campaign 1976. Vol. 2: *President Gerald R. Ford*. 1979. Washington, D.C.: U.S. Government Printing Office.

The Presidential Campaign 1976. Vol. 3: *The Debates*. 1979. Washington, D.C.: U.S. Government Printing Office.

Tow, William T., and Douglas T. Stuart. 1981. "China's Military Turns to the West." *International Affairs* 57, no. 2: 286–300.

Treml, Vladimir G. 1980. "Foreign Trade and the Soviet Economy: Changing Parameters and Interrelations." In Egon Neuberger and Laura D'Andrea Tyson, eds., *The Impact of International Economic Disturbances on the Soviet Union and Eastern Europe: Transmission and Response*. New York: Pergamon.

Treverton, Gregory. 1980. *China's Nuclear Forces and the Stability of Soviet-American Deterrence*. Adelphi Papers, no. 160. London: International Institute for Strategic Studies.

Turpin, William Nelson. 1977. *Soviet Foreign Trade: Purpose and Performance*. Lexington, Mass.: D. C. Heath.

UD (Utrikesdepartementet). 1975. *Konferensen om säkerhet och samarbete i Europa, 1973–1975*. Ny serie 2:29. Stockholm.

———. 1978. *Konferensen om säkerhet och samarbete i Europa (ESK): Uppföljningsmötet i Belgrad, 1977*. Ny serie II:35. Stockholm.

United Nations. 1980. *Yearbook of International Trade Statistics, 1979.* New York.

United Nations. 1982. *Yearbook of International Trade Statistics, 1981.* New York.

Valenta, Jiri. 1979. *Soviet Intervention in Czechoslovakia, 1968: Anatomy of a Decision.* Baltimore: Johns Hopkins University Press.

Väyrynen, Raimo. 1987. "Adaptation of a Small Power to International Tensions: The Case of Finland." In Bengt Sundelius, ed., *The Neutral Democracies and the New Cold War.* Boulder, Colo.: Westview.

Verhengen, Günter, ed. 1980. *Das Programm der Liberalen.* Baden-Baden: Nomos.

Volten, Peter M. E. 1982. *Brezhnev's Peace Program: A Study of Soviet Domestic Political Process and Power.* Boulder, Colo.: Westview.

Wallace, William. 1971. *Foreign Policy and the Political Process.* London: Macmillan.

Waltz, Kenneth N. 1979. *Theory of International Politics.* Reading, Mass.: Addison Wesley.

Watts, William, and Lloyd A. Free. 1978. *State of the Nation III.* Lexington, Mass.: Lexington Books.

Wilson, Dick. 1980. "China's Affair with Russia." *Asia Pacific Community* 7: 66–78.

Witcover, Jules. 1977. *Marathon: The Pursuit of the Presidency, 1972–1976.* New York: Viking Press.

Wolf, Thomas A. 1979. "The Distribution of Economic Costs and Benefits in U.S.-Soviet Trade." In U.S. Congress, Joint Economic Committee, *Soviet Economy in a Time of Change*, vol. 2. Washington, D.C.: U.S. Government Printing Office.

Zagare, Frank C. 1985. "Toward a Reformulation of the Theory of Mutual Deterrence." *International Studies Quarterly* 29, no. 2: 155–69.